User Experience in Libr

G000162966

Modern library services can be incredibly complex. Much more so than their forebears, modern librarians must grapple daily with questions of how best to implement innovative new services, while also maintaining and updating the old. The efforts undertaken are immense, but how best to evaluate their success?

In this groundbreaking new book from Routledge, library practitioners, anthropologists, and design experts combine to advocate a new focus on User Experience (or 'UX') research methods. Through a combination of theoretical discussion and applied case studies, they argue that this ethnographic and human-centred design approach enables library professionals to gather rich evidence-based insights into what is really going on in their libraries, allowing them to look beyond what library users say they do to what they actually do.

Edited by the team behind the international UX in Libraries conference, *User Experience in Libraries* will ignite new interest in a rapidly emerging and game-changing area of research. Clearly written and passionately argued, it is essential reading for all library professionals and students of Library and Information Science. It will also be welcomed by anthropologists and design professionals working in related fields.

Andy Priestner manages Cambridge University's pioneering FutureLib innovation programme, employing user experience and design thinking to develop new library services across the university. He is the founder of the UX in Libraries Conference and provides training and consultancy on the subject to institutions across Europe.

Matt Borg was an academic librarian at Sheffield Hallam University for fourteen years, during which time he was responsible for a new research-based approach to user experience. He is now a Solutions Expert at ProQuest's Ex Libris, where he works to bring new technology to libraries across Europe, as well as a freelance trainer in UX techniques.

User Experience in Libraries

Applying Ethnography and
Human-Centred Design

Edited by
Andy Priestner and Matt Borg

NEW YORK AND LONDON

First published 2016
by Routledge
2 Park Square, Milton Park, Abingdon, Oxon OX14 4RN

and by Routledge
711 Third Avenue, New York, NY 10017

Routledge is an imprint of the Taylor & Francis Group, an informa business

British Library Cataloguing in Publication Data
A catalogue record for this book is available from the British Library

Library of Congress Cataloging-in-Publication Data
A catalog record for this title has been requested

ISBN: 9781472451002 (hbk)
ISBN: 9781472484727 (pbk)
ISBN: 9781315548609 (ebk)

Typeset in Times New Roman
by Apex CoVantage, LLC

Contents

Tables

Figures

Preface and acknowledgements

We came up with the idea of this book at the 2014 LILAC conference, by which point we had already started to promote the inaugural UX in Libraries conference planned for the following year. There was some trepidation at the thought of putting together a book as well as the conference given how groundbreaking and interactive we were planning the latter to be – to say nothing of our respective day jobs. As soon as we started talking about such a tome, we realised how valuable it would be to gather together great stories about UX in libraries – stories which would advocate for more ethnography and design thinking, encourage discussion and debate, and help kick-start library UX projects, big and small. Whether we have achieved our aim or not we will have to wait and see, but the contributors to this volume remain convinced that in today's highly complex library and information world we must adopt user experience research methods to observe, listen to and question our users if we are to understand them more fully and offer services that they need.

We are hugely grateful to all of our contributors, not only for their mindful chapters, but also for their patience – suffice to say we embarked on this book in different jobs to the ones we have now. Thanks also to Dymphna Evans for readily agreeing to publish the book and immediately recognising the need for it in the library literature. One person whose name should probably be on the cover alongside ours is Marisa Priestner, who proved indispensable as eagle-eyed second proofer, queen of reference checking and manuscript preparation – thank you!

Matt's acknowledgements

I'd like to thank those I've worked with in all walks of my professional life. Thanks to Andy for being a genuine friend, supporter and collaborator. Above all, thanks to my family; Rachel, Dylan and Oz. You are, as they say, the best.

Andy's acknowledgements

I'd like to thank Bryony Ramsden who I hold directly responsible for igniting my ethnography flame, and Donna 'force of nature' Lanclos for fanning it. Grateful thanks also to everyone who made UXLibs such a success, especially Georgina

Cronin who shared most of the pain. I'd also like to thank her and Ange Fitzpatrick for starting the UX journey with me, for singing with me in the office and for otters. As for Matt – back atcha fella!

Matt Borg
Andy Priestner

Contributors

Andy Priestner (editor) is a freelance trainer and consultant specialising in user experience, social media, storytelling, marketing, communications and team-building, working with libraries (academic and public), universities and the private sector in the UK and mainland Europe. He originated the UX in Libraries conference after embarking on several ethnographic research projects at Cambridge University's Judge Business School, where he was Head of Information & Library Services between 2007 and 2015. His interest and expertise in user experience has most recently led to his appointment as manager of Cambridge University Library's FutureLib innovation programme, which employs ethnography and human-centred design to explore and deliver innovative new services and products across Cambridge's many libraries. This is his second co-edited academic volume; the first, with Elizabeth Tilley, was *Personalising Library Services in Higher Education* (Ashgate, 2012). Andy was President of the European Business Schools Librarians Group (2014–2015) and Chair of the Business Librarians Association (2006–2010). He is a trained LEGO Serious Play facilitator and blogs regularly as 'Constructivist'.

Matt Borg (editor) is a librarian, trainer, geek and troublemaker. For over 14 years he worked in academic libraries in a variety of roles. At Sheffield Hallam University he was an academic librarian, where he coded and designed the library website and was a lecturer in the Business School on information management. He also co-created the Information and Creativity in Libraries conference (I2C2). His passion for UX enabled him to initiate a research-based approach to user engagement at Sheffield Hallam, focusing on interaction with library tools. This led to a number of talks and keynotes on the topic, and an invitation to collaborate with Andy by joining the organising committee for the UX in Libraries conference. In September 2014 he moved to ProQuest Workflow Solutions. He works with libraries across Europe on library technologies including discovery systems and library services platforms. Previous academic publications include chapters on responsive web design for libraries ('Best of Both Worlds' in *M-libraries 4: From Margin to Mainstream*, Facet, 2013) and information literacy and discovery systems (*The Road to Information Literacy: Librarians as Facilitators of Learning*, IFLA, 2012). Matt is also a part-time freelance trainer and a LEGO Serious Play facilitator, and can often be found trawling his kids' LEGO sets for neat pieces to use.

Penny Andrews is a writer, performer, para-athlete and librarian. She'd call herself a polymath, but that would imply a greater objective level of success at these things, when she's probably better known for deconstructing popular culture and engaging in professional debate via social media. She managed not to swear or stutter that one time she performed on BBC Radio 4. *Doctor Who* is one of Penny's special interests (she's autistic, so that implies a very special level of interest), but she can often be persuaded to talk about libraries, Open Access to research, accessibility and other slightly less cultish topics.

Andrew D. Asher is the Assessment Librarian at Indiana University Bloomington, where he leads the libraries' qualitative and quantitative assessment programs and conducts research on the information practices of students and faculty. His most recent projects have examined how 'discovery' search tools influence undergraduates' research processes, how students locate, evaluate, and utilise information on research assignments, and how university researchers manage and preserve their research data. From 2008–2010, Andrew was the Lead Research Anthropologist for the Ethnographic Research in Illinois Academic Libraries (ERIAL) Project (http://www.erialproject.org/), a two-year study of student research processes at five Illinois universities and the largest ethnographic study of libraries undertaken to date. An ethnographer and anthropologist by vocation, Andrew holds a PhD in sociocultural anthropology from the University of Illinois at Urbana-Champaign, and has written and presented widely on using ethnography in academic libraries, including the co-edited volume, *College Libraries and Student Cultures* (ALA Editions, 2012). He is also currently writing a methodological handbook for librarians on developing and implementing anthropological and other qualitative research methods in libraries.

Michael Courtney is the Outreach and Engagement Librarian for the Indiana University Libraries. Michael is also an adjunct faculty member in the Department of Information and Library Science, School of Informatics and Computing (IUB) where he teaches the reference course. Prior to coming to IUB, he has worked in many facets of librarianship, in both public and technical service positions within public and academic libraries over the past 20 years. Current areas of scholarship and publishing include future trends in academic reference service, library history, instructional design in online learning, and the connections between service learning and libraries. He credits his formative years at Barningham CEVC Primary School (Suffolk) as the foundation for a lifetime of inquiry.

Carrie Donovan is Head of Teaching & Learning for the Indiana University Libraries, where she works with students, faculty and instructors to connect the libraries to student learning. Carrie's contribution to information literacy and learning assessment is made evident through her publications and presentations on the topic, as well as her engagement in professional organisations. She currently serves as a facilitator and curriculum designer for the Association of College & Research Libraries' Assessment in Action initiative. At IU, Carrie advocates for information literacy assessment across the curriculum to ensure the libraries' centrality to disciplinary discourse and student learning. Carrie's own research areas of interest include the review and reward of librarians' teaching, student-centred learning for library instruction, and critical information literacy. Carrie received her Master of Library Science degree from Indiana University.

Leah Rosenblum Emary is an American librarian who has worked in libraries in Brussels, Berlin, San Francisco and San Diego. Her main research interests are information literacy, user-centred design in libraries, and scholarly communication. She is now an Academic Liaison Librarian at York St John University in the UK, where she lives with her husband and two sons.

Nicola Grayson has worked in academic libraries since 2005. In 2012 she secured a post at the Alan Gilbert Learning Commons which is part of the University of Manchester Library. Nicola is currently a part of the Learning Development Team, responsible for developing the award-winning 'My Learning Essentials' Open Training Programme. She focuses on academic skills and broader student support in her work, designing and delivering workshops, and is also responsible for the library's team of 'Student Rovers' and their research. In 2015 Nicola completed her doctorate in the subject area of philosophy and her research centred heavily on the communication of ideas in the works of Immanuel Kant. In her current position she contributes to key library and strategic projects and works generally to promote and sustain student skills support at the University of Manchester.

Paul-Jervis Heath leads the design studio at Modern Human, a design practice and innovation consultancy. He and his team of researchers, designers and technologists apply human-centred design to imagine future services and meaningful digital products. He is a designer and innovation consultant with 17 years' experience of helping companies make fundamental changes to their business by combining design thinking with business strategy and cutting-edge technology. He has led design on a wide variety of projects including in-car information systems for driverless cars, smart home appliances, future libraries and retail stores of the future, as well as many multichannel services and digital products. Paul works closely with the University of Cambridge on their FutureLib programme, which explores the future of academic libraries at the institution. He continues to be involved in designing future libraries around the changing needs of their patrons through a variety of design and strategy projects.

Helen Jamieson is Customer Services Manager within Learning Services at Edge Hill University, Lancashire, UK. Her current role involves overall responsibility for the libraries' learning spaces as well as managing and developing all physical and virtual enquiry services. Helen has worked in higher education libraries for nearly 20 years. Her roles have been varied and have included managing services for distance learners and delivering learner support. Recent management roles have focused more on operational and strategic responsibilities in relation to learning spaces and service provision. A particular interest for Helen is the area of customer service and she is the service lead for the Customer Service Excellence award.

Rosie Jones has worked in academic libraries since 2001. In 2011 she moved into a specialist role, project-managing the development and implementation of the award-winning Alan Gilbert Learning Commons at the University of Manchester Library. After the success of this project her remit grew to planning, initiating and managing a wider range of complex library projects covering all library spaces and any plans for library management of a learning and study space. She is now Associate Director of Library Services at Liverpool John Moores University, where she continues to develop her expertise in this area through the new Copperas Hill development, an ambitious project to create a community for learning and knowledge in the heart of Liverpool city centre.

Donna M. Lanclos is an anthropologist working with ethnographic methods and analysis to inform and change policy in higher education, in particular in and around libraries, learning spaces, and teaching and learning practices. She is Associate Professor for Anthropological Research at the J. Murrey Atkins Library at UNC Charlotte. Her research includes how students and staff engage with the nature of information and knowledge, how ethnography and anthropology can be used as tools in academic development and can influence policy and practice in higher education, physical and virtual spaces in academia, and how technology impacts learning, teaching and research. She collaborates with librarians, engineers, anthropologists, sociologists, education technology professionals, architects and designers. Donna has conducted anthropological research on academic practice in libraries not only at UNC Charlotte, but also University College, London. She collaborates with colleagues in the US and the UK, investigating the nature of learning landscapes and academic taskscapes, so as to better contextualize the behaviors that take place and problems that erupt in library spaces. She has conducted workshops for professional development at Imperial College, Kingston University, NUI Galway, Parsons the New School (NYC) and Carnegie Mellon University. Details about this work and other projects can be found at http://www.donnalanclos.com.

Helen Murphy is Assistant Librarian at the English Faculty Library, University of Cambridge, where she co-runs the library's ever-expanding teaching programme and takes a leading role in new initiatives, especially those that involve fabricating spurious excuses for the rest of the staff to do fancy dress. She likes talking to students and academics, fixing broken things, her cats, watching *Murder, She Wrote*, and avoiding writing biographies like this one. UX appeals to her because it's about making libraries better for the always complex and often brilliant human beings who might use them and because – until now at least – it hasn't involved writing any biographies at all.

Bryony Ramsden is a Subject Librarian at the University of Huddersfield, and has worked in libraries since the late 1990s. She was research assistant on the first phase of the 'Library Impact Data Project' (https://library3.hud.ac.uk/blogs/lidp/) which proved a correlation between library use and level of degree attained. She has also worked as a research assistant on an internally funded library project investigating post-occupancy informal learning space use. The results of the project led to her current research for her PhD on user behaviour in academic libraries, which utilises ethnographic methods to collect the data from a number of universities.

Matthew Reidsma is the Web Services Librarian at Grand Valley State University in Allendale, Michigan. He is the co-founder and Editor-in-Chief of *Weave: Journal of Library User Experience*, a peer-reviewed, open access journal for Library User Experience professionals. He is the author of *Responsive Web Design for Libraries* published by ALA TechSource, and the forthcoming *Customizing Library Vendor Tools for Better UX* from Libraries Unlimited. He speaks about library websites, user experience, and usability around the world. *Library Journal* named him a 'Mover and Shaker' in 2013, which led to many unfortunate dance-related jokes in the Reidsma household. He writes about libraries and technology at http://matthewreidsma.com.

Elizabeth (Libby) Tilley has successfully managed both a science library and an arts library at the University of Cambridge and has been regarded, in both places, as an expert in the subject. This expertise has come about by being embedded in the life of the discipline, observing what students and researchers 'do', and subsequently leading and adapting library services to better suit user need. A PGCE from an earlier life, librarianship qualifications, and being a Fellow of the Higher Education Academy have contributed to her focus on teaching in addressing the user experience. She currently also manages the School of Arts and Humanities libraries at Cambridge. However, tea@three at the English Library remains her self-confessed number-one opportunity for building relationships with students. A recipient of tea and cake commented recently: 'Thank you for being such a good listener and discussant; I really appreciate your sense of humour and taste in cakes.' It's clearly all about the stories.

Bea Turpin, Deborah Harrop, Edward Oyston, Maurice Teasdale and John McNamara were all colleagues at Sheffield Hallam University and members of the learning centres redevelopment project team. This team, along with others, was responsible for the redevelopment project which radically changed and updated the way learning centre spaces function and feel. The team was also responsible for developing the evidence-based approach which underpinned the project. Edward and Maurice led the project, provided the strategic vision and, working with John in the Estates department, ensured the project's successful implementation. Bea and Deborah led the research into learners' preferences.

David Jenkin, Design Director at Alexi Marmot Associates (AMA), worked in a collaborative way with the SHU team to develop the learning centres. He is a highly experienced architect known for his design and planning of interior space. His skill is as an enabler, matching the complex and changing requirements of users to the building design, recognising the need to be pragmatic whilst maintaining a vision for possible future needs.

Margaret Westbury is the Librarian for Wolfson College, University of Cambridge. She has worked in a variety of libraries and library services during her career, including the Bill & Melinda Gates Foundation, the University of California at San Diego, and Jones International University (a 100% online university) in various capacities, most of them technology related. She has a passion for UX, using social media and creating usable library spaces, and is keen to find ways to make the academic libraries relevant for twenty-first-century researchers. She is currently working on a PhD in technology-enhanced learning which explores the implications of new educational technologies on library services and spaces.

1   Uncovering complexity and detail

The UX proposition

Andy Priestner and Matt Borg

Today's library services are incredibly complex. Long gone are the days when librarians were only questioning how to arrange their stock and have it circulate appropriately amongst their users. Now we also grapple with striking the right balance between print and electronic media, seamlessly serving both physical and remote users, actively embracing technology and research data, and delivering effective teaching and learning. The list goes on, it is only getting longer and rarely, if ever, is anything removed from it. For every new service we offer, we have to consider how it will be implemented, to whom it will be promoted, and from where it will be accessed. In most cases, this means considering myriad approaches, time-consuming tailoring of messages for different platforms and users, and offering a variety of alternative delivery methods. The efforts undertaken are immense and the services we deliver are fiendishly complicated to manage and sustain. Unfortunately, however, far fewer efforts are directed towards evaluating the success and efficacy of the services we provide: how well they meet user needs; whether user experience of them is good, bad, or average; and what values these touchpoints lead our users to ascribe to libraries.

There are probably a number of reasons why user experience (UX) of our spaces, services and products has been so neglected before now. One is simply that for the past 10 years and more many of us have just been trying to keep up with the pace of change, with the demands of ever-advancing technology and opportunity. While focused on these demands and the pursuit of relevance and understanding in an age where our purpose and value has to be constantly proved, we have perhaps paid less attention to the finer details and to the actual day-to-day experiences of the users of our services.

We librarians have always prided ourselves on excellent customer service and putting the user first, but most of us have never been trained to think about users to the level of detail that true UX research methods ask of us. Neither have we actually been trained in these methods. Surveys and questionnaires have been almost the only user research tool that most of us have been (self-)schooled in, and we have come to cling to them as if they were our sole means of gathering data from our user populations – a panacea for all library ills.

And this despite our open recognition that the traditional survey has many inherent flaws, not least of which are the facts that they are largely completed by pro-library users and that self-reporting is commonly understood to be unreliable. Our users have been telling us what they think we want to hear and we have been all too eager to lap it up and promote these results – and why wouldn't we, when we're so regularly faced with threats of cuts to our services and increasingly inaccurate perceptions of our value? Surveys aside, through automated means we have slavishly and accurately (we *are* librarians, after all) measured and collated quantitative statistics on footfall, holdings, loans and renewals, database use, e-book views and downloads and, more recently, social media followers and likes, but rarely have we embarked on any initiatives to look beyond the spreadsheet totals.

Most of us can anonymously follow the user from the start of their information search, see what they have searched for in the discovery system, observe what database they ended up in, and whether they opened a PDF. But we have no idea whether this was a *successful* search experience. Did that article view answer a pressing research question?

Similarly, a library gate stat does not mean that a user has made a valuable trip to our library space – the resource they needed might not have been available, they may have visited the wrong library, they may even have had a less than satisfactory encounter with a member of library staff, but we just don't know. And for the most part we have been quite content not to find out. This is perhaps because we have felt confident that our services were generally appreciated and as good as they could be (as evidenced by high survey scores), or conversely because we have not wanted to explore the messy detail as we know some procedures are difficult (some even baffle us librarians – transferring an e-book to a device, for instance!). It could also be because we don't have the time, staffing, or motivation to uncover yet more problems to deal with. There are no doubt a few of you reading this first chapter who have behaved more intrepidly and run the occasional focus group around a particular topic or undertaken usability studies of your library website, but for the most part, until recently, comprehensive attitudinal and behavioural user research of the type and scale that this book advocates has been almost non-existent. Most of us had zero concept of what taking an anthropological approach might look like or what an ethnographic or participatory research technique might be.

Whatever the explanation as to why we librarians have chosen not to delve too deeply into how our users are 'experiencing libraries' – in terms of actually employing anthropological and design research methods – there is a strong argument that this gap cannot be ignored for very much longer. In the academic environment 'student experience' is talked about more and more as central administration seeks to explore all aspects of university life through student eyes, identifying barriers and inconveniences and moments at which their experience is less than satisfactory. In the UK even the behemoth that is the National Student Survey now claims to want to assist institutions and student unions to 'better understand the experience of its students and to help inform change' (NSS, 2015). This does not get away from the fact that it is a survey and therefore limited in what it can hope to reveal, but it speaks at least of a wider appetite for experiential data. The student experience boom is an opportunity for librarians to prove their worth, not just in terms of services and resources, but in a pastoral and social sense too. UX methods can help us collect the evidence that reveals our crucial role in student lives that we have always known but rarely shared formally.

This deeper interest from universities in student experience is naturally in part monetary, due to competition to fill university places, but a shift in societal expectations of service has also played its part. The choices that new technology, online retail and social media have given us has markedly increased all of our expectations, not only of how much better a service should be and the range of products available to us, but also of our ability to influence and interact with service providers. It is more than just a shift from writing letters of complaint to writing reviews on TripAdvisor or sending disgruntled tweets; it is a fundamental change in how individuals perceive their power and how they expect to be treated. The opportunity to have one's voice heard is now actively anticipated, as is the immediacy and seamlessness of the platform through which one can do that.

Today's users are incredibly complex. Their information-seeking behaviours have changed, and their engagement with and perception of our services are vastly different. By adopting UX research techniques (by which we chiefly mean ethnography, usability, and service design) we can uncover the sort of users our libraries have today: users who do things in ways that we do not understand, that we find frustrating, or even condemn. The crucial point is that we are not our users, and just because they carry out tasks in a way that is alien to us does not mean that their way is wrong or broken. Instead, we need to see their approach as an opportunity to learn and discover. A user choosing to sit and photograph a 300-page reference-only book with a smartphone, thereby effectively creating their own unwieldy e-book, might seem ludicrous to us when they alternatively could sit and read it in the library or photocopy it (within legal limits, naturally). However, it is a scenario that bears some analysis and would reveal significant issues around convenience and preferred study environments were follow-up explorations to take place.

It is precisely scenarios like this that UX can help to inform, leading us in turn to better delivery solutions that accept rather than question user practices. In this way these research methods are as much about a mindset as a practical approach, as they prompt us to acknowledge *what is* rather than how we think things *should be* or how people *should behave*. As this is the case, there is inherent in these methods a necessity for us to be less precious about the services we manage and less tempted to assume we know better than the user. This is not to say that sometimes the user could be approaching a library research need in a better way – a way that we could have a hand in influencing – but that we should accept and learn from the behaviour we observe.

Observing other people, the crux of ethnography, is an activity at which many of us are naturally adept. Indeed, if you ask a roomful of librarians whether they enjoy people-watching, inevitably the hands of around three-quarters of the audience shoot up, and yet it does not naturally occur to us to undertake it as an illuminating research option in our libraries. Concentrated observation can uncover fascinating insights into how our users relate to library spaces, other users, and our resources. Of course as natural people-watchers we have to be careful not to record activities too subjectively, creating wild love affairs between users or back-stories suitable for soap operas, but rather seek to objectively note activities, users' preferred study styles, use of facilities, and other crucial behaviours.

It is our assertion that exploration of user behaviour of our spaces and services stands as perhaps the most completely neglected aspect of libraries today. And yet it is an endeavour that promises riches and insights that multitudinous library surveys could never seek to offer – detailing as it can how broken our signage and wayfinding is; how poorly laid out our spaces are; and, perhaps most significantly, what users are actually doing rather than what they tell us they are doing – and much, much more.

For far too long we have been relying on our intuition as information professionals, but our intuition can often be wrong. By participating in library spaces ourselves we can learn first-hand what it is like to be in that space as a library user, irritated by that constantly banging door, uncomfortable chair, or suffocating heat. Participant observation is just one of a wide array of ethnographic techniques that can help us to derive real, and often uncommunicated, user needs and perspectives that otherwise would have remained hidden. Like most other UX research it is time-consuming to undertake if done well (and enough data is gathered to inform changes), but the results – which reveal a more holistic and detailed picture of the study lives of our users – are unquestionably worth the investment.

There is far more to UX approaches and ethnography than observation of behaviour. It also involves seeking user attitudes and opinions, an activity with which we are more familiar and comfortable. However, our current approaches to attitudinal user research do not go nearly far enough. Directed storytelling, contextual enquiry, or unstructured in-depth interviews are all ethnographic research methods which provide a framework for us to listen and learn from our users, to understand why and when and how they do things. When supplemented by methods like diary studies, photo studies, or cultural probes through which students detail their study lives and the library's place in it, we have the opportunity to possess a more complete picture of user experience than ever before – and crucially, a picture that is evidence-based, gathered through internationally recognised research methods. Many of these methods are, of course, detailed within the chapters of this book.

Our chapters come from a wide range of contributors. When we sat down to sketch out whom we wanted to invite on board, our aim was to create a useful, authoritative book on UX in libraries. We knew there was a fascinating array of UX research and activity taking place; it was simply a question of bringing it all together in one volume. You will find stories from practitioners, library UX professionals, theorists and anthropologists.

The chapters are not grouped by themes as such. Using metrics such as location or type of university or the role that the author has at the institution just did not feel right in a book that exists chiefly to bring together excellent stories around UX in libraries. Some chapters serve as practical case studies, others explore the topic from a more theoretical angle, still others offer advice and information on techniques and processes, but all collectively invite you to join the authors on a journey examining UX from various points of view.

Bryony Ramsden of Huddersfield University starts us off, asking a question that, in some ways, sums up the entire book: 'As a librarian, how much time do you spend in the library?' She explains why utilising ethnographic techniques is the best and most appropriate way to learn about the culture of the people using our spaces and can help us understand why they behave in them as they do. Her exploration of ethnographic methods neatly outlines the reasons and rationale for making this a fundamental part of our roles.

Donna Lanclos, Library Ethnographer at UNC Charlotte, North Carolina, explores the ethnographic agenda more widely, presenting it as a means of transforming institutional practices and increasing the role of library voices in shaping them. She calls for an increased openness to an anthropological worldview – a mindset which should lead us to generate and ask more questions. She explains how by gathering stories we can start to speak with ethnographic authority about our users' day-to-day realities, and how collaboration is the key to finding successful solutions to these realities and to forging a new educational agenda.

Matt Borg and Matthew Reidsma examine how leveraging the fetish we librarians have for gathering and curating data can actually help us once we have asked the right questions. They argue that we need to rely less on our 'expert intuition' and move to a model of 'expert listening', thereby gaining a more holistic view of user needs. It starts with Douglas Adams, ends with the magician Teller (of Penn and Teller), and there are some insightful musings around usability in between.

Designer Paul-Jervis Heath, who joined Matthew Reidsma and Donna Lanclos as a keynote speaker at the UX in Libraries conference, focuses on how we can apply a human-centred design process to the library experience. He details the modes of design that he and his colleagues move between as they explore context, identify opportunities, and develop and experiment with ideas, and also outlines the methods and techniques that can be employed at each stage. He argues that you do not need to be a professional designer to apply human-centred design and design thinking, and encourages librarians to embrace these principles when seeking to develop new ideas for their users.

Academic librarian Leah Emary, from York St John University, explores how using ethnography can contribute to designing improved user experience of libraries. She argues that librarians are well suited to collecting ethnographic data, examines what types of questions are best answered using these methods, and highlights some common pitfalls and ways to avoid them. As well as exploring practical techniques such as cultural probes and participant observation, Leah details the core components of good research design and the importance of objectivity and reliability.

Our next chapter is from Andrew Asher, anthropologist and Assessment Librarian at Indiana University, Bloomington; he was also lead research anthropologist (2008–2010) on the seminal ERIAL (Ethnographic Research in Illinois Academic Libraries) Project from which his chapter draws its data. Andrew introduces the reader to 'taskscapes', advocating that we obtain a broad, holistic view of our users that specifically looks at their social and educational landscapes, with a view to designing a more relevant user experience. He examines how social context affects the academic practice of students in the library and the importance of examining the local realities of a university campus when we design and plan library services.

Two case study chapters follow, which focus on pilot projects that are part of Cambridge University Library's FutureLib programme, which is seeking to design products and services to answer user needs that were derived from a long period of ethnographic research. Andy Priestner explains the premise behind Spacefinder, a pilot service which aims to match student study preferences with available study spaces and seeks to offers a 'big picture' solution to the problems that their research identified. Meanwhile Helen Murphy examines the WhoHas? pilot, a bold attempt to legitimise the practice of peer-to-peer sub-lending of books. Despite being inspired, well planned, and underpinned by user experience research, this prototype service was ultimately unsuccessful. Helen details how failure proved to be a useful experience nonetheless.

Penny Andrews explores good user experience design from an autoethnographic point of view. Her chapter offers a refreshingly honest look at how, in general, we focus on the overall view or 'best fit' in terms of library provision – often to the detriment of minority groups or individual cases – the 'Special Case' of her title. She argues that everyone is entitled to a good user experience, and no user is any less than another.

In their chapter, Rosie Jones (University of Liverpool) and Nicola Grayson (University of Manchester) explain how the design and development of the award-winning Alan Gilbert Learning Commons at the University of Manchester was shaped by changing the focus of how the library engaged in open dialogue with its students, seeing them as partners who would co-create and take collective responsibility for the space. The pair also explain how library staff now seek to accept and respond to user behaviour and to understand what they value.

Margaret Westbury's case study of ethnographic techniques carried out at her college library (Wolfson, Cambridge) shows how adopting a UX mindset on a small scale helped her move beyond assumptions and intuition. Her efforts revealed the complexity of her users' lives and their hidden needs and prompted her to alter many long-standing policies accordingly.

Michael Courtney and Carrie Donovan talk about their work at Indiana University, where they have applied ethnographic methods to library instruction in order to investigate students' understanding of the processes of information seeking. They reflect on how the experience created opportunities for them to think, and act, like anthropologists in other aspects of their professional practice as well, and how examining the ever-changing variable of students' behaviour can be challenging and unpredictable, but most of all, rewarding.

The next chapter by Beatrice Turpin, Deborah Harrop, et al. from Sheffield Hallam University, explains how a robust research methodology, incorporating coordinate and photographic mapping and semi-structured interviews, illuminated user behaviours and attitudes towards informal learning spaces ahead of a significant site redevelopment project. They detail how their research data translated into practical design solutions and how and why they created a typology of learning space preference attributes.

Edge Hill University's Helen Jamieson contributes a case study which offers a valuable insight into how ethnographic techniques can add context to the statistics and figures which her department already generated. She explains how student diary entries and photo studies offered library staff a new perspective on library use and led to many space improvements.

Cambridge University's English Faculty librarian Elizabeth Tilley uses her chapter to tell a story about stories; specifically, how they might be able to improve user learning experiences. She explains how, after gathering stories ethnographically, the Stories in Teaching project sought to explore their impact and value to student learning, and also whether they could engender a sense of community. She details how ethnographic research teaches us to observe and to get under the skin of those we study, and that stories can improve user experience.

In our final chapter, we seek to draw together the various strands that have been explored throughout the book, and examine how user experience research can be conducted on either a small or large scale. We explore the influence and impact of the UX in Libraries conference and the task ahead – that of convincing other members of the library profession of the value of UX research methods. We also debate who should be conducting this kind of research: librarians, trained anthropologists, designers, or all three? We end by considering the compelling opportunity which UX now offers us: to better understand user behaviour and illuminate an ever more complex landscape of learning.

We intimated earlier that we may have continued to persist with surveys because libraries score very well in them. However, it is our contention that we could score even more highly were we to engage with these more intensive and revealing methods to truly understand user need. This is not to suggest that we should dispense with surveys or indeed with quantitative data altogether, but instead that we accept that they cannot give us much valuable information about how our users feel about our services and whether they actually assist them to fulfil their learning goals.

A quick but important word on definitions and language. Just as our users arrive at our libraries having had different experiences and perspectives, so too do we all approach user experience and what it means to us from different angles. There are contributors to this book who prefer to talk about ethnography and others human-centred design; there are still others who are not completely at ease with the term 'user experience' and adopt it sparingly or just see it as part of a wider picture. Some see anthropology at the top of the tree whereas others design. We editors, who have been librarians for most of our working lives, are inclined to sit somewhere between these points of view. We can see the value of both and engage in these methods, but ultimately argue that a great user experience is at the centre of the model as it is our ultimate goal, and that ethnography and design are tools we can employ to successfully achieve that.

This book is titled *User Experience in Libraries* not merely to tie it in with the conference of the same name last year, but because we believe user experience should naturally sit front and centre for us librarians as our number-one priority. We firmly believe that it is high time that we all engage in UX research. If you are not ensuring that your users' experience of information, of research and study, of your library, is the best that it can be, you could well be in the wrong profession.

Reference

NSS, 2015. *The National Student Survey*. [online] Available at: <http://www.thestudentsurvey.com/> [Accessed 10 August 2015].

2 Using ethnographic methods to study library use

Bryony Ramsden

As a librarian, how much time do you spend in the library? Not in the office, or on the enquiries desk, but actually in the areas your visitors use. Do you use your own library? The chances are that you don't get to see much of what goes on in your library, and that much of what you know about visitor use comes from surveys, complaints or from briefly spotting something as you walk through the building. Using information from surveys and responding to direct user feedback are both important ways of learning about what's happening in your library, but they don't always produce the level of data that tell you enough about usage requirements. They might tell you that your visitors want silent areas, but not necessarily where they'd like to see them; whether they work once installed; what kind of people use the areas and whether they follow the rules. The example of silent use preference is a simple one, but demonstrates that there is a need to go beyond the kind of data surveys provide. As Given (2006) so concisely puts it, quantitative research can give you information on the characteristics of usage, but it can't tell you the 'why' of usage patterns. Surveys also rely on self-reporting, and respondents won't necessarily say what they actually do (or may even hide it if they know it is against library policy).

An excellent way to learn more about use is to utilise ethnographic methods. Ethnography is a term often connected to qualitative research in general, but its primary aim is to learn about cultures. The methods associated with ethnography can help you get more detailed, real-time, in-depth qualitative data that can be much more representative of what happens in libraries. Use of ethnographic methods is still comparatively new in the library world, considering how long they've been used in other disciplines, and fairly underused because they can be time-consuming and complex. However, they are also extremely revealing and can provide access to data unavailable via other more commonly used methods. Libraries in the US have been working with anthropologists and utilising ethnography for some time: in particular, see work by Delcore et al. (2009), Duke and Asher (2012), Foster and Gibbons (2007), Kim Wu and Lanclos (2011), McKechnie et al. (2006) and Suarez (2007). The methods are starting to be adopted in libraries in the UK, though: Bryant et al. (2009) conducted an ethnography at Loughborough University Library; Atton (1998) was talking about using the principles of ethnography to learn about and develop library collections as a fairly early adopter;

while ethnographers were already conducting research in schools, with school libraries featuring in work by Shilling and Cousins (1990).

Why ethnographic methods?

So, if so many people are doing some kind of ethnographic work, why isn't it happening more? The benefits outweigh the costs, but there are quite a few reasons why it may be overlooked, with the first being a misunderstanding of what ethnography is for or about. On a very basic level, you are probably already aware of ethnography, perhaps without even realising it, and its roots can create some level of preconception. Anthropologists have been using it for years to learn about cultures different to their own, which may make you think of people studying small island cultures in far-off countries (the colonial white man looking at the 'other' is a common perception that many anthropologists are trying to renegotiate) rather than your own library visitors. However, the key term here is learning about cultures: our libraries have visitors that form a specific user group, which can be viewed as constituting a 'culture', that is, a collection of ideas, values, experiences and attitudes linked to a particular group of people. There will be subcultures within it, such as teenagers, students, researchers, the elderly, parents with children, or librarians as library visitors. Library users are a culture and have specific identities that can inform on their usage patterns (and in turn cycle back to inform the culture's identities), and thus show us how each culture responds to the library's policies, designs, resources or anything else we as library staff might provide. And that's something we really have to remember: we are library staff. We use libraries as library staff, whether we are working at the time in the library we are visiting or not. That differentiates us somewhat from the people we are providing for and supporting, although we might not always realise it. Using ethnographic methods helps us learn about the people using our libraries because we start to understand how they use them, in ways they might not even be conscious of themselves. In addition, using a critical approach to looking at the data collected will potentially help create an environment that enables and empowers the people who visit it – but that will be discussed later.

Looking beyond the surface

There are other reasons why ethnographic methods aren't as popular as they could be in library research. To carry them out potentially means dedicating a lot of time to data collection and analysis. If you choose to conduct observations and interviews, that's a lot of time to commit, which in turn can cost money in staff hours (and probably reimbursement to participants and interviewees). However, it is time and money worth investing. Let's say you decide that you want to buy a full set of replacement furniture for the library. The old stuff is looking tired, so you need to buy some new pieces anyway, and you successfully win funding to do so. Rather than replacing the furniture with like for like, you decide to be a bit more adventurous and buy some new fancy things to try and encourage new visitors and to brighten the place up a bit. However, you find that once the new furniture is in place people aren't using it, or they complain about it at the desk. So you decide to change things back and rethink the layout, as you still have the old furniture lurking about. You get more complaints from other people who liked using the new stuff. Aside from totally missing out on an initial consultation with current library visitors, you've also forgotten to try and ask why people aren't visiting, and you haven't looked at what people are actually doing in the library with each furniture set. Conducting some research would definitely have made a difference in this rather simplistic and frankly highly unlikely scenario (you wouldn't buy new furniture without asking people what they wanted, didn't like about what they had, or how they used the library, would you?). As a bonus, ethnographic methods would have helped you learn more about *how* people use the library furniture before you even started the process of bidding for funding. Additionally, you don't have to approach ethnographic methods as if you are going to do a full-blown ethnography, which traditionally can involve spending years studying a particular group of people. Without the full training anthropologists have, you are more likely to be doing something much smaller in scale, which doesn't require you to spend a solid year of observational data collection instead of your normal job. Ideally you would be able to employ an anthropologist to work alongside you on a permanent basis and help you learn about your visitors, but what if that isn't an option? You can utilise methods drawn from ethnography and gather data that is extremely useful to you without having to dedicate months or years of time to the research.

Which leads to one more reason why people might decide not to take the ethnographic method route: they've never done anything like it before. They may have conducted some research or run some surveys, but they haven't ventured into what can appear to be a slightly intimidating practice because of the amount of data and analysis it might involve. Ethnographic methods are what you make of them, and even more so if it is you who gets to make the decisions in your library. Smaller scale use of some of the methods can be quite similar to research already in common use, so it's a matter of piloting a method to see if it can work for your purpose. In some cases, you might already be using ethnographic methods without realising it, including that moment when you spot something happening as you walk through the building.

When to use ethnographic methods

To start off with, you probably already have an idea of something you want to find out, and you need to consider what method is best for your research question. It might seem obvious, but don't dive in assuming ethnographic methods will work to answer all your questions. If you want to know whether people are for or against opening on a Sunday, then that's more of a survey question. If you want to find out what purpose people have when they visit on a weekend, that could be a mixed methods piece of research: that is, you'll probably want to use a combination of statistics to measure how many people use the library, and some qualitative data to find out the purpose of their visits. If you want to learn more about what's actually happening in the library when you are open, you might want to start applying ethnographic methods.

Using ethnographic methods to study library use can give you more detail of what often goes unseen, things that you might even be aware are happening but are effectively hidden when you try to research them because you don't get the answers you were expecting. There are all kinds of ways you can use the methods to find out more, as the literature mentioned earlier demonstrates: website usability, building usage patterns and wayfinding, and information-seeking behaviours are just a few examples of research where ethnographic methods can be particularly useful.

Types of method

Methods used in ethnography are numerous, so this is a starter guide with lots of information on where you can learn more.

Observation

Observation is the one people will most likely be aware of. Spending time with the culture you want to study is a great way to learn more about it. There are a few ways you can conduct observations, but these are two of the main ones:

- *Active participant.* This is where you join the group you want to learn more about and take part in their activities as if you were a member. Active participant observation (like all observation methods) is conducted without making judgment on the behaviours that appear as you observe. This kind of observation can make a difference to how the people you are observing behave if they are aware you are observing them: they may try to impress you, or shut you out of their normal activity.
- *Non-participant.* You might spend time 'in the field' observing what happens, but in contrast to active participation you don't get involved at all in what is going on, and remain a detached observer.

There are a couple of ways of conducting observations whether you are a participant or not. You can either overtly observe, ensuring you tell everyone you can that you will be collecting data, or covertly observe people, observing without telling anyone what you are doing. To make things a bit more complicated you can also be semi-covert, and notify people that you will be undertaking observations but not tell them exactly where or when you will be doing it.

In all types of observation you need to be aware of the ethical implications of what you are doing, so think carefully about what is the most appropriate method. Approach observation in the wrong way and you can walk into a minefield of problems. Think of your legal responsibility to participants in the first instance. Get ethical approval for observation from both the people who run the place you want to observe in, and from an ethical panel (if you work in education) or legal advisor (if you work in public libraries) if possible. Theoretically, libraries of all kinds are public spaces, and in the US and Canada regulations will allow you to conduct observations in public places as long as you don't endanger anyone (for an example, see work by McKechnie et al. [2006]). In the UK it's a bit different because of English and European human rights laws, and because of research guidelines such as those published by the British Educational Research Association (2011) and the Social Research Association (2003), so check with whomever is funding the research. They will usually conduct ethical checks on your research plans, or obtain legal advice if necessary. Make sure you write up an information sheet for anyone who may have any questions. These are useful for all kinds of observation, whether they are handed out or displayed at the library entrance, uploaded to the library website for information, or distributed during covert/unobtrusive observation if you are spotted and asked questions. Include an opt-out clause with information on whom to contact if they want to be excluded from the data collection.

You also need to decide what kind of observation data collection process to follow. One option is to note down pretty much everything you can about what's going on within ethical remits: you don't want to be noting lots of personal conversation if you don't have permission to do so from the people you are observing! Otherwise, noting down everything does mean *everything* with as much detail as possible, whether it seems important or not at the time. While quite hard going to carry out, it is extremely revealing and can generate useful extensive data: you learn a huge amount about all the ways people use your building and spaces. When making notes, it might be useful to follow the double-entry notes style to aid logging what happens without making assumptions or judgements on actions. It's important to try and avoid judging what's happening while it happens, as unless you speak to people directly you don't really know what their motivations or feelings are; you only know your own interpretations. Naturally it isn't possible to be totally independent of your own assumptions, however, so using the double-entry system will help you work with that. You use one column for describing actions as they occur, and one for your own thoughts, feelings and ideas about what is happening. That way the two are separate, but you have prompts as to how things appeared at the time, and you have an increased awareness of how much conjecture you are making about the data.

The other option is to collect structured observation notes, creating a list of things you want to look for and chart when and how often they occur, as well as potentially logging details of them (as in Paretta and Catalano [2013]). This ventures a bit more into a mixed method approach, as it involves some level of counting incidents, and you may be limiting yourself to only the items in the list without noting other behaviours or occurrences. However, it is much simpler than detailing everything and makes the process much more focussed if you are conducting smaller-scale research. Whichever method you choose, you'll need to start by piloting and practising data collection, and refining the list of items you want to include if you use structured observation.

Interviews

Interviews are an excellent way to learn about how and why people use or don't use your facilities, and yes, you will want to try and learn about those people who rarely visit. If you have been conducting observations they will link directly into your interview process, generating questions and discussion points. If not, you'll need to start from scratch at creating some questions that will be open enough to prompt discussion and inform but closed enough to get the answers you need. There are a few routes you can take for your interview design:

- *Open-ended/unstructured interviews*. As the name suggests, these are very open and exploratory, and involve allowing the interviewee to lead the discussion. However, you will need to plan out how you want to guide the interviewees through the process so that it doesn't just end up as a conversation that doesn't tell you anything: create a list of goals for what you want to learn about by the end of the interview. Questions might involve asking the interviewee to describe a typical day that features a library visit, or telling you about what they do when they visit the library.
- *Semi-structured interviews*. These are fairly open and work well when used in conjunction with observation data. Design questions to discuss what you've noticed when observing, but leave them open enough for the interviewee to talk about their own usage. For example, to learn about specific incidents you have observed, or a particular kind of library use, design questions based around these topics. Questions could be along the lines of asking the interviewee to describe what happens when they want to borrow a book from the point of trying to find out if the library stocks it to returning it; or you might ask about how they use a specific area of the library, if at all, and why they do or don't use it. The questions can be moved around if they fall naturally into a different order, and can be added to during the interview process to learn more about a specific comment the interviewee makes.
- *Structured interviews*. These involve highly specific questions that will directly ask about the issues you want to learn about in a very prescriptive way. You'll probably already have some very clear ideas about what you want to learn about, and structured interviews provide a method to learn about just those subjects without moving away from them. The interviewer still needs to guide the process without being too closed, as there's a risk that no useful data is collected. Questions for structured interviews will always be the same for each interviewee, regardless of their use or non-use of the library, and asked in the same order. This style of interviewing could involve asking participants about how they would score a specific library service and why, or about how satisfied they are with staffing levels. Structured interview questions can often be conducted as printed questionnaires, but the interview process provides the opportunity to prompt for clarification or more detail, thus differentiating itself from the problematic survey process mentioned at the start of this chapter.

The trick in interviews is to avoid closed questions that only prompt a yes or no answer, because they won't tell you anything much. Also be aware that while it is good practice to try and build rapport with your interviewee so that they feel they can talk openly to you, avoid putting words into their mouths by encouraging them to respond in a certain direction. Expressing your own opinion on a topic may influence their answers, whether they agree with you or not, so try and be friendly, non-judgmental and receptive without prompting in a particular direction. To learn more about interviewing, try Hammersley and Atkinson (2007), Schensul et al. (1999) and Spradley (1979).

For interviews, you'll need to create a consent form and an information sheet including the contact details of the researcher to make sure interviewees are aware of your research intentions and their rights. Examples of consent forms and information sheets can be found on most university ethics websites (useful resources no matter what kind of library is being researched), so modify content to suit the circumstances. They usually need to contain check boxes to confirm that participants understand the important details about the research, including (at the very least) the way the interview is recorded, how the data will be stored and the option to withdraw from the research at any point.

Cognitive mapping

Developed from a concept used in psychology, cognitive mapping is a deceptively simple process that can provide a wide range of data for a variety of use and non-use patterns, and has been used to great success by the ERIAL (Ethnographic Research in Illinois Academic Libraries) Project (Duke and Asher, 2012; Green et al., 2014), Donna Lanclos (2013) and many more. The participant is given a sheet of paper with the research question at the top of the sheet (usually landscape-oriented), and asked to create a 'map' of their answer over 6 minutes, changing the colour of their pen every 2 minutes. They then label up what they included in the map, and describe and discuss what they have created. The word 'map' can be interpreted as the participant wishes, so it could be a mind map and text based; it could be something closer to a geographical map, detailing various spaces in relation to each other; or it could be a drawing of specific places and objects.

Because the participant has used different coloured pens during the process, you can draw some rough conclusions immediately about what is potentially the most important to them or the first place they go to. The labelling and discussion will provide more information about why exactly they were drawn first, why things included later in the map were left until that point, and what was omitted and why: certainly the omissions can be as interesting as what was included. The map is used to prompt questions and discover talking points, but having a few themes and questions prepared prior to data collection will help focus the discussion in the direction you want it to. Using this method will help you learn about what works for your participants outside of the library as well as inside it, and while you may not wish to replicate other kinds of environments within the library, you can consider borrowing from their features to modify the library.

Focus groups

This is pretty much what it says on the tin, and not purely ethnographic as such: getting a number of people together to talk about using or not using the library is a potentially useful way to learn more about what works and doesn't work in it. The focus group method is listed last, as while it is a useful, it is also a bit problematic. Approaching focus groups from an ethnographic perspective means they can be used as a way of collecting observational data, focussing on the participants' experiences. Be aware that responses may differ in comparison to interviews depending on the personalities of the participants: they may influence each other's opinions and responses somewhat, but that kind of interaction could be useful.

What the focus groups have that interviewing doesn't is that level of conversation and discussion that can arise between multiple participants. They may feel more relaxed discussing things amongst each other rather than directly with the interviewer, but naturally this may also swing towards feeling less comfortable discussing things if there is a dominant opinion/speaker. That's where your level of control over the discussion comes in, where you need to attempt to bring the quieter participants to the front of the discussion and give them the opportunity to speak as openly as possible. That's not an easy task, as it depends on the individuals as to whether they would feel comfortable enough to say something that contradicts what others have said, and it may be worth considering using focus groups before the interview process and then asking some of the participants to return for one-to-one interviewing.

One of the ways to help stop participants feeling that they can't speak out easily is to start the group with a task. Delcore et al. (2009) used 'bootlegging' workshops, providing participants with a theme to focus on before asking them to break into smaller groups and create a skit about the related issues, or offering them the opportunity to design library spaces. Foster and Gibbons (2007) asked students to create their own designs for the library refurbishment, something that I've also done in my own research using LEGO, drawing materials and modelling clay. There's still some level of difficulty in encouraging equal participation, but providing a specific task to work on in groups or individually and then gathering together to discuss what they worked on or created can generate discussion and provide more opportunities for each participant to speak.

What do you do with the data?

Once you've conducted your research, you should have a ton of data to go through. Many others have covered how to analyse the data collected (see the ERIAL Project in particular, which provides an excellent toolkit on its website [Asher and Miller, 2011]; also see Saldana [2013]), so I won't go into too much detail here. There are as many routes for data analysis as there are for data collection, if not more: grounded theory, statistical analysis (in some cases), and thematic analysis, to name but a few, but here I'll just talk more generally about 'coding' your data. Do you want to let the data drive your analysis, or do you want to look for specific themes or incidents? This choice will narrow down your approach straight away, but using an approach to data analysis like the routes listed earlier may be beyond the time and scope of your project.

The simple starting point is to begin coding: looking for and labelling any themes or concepts that appear in your data. Themes and concepts could be anything that is discussed, such as noise, food and drink, proximity to resources and so forth. Start broad, picking out as many concepts as you can and tracking their frequency, looking for commonality between them as well as the more unusual or unique occurrences. Then start refining them: look for duplication where themes are too close to be kept separate. You can still tag them as points of interest, variation or discussion. Once you have a set of codes to work with, start formally tagging your data with them, either manually using a highlighting technique, or automatically by using software. Which of these methods to use is very much a personal preference. I originally started coding my data using software, and found that I lost track of the content and got too concerned about the codes themselves. I found working in word processing software let me highlight and comment on the data just as well, but events and points of interest felt more overt and part of a bigger picture when I was reading through, rather than standalone moments separate from the rest. However, it is definitely down to what works best for the individual. Make sure you keep a record of how you code your data so that you can recreate the process and find your codes later more easily. After you've coded all your data, you need to collate the codes into themes, and then you can start to consider what the codes and themes tell you about the use of your library.

If you took the structured approach you will probably find the data guides you through the analytical process, as you've been focussed on what you want to find out from the start, and it is more a question of deciding what to do with what it shows you. Most of the data you collected from structured observations will often be number-based: counting the number of actions and when and where they happened will factor into some level of statistical analysis, often using software. However, you will probably also have additional notes and data related to the actions that will need some consideration, and will need to be examined alongside the statistics. If you carried out interviews as well, you can start to link up the behaviours and actions you've observed with the interview data and see if they contradict or confirm each other.

In the less structured approaches, you may find an inductive process more appropriate (i.e. letting the data lead how you code), or you may already have some ideas about the data you've collected and decide to focus on looking for specific issues or elements. You probably have already developed a sense of the data by this stage from preparing for interviews and possibly even have some preliminary coding completed, which should help start the analytical process proper.

Critical approaches to your data

I'd like to suggest at this point that you consider taking a critical standpoint when you are investigating your data during the coding process. A critical standpoint here means approaching the data from a specific sociopolitical perspective, so you could look at your data for any issues related to inequalities with regard to disability, gender, race, or social background (if you have engaged library users to allow you to conduct active participant observations). The landscape in libraries in the UK, be they public or academic, is shifting towards concerns over money rather than the needs of the library's visitors. Library users are also changing, particularly in the higher education sector; we need only read the Higher Education Academy's report (Temple et al., 2014) on the student experience following the introduction of fees to see how usage patterns are changing for some institutions. Public libraries in the UK are facing closures, which potentially removes access to information, both on- and offline, for many people who don't have access to information, computers or the Internet elsewhere, which in turn can lead to a reduction in agency. Studying use or non-use of your library spaces can be used to help improve agency of users, be they public or academic library visitors, and help curb inequalities between different cultural groups. If you decide this is a route you want to take, I recommend looking at Schostak and Schostak (2008), but there is a lot of research out there that takes a critical standpoint and can help lead your planning and analysis, even if it isn't based in libraries.

Using your data

However you look at your data, it's important not to have a knee-jerk reaction and change everything immediately. I'd also suggest that if the data shows something you don't like about usage patterns, remember that it isn't you using the library and that, depending on the usage patterns (obviously some types of behaviour are not acceptable at all!), you consider whether you need to rethink your perceptions of library use. Any changes that you decide need to be considered for implementation should be fed back to the library users for their opinions before you take any further action and potentially spend money on them. Keep collecting data regularly if possible so that you can compare it over time, see if anything changes and whether any change might stem from any actions you take.

I'd also recommend very carefully considering changes where you borrow design features and service ethos from commercial ventures like coffee shops and book shops. Those companies exist to make money rather than provide a service, and while library users may like the environments they provide, you are also potentially communicating a specific message based on that commercial ethos that will influence how your library users interpret and use the spaces you provide. It isn't to say that you should completely discard any changes that match the kind of designs they have, but the implications of incorporating that style on a wide scale need to be reflected upon.

Conclusion

I've summarised a few different routes you can take to conduct ethnographic-based research in your workplace, and hopefully whetted your appetite to try them. I've also made you aware of the complexities of the process. The data you can collect using ethnographic techniques are extremely revealing, intriguing, exciting and often difficult to obtain by other methods. There are lots of places you can learn more, and I provide some in the references. Look beyond the numbers to seek out the information that usually matters the most to the people using our libraries – what happens when they are in our buildings using them.

References

Asher, A. and Miller, S., 2011. *So You Want to Do Anthropology in Your Library? Or a Practical Guide to Ethnographic Research in Academic Libraries*. [pdf] Available at: <http://www.erialproject.org/wp-content/uploads/2011/03/Toolkit-3.22.11.pdf> [Accessed 1 November 2014].

Atton, C., 1998. The librarian as ethnographer: Notes towards a strategy for the exploitation of cultural collections. *Collection Building*, [e-journal] 17(4), pp. 154–8. Available at: <http://www.emeraldinsight.com/10.1108/01604959810238293> [Accessed 15 October 2014].

British Educational Research Association, 2011. *Guidelines for Educational Research*. [pdf] Available at: <https://www.bera.ac.uk/researchers-resources/publications/ethical-guidelines-for-educational-research-2011> [Accessed 15 November 2014].

Bryant, J., Matthews, G. and Walton, G., 2009. Academic libraries and social and learning space: A case study of Loughborough University Library, UK. *Journal of Librarianship and Information Science*, [e-journal] 41(1), pp. 7–18. Available at: <http://lis.sagepub.com/cgi/doi/10.1177/0961000608099895> [Accessed 9 September 2014].

Delcore, H.D., Mullooly, J., Scroggins, M., Arnold, K., Franco, E. and Gaspar, J., 2009. *The Library Study at Fresno State*. [pdf] Available at: <http://www.csufresno.edu/anthropology/ipa/TheLibraryStudy(DelcoreMulloolyScroggins).pdf> [Accessed 31 October 2014].

Duke, L.M. and Asher, A.D. eds, 2012. *College Libraries and Student Culture: What We Now Know*. Chicago: American Library Association.

Foster, N.F. and Gibbons, S. eds, 2007. *Studying Students: The Undergraduate Research Project at the University of Rochester*. [pdf] Chicago: Association of College and Research Libraries. Available at: <http://www.ala.org/acrl/sites/ala.org.acrl/files/content/publications/booksanddigitalresources/digital/Foster-Gibbons_cmpd.pdf> [Accessed 31 October 2014].

Given, L., 2006. Qualitative research in evidence-based practice: A valuable partnership. *Library Hi Tech*, [e-journal] 24(3), pp. 376–86. Available at: <http://www.emeraldinsight.com/10.1108/07378830610692145> [Accessed 2 September 2014].

Green, D., Asher, A. and Miller, S., 2014. *ERIAL Project*. [online] Available at: <http://www.erialproject.org/> [Accessed 23 November 2014].

Hammersley, M. and Atkinson, P., 2007. *Ethnography: Principles in Practice*. 3rd ed. Oxon: Routledge.

Kim Wu, S. and Lanclos, D., 2011. Re-imagining the users' experience: An ethnographic approach to web usability and space design. *Reference Services Review*, [e-journal] 39(3), pp. 369–89. Available at: <http://www.emeraldinsight.com/10.1108/00907321111161386> [Accessed 31 October 2014].

Lanclos, D., 2013. *The Anthropologist in the Stacks: Playing with Cognitive Mapping*. [online] Available at: <http://atkinsanthro.blogspot.co.uk/2013/11/playing-with-cognitive-mapping.html> [Accessed 23 November 2014].

McKechnie, L., Dixon, C., Fear, J. and Pollak, A., 2006. Rules of (mis)conduct: User behaviour in public libraries. In: H. Moukdad, ed. 2006. *Information Science Revisited: Approaches to Innovation*. Proceedings of the 34th Annual Conference of the Canadian Association for Information Science, June 1–3, York University, Toronto, Ontario. pp. 1–10. Available at: <http://www.cais-acsi.ca/proceedings/2006/mckechnie_2006. pdf> [Accessed 11 October 2014].

Paretta, L. T. and Catalano, A., 2013. What students really do in the library: An observational study. *The Reference Librarian*, [e-journal] 54(2), pp. 157–67. Available at: <http://www.tandfonline.com/doi/abs/10.1080/02763877.2013.755033> [Accessed 31 October 2014].

Saldana, J., 2013. *The Coding Manual for Qualitative Researchers*. Los Angeles: Sage.

Schensul, S. L., Schensul, J. J. and LeCompte, M. D., 1999. *Essential Ethnographic Methods: Observations, Interviews and Questionnaires*. Walnut Creek: Altamira Press.

Schostak, J. and Schostak, J., 2008. *Radical Research: Designing, Developing and Writing Research to Make a Difference*. New York: Routledge.

Shilling, C. and Cousins, F., 1990. Social use of the school library: The colonisation and regulation of educational space. *British Journal of Sociology of Education*, [e-journal] 11(4), pp. 411–30. Available at: <http://www.jstor.org.libaccess.hud.ac.uk/stable/ 1392876?seq=1> [Accessed 31 October 2014].

Social Research Association, 2003. *Ethical Guidelines*. [pdf] Available at: <http://the-sra. org.uk/research-ethics/ethics-guidelines/> [Accessed 4 November 2014].

Spradley, J. P., 1979. *The Ethnographic Interview*. New York: Holt, Rinehart and Winston.

Suarez, D., 2007. What students do when they study in the library: Using ethnographic methods to observe student behavior. *Electronic Journal of Academic and Special Librarianship*, [e-journal] 8(3), pp. 1–19. Available at: <http://southernlibrarianship. icaap.org/content/v08n03/suarez_d01.html> [Accessed 15 October 2014].

Temple, P., Callender, C., Grove, L. and Kersh, N., 2014. *Managing the Student Experience in a Shifting Higher Education Landscape*. York: Higher Education Academy. Available at: <https://www.heacademy.ac.uk/node/10145> [Accessed 23 November 2014].

3 Embracing an ethnographic agenda

Context, collaboration, and complexity

Donna M. Lanclos

The decision to incorporate ethnography and other qualitative methodologies into the work of libraries can have a transformative effect on institutional practices. Adopting such an approach signals the conviction that institutional spaces should be comprehensible, and not just to insiders. Qualitative approaches to understanding library users provide opportunities, provide space, give chances for breath, reflections, possibilities, and perhaps most important of all, for persuasion.

Libraries are portals today – as they have always been – to content, to information. They are also increasingly locations that provide access to people and tools and places for the creation of something new. As locations for collaboration – among students, among staff, among community members – libraries stake a claim to something new, and something terrifically difficult to quantify. Universities are not just in the business of reproducing their faculty, nor should they be, not any more than they are simply vocational training grounds. Thus, libraries must be about access for all, not about the narrow range of users who will go on to be professional scholars.

Here I discuss traditional usability (UX) work as a subset of ethnographic practices, as one particular way among many of eliciting qualitative data about user behavior, and more importantly as an avenue to transforming institutional practices and increasing the role of library voices in shaping such practices. Taking a policy stance grounded in qualitative research requires reflection, backing away from assumptions and accepting the risk that what is revealed might be uncomfortable or contradict long-standing practices and beliefs about user needs and priorities. Institutions willing to take on those complications can thrive. Institutions that want the publicity that comes from ethnography but not the work, not the ambiguity, and not the full-time commitment will fall short. They will miss the opportunity to transform their practices and fail to find new ways of making arguments about how and why to spend money, resources, and time effectively. However, a methodological turn to the qualitative is not enough; insight also requires an openness to an anthropological worldview, and a willingness to not-know on the way to greater comprehension (Harouni, 2009, 2013; Stommel, 2014).

Ethnography is literally 'writing culture' (Clifford and Marcus, 1986), but is often taken to mean the cluster of techniques that researchers engage in to gather detailed descriptions of everyday behavior. Ethnographic techniques can include but are not limited to participant (or immersive) observation, structured and unstructured interviews, visually based instruments such as photo diaries, and mapping techniques intended to elicit people's interpretations of landscapes and social structures. They provide ways for researchers to gain insight into the logics behind people's behavior by situating their choices in broader social and cultural contexts.

Via ethnographic work, we gather stories, we gather what anthropologists call 'ethnographic authority' – the authority to speak that is grounded in 'being there', in effective representations of our users' realities, because we did the work. Stories can be ambiguous and powerful. Stories can encourage us to learn more. Stories, taken together, can begin to reveal patterns. Those patterns emerge from a better and better known past and present, as revealed in the qualitative data. Interpreting such qualitative data is risky, and opens us up for uncomfortable moments, debates, and possibilities that we might be wrong. I would argue that it is less important to accurately predict changes, for example, than to be able to recognize what is a change, as it is happening, and not be so locked into 'The Way We Do Things' that it's impossible to respond to changes. This is what 'agile' should mean; libraries that purchase furniture, or build a website, or take any other decision thinking that they are establishing something that will last 10 years, cannot respond as effectively to change as those who accept that they may need to change things in 6 months, a week, a year. Perhaps if institutions think decisions should stand for 10 years it does feel more important to predict the future. But a better path is to be plugged in to the present, so that responding quickly to conditions on the ground is more possible, and more effective. 'Agile' then comes from a genuine connection to what is going on, a recognition that sometimes our understanding of what is going on is incomplete, or incorrect, or both, and then a willingness to act on that recognition.

The problem of library legibility, visibility, and voice

Historically, libraries in Western culture have been heavily mediated spaces, with collections/materials as well as buildings that were configured to facilitate that mediation – gates, desks, collections behind doors that could only be accessed by the professionals. Academic buildings, libraries included, are not generally laid out for the benefit of the people who will be using them. They are designed by architects hoping to make a statement about themselves and the institution they are working for; the rooms are numbered by facilities managers who organize the space according to the work their staff need to do. The locations of the buildings are often determined as much by where available space to build exists as by where it would 'make sense' to have the buildings constructed. The ways in which such buildings as libraries, classrooms, and student unions (among others) 'make sense' are not uniform, and depend very much on who is navigating those buildings, and for what purpose. We are now in a time when people are increasingly accustomed to using digital tools (such as Google Maps) and mobile devices (like smartphones) to navigate physical spaces. When they enter most academic buildings, those expectations are thwarted. Library buildings (and, not incidentally, library websites) are traditionally not terrifically intuitive, except to people who have been trained to use them. Unfamiliar buildings and websites can read as unfriendly. And places perceived as unfriendly swiftly become invisible, as they are avoided in favor of places that are familiar and comfortable, such as cafés, bookstores, and the open web.

What makes libraries visible to students? Research indicates that it is not librarians, or library websites (Connaway, White and Lanclos, 2011; Connaway, Hood et al., 2013; Connaway, Lanclos and Hood, 2013; Schoenfeld, 2014). Library resources and the people who work within the library are made visible when attention is paid to the ways that people already search, the cues that they are looking for, and the conventions of the open web. Leveraging relationships that people already have with each other, with their instructors, and with familiar digital tools and places such as Wikipedia, Google, Facebook and Twitter can then make all of the different possibilities within libraries (as spaces, as collections, as communities) visible in the wider web. For libraries to be visible to their communities, discovery cannot depend on prior knowledge of specialized systems. Rather, those specialized systems should become natural extensions of the networks people bring with them to university, and build and extend while they are there.

Library websites are perceived as useful or usable according to the vernacular of the wider web, not just our own local environments. This is likewise true for our physical places – useful places are comprehensive and navigable, not just by expert users but by most people who walk through the doors. Library spaces become more visible as they are more easily discoverable, whether it is through face-to-face opportunities or digital proxies such as virtual tours. Tours, events, classes, and digital tools such as wayfinders and study room booking software can be leveraged to make the library building familiar and more friendly long before students need to use it (and the resources within) during exams, research projects, and collaborative projects. And the tools and spaces in libraries can be made familiar by paying attention to the kinds of places, libraries or otherwise, that attract people. In the same way that the conventions of the open web should inform library (or any institutional) web design, the conventions of comfortable productive 'third places' (public gathering places that are neither homes nor institutions, but in between [Oldenburg, 1989]), such as cafés, can help libraries feel accessible to people who have never been in academic spaces before. When I collect photo diaries from undergraduate students, one common response to 'favorite place in the library' or 'most useful place in the library' is a photo of the library café. This contrasts with the many photos of library stacks filled with books submitted in response to 'most confusing place in the library' or 'least favorite'. If people think there is a café in the library, they have something comforting and known to ease them towards the rest of the less familiar components.

There are increasing numbers of libraries in higher education whose agendas have been taken over by information technology (IT), or dictated by central administration, rather than being approached as partners in the work of the university. But traditionally, library reporting and analytics are largely responses to interlibrary queries and library-centered accreditation processes. Library staff are talking in tight loops to staff in other libraries, or to themselves, with and about their data (ACRL, 2010). The near-frantic levels of quantitative data collecting are therefore going into reports that may or may not get to the people who libraries need to influence. These data reports are the equivalent of LibGuides: tools used by librarians that primarily communicate with other librarians – even if, in the case of LibGuides and quantitative data, they are assembled with the intention of also communicating outside of the library. At the same time, people who run and work in libraries are worried (and rightfully so) about getting the right sort of attention, generally in the form of resources, from their universities.

The kind of quantitative data traditionally collected by libraries has not proved effective for talking outside of the library, not for reaching the people they need to reach within and outside of their institutions. The problem of library visibility is evident from the persistent anxious discourses about the Future of Libraries, the Threats to Libraries (especially the Threats to Funding of Libraries), and the Utility of MLIS Degrees, and the problem of the lack of library voices in higher education policy made evident in the examples of academic libraries being radically cut, or taken over by non-library parts of the university – their voices muffled if not silenced altogether. Too many libraries have lost their voices, or are only using them to talk to individuals or parts of the institution who cannot help with their agenda. Buildings being built or spaces being planned on university campuses powerfully resemble things that I would call 'libraries', but many are not called that. There are 'hubs' and 'learning centers' and 'commons'. 'Library' is a word that has associations that some people think should be left behind, but part of the power of the word library is that it can mean so much:

> Books. Quiet. Shelves. Distraction. Friends. Computers. Space. Librarians. Refuge. Anxiety. Café. Printing. Scholarship. Community.

Qualitative data and the research agendas that yield such data can provide paths towards a stronger voice for libraries in higher education, and more effective policies on behalf of library users. Qualitative approaches point the way to building the relationships necessary to demonstrate and further develop the important role of academic libraries within higher education. Libraries cannot build relationships by counting things. Rather, connections emerge from work, with collaboration, from being embedded into the work of higher education. This is work that has always been done within libraries, and it is more important than ever to make that work visible and explicitly connected.

The complicated strengths of qualitative research techniques

Qualitative research in libraries has two primary purposes: to improve user experiences and to more effectively communicate with those who fund and otherwise support libraries. Qualitative research is messy, in execution as well as in the data it yields. The stories it can tell may be unclear or contradictory. Paradoxically, this can lead to simpler policies, less messy procedures, a clarity of configurations born from a sense of the sheer variety of human behavior, and the need for flexibility to accommodate that variability. Telling stories, using the data to tell stories, can sound trivial, and can be rejected as 'anecdotal'. But there is a power in stories, in their relationships with one another, their resonance with a lived reality that is not effectively represented in spreadsheets and bar charts. Qualitative data gives us a chance to represent our patrons as people. This is not trivial. Numbers get in the way of our recognizing that we work with people. Being forced to transform human experiences into numbers by the institutional assessment requirements is not just awkward and time-consuming, but frequently does not facilitate effective arguments for human-centered, grounded policy.

Qualitative practitioners such as anthropologists should ideally be embedded in libraries as full-time members of staff: capturing, collecting, collating and disseminating those stories is far more possible in a situation where one is consistently present, capable of seeing things as they happen, capable of absorbing and collecting more context. This is the model for my own position at UNC Charlotte, and was for Nancy Foster's position at Rochester (Foster and Gibbons, 2007). Allocating a full-time position to such work can be a challenge to resources, but can yield benefits in voice, in influence, and ultimately in potential for more and different resources in the long term.

For example, on the ground floor of my workplace, the J. Murrey Atkins Library, ethnographic methods helped give us the information we needed to tell effective stories to administrators about the kinds of spaces we needed to configure for our students (Lanclos, 2015). Taking photos of student workspaces in the library revealed the amount of 'spread' they required for all of the materials that they have with them while studying: books, tablets, laptops, paper notebooks, phones, calculators, food and drinks. Observations on the main floors of the library revealed that students working together at computer tables didn't have enough space to sit, and could not easily share materials on one regular desktop computer screen. Photo diaries we collected over several semesters revealed that students do not just sit at desks in task chairs when they are writing research papers, but sit on couches, or even in their beds. Academic workspaces are varied outside of the library, but were fairly homogenous in Atkins pre-2009: there was only one couch, and the two modes were either at hard furniture (tables or carrels) or in soft (single) seating with coffee tables. Group study was only possible in a few bookable rooms. Our new ground-floor study commons has varied types of furniture; bookable spaces for small and large groups; and many screens with integrated computers, so that students can either plug in their own device or walk into the library without any technology and still be able to do the work they need for their classes. Glass walls throughout ensure that students can see the work that their peers at the university are doing, providing a visual for the academic community of practice of which they are members. The library has become more usable, in adding this space that did not exist before. The students have more access, institutionally, to the resources they need for their studies.

Institutions that do not have the resources to dedicate a full-time position to qualitative data collection and analysis would do well to carefully consider how they can incorporate qualitative practices into the workflow of their current staff – what are they currently doing that is less effective than qualitative approaches? What more can be gained, substituting or supplementing current library work for some of these techniques? In addition to providing an opportunity for more and better learning places for our students, the attention paid to UX and ethnography has made Atkins Library, at this point 5 years after we started with agendas, an authoritative voice in our university around physical and digital policies. The library is not just in the library anymore. Our engagement with these methods has given us a voice that is heard, a place at the table, and resources for our community.

Usability as a motive

Why do we care about usability? Institutions can care about usability in the service of selling more things to more people. They can care about the behavioral logic of their 'customers' so that there are increasing levels of satisfaction with what is bought or consumed, and also a loyalty to institutions who provide good experiences. That is the marketing approach: 'Try us, you'll like it, we're easy.'

Usability is a perspective, a philosophy, a conviction that systems and buildings and signs can be created that are self-evident, widely intelligible, and do not require mediation. Being motivated by usability signals a concern for access – if the environment surrounding resources is not usable, then it does not matter how high a quality the resources are, they will not benefit any user, because they will not be engaging with those resources. If patrons cannot figure out how to navigate EBSCO, it does not matter how much libraries have paid for access to the peer-reviewed articles in those databases; the articles will not be used.

Higher education is a public service. Universities are portals of information, and resources for people who need more than information. Education should ideally facilitate the development of people who can use information effectively and think critically about information. Such people need partners in navigating the information landscape – libraries can be those partners, and can also contribute to building the information landscape so that it is as accessible and usable as possible.

If libraries are about access, then usability is a crucial part of that mission. One has to only think about all of the things public libraries are used for – medical knowledge, legal knowledge, job seeking, psychological seeking, social reaching-out. Some things people will not do if they have to be mediated; they will just give up. Making sure that library resources are accessible is the reason that it is important to take the risk of de-centering our expertise, to allow people who are not librarians to speak to what libraries mean for them, independent of our individual or institutional intentions. This is not to say that libraries should give up their voices, but that they make an awareness of the priorities of all of the people using their physical and digital spaces a central part of policy discussions, and so inform the library voice with a grounded knowledge of the priorities and behaviors of their academic community.

Usability is about more than our own places and how they work, and also far more than the digital. It is about the places our users go, and what they need to do in the course of their academic work, and how our resources do or don't articulate well with those environments. The persistence of books as resources that students want and need (either as library resources or bought to own) is in part because of the places where they need to work – not necessarily with Wi-Fi, not necessarily with electricity, not necessarily with the resources themselves to buy the devices that require Wi-Fi and electricity, and that can also serve as e-readers. To what degree can buses and trains be seen as learning spaces? Why or why not? If you are concerned about usability of websites on mobile devices, are you paying attention to whether or not people have access to mobile devices at all? Do they have access to the textbooks they need? What impact do electronic texts have on access? Usability is implicated in all of these questions.

For example, when we in Atkins Library committed to only buying electronic book packages that are unlimited use and DRM-free, that was a decision that facilitated access for students and instructors to materials they use for teaching and learning (http://library.uncc.edu/etextbooks). At least 100 textbooks per semester are available through the library, at no additional cost to our students or faculty, because of proactive policy decisions around vendor contracts and electronic resources. Simply making sure that the contracts allowed for the sort of use of these materials that we know our patrons need is paying attention to usability and to access.

Effective usability: time-wasting and accessibility

Digital spaces such as library websites are operational spaces where information has been organized according to principles that are likely to be unfamiliar to non-expert users (Kim Wu and Lanclos, 2011). Even outside of academia, the need for attention to usability looms large in an environment of increasing expectations by everyday users of those digital spaces for easy navigability and intuitive content – think about the difference between the interfaces of the Google search page and that of EBSCOhost. Corporate and commercial spaces engage in wayfinding practices to drive their customers into places that the company wants them to go. In IKEA, for example (Potente and Salvini, 2009, pp. 38–41), the path is clear, and laden with things the people could buy; the directional pathmaking is masterful, clearly intended to walk customers past as much merchandise as possible, so they can be maximally encouraged to purchase something. Recall, too, that the motives of entities such as Google and IKEA are not the same things that motivate libraries (increased access to knowledge) but by increased access, ultimately, to money.

Those working within academic spaces should not be in the business of directing people to where we think they should go, or in profiting from the information we gather about their behavior, but we should be invested in in helping people find where they need to be. Individuals enter university spaces with their own priorities. Effective usability, in this context, is about allowing students and faculty to find their own way to the resources important to them, swiftly and effectively, in physical and digital environments alike.

If our systems are so complicated and our buildings so illegible that they require mediation, that people walking into our libraries or encountering our web environments for the first time have to come to us for help in navigating links or hallways, we are wasting everyone's time. We are wasting time being tour guides, traffic cops, gatekeepers, that could otherwise be spent having conversations, picking things apart, writing things, producing content, analyzing thoughts, or making something new.

Universities and their libraries have a responsibility to be accessible. The purpose of education is not to produce people to work at jobs. It is to produce effective citizens, engaged human beings, people not just capable of independent thought but people who revel in it, who are so good at it that they come up with solutions to problems, that we make the world around us a more engaging, more constructive, more supportive, better place. If the only people who can comprehend what we are doing are the people who already know the ways to navigate complicated institutional places, then we are not educating, but sorting.

Critical thinking happens in groups – distributed critical cognition about value and authority happens all around us. It is particularly visible on the web in the form of reviews of things such as books, movies, and products to purchase, but is also present in blog conversations about theory, in Twitter discussions of policy, in Facebook fights about inappropriate jokes and memes. Libraries and universities provide nodes where people can come together to think, to argue, to consume with an eye to produce. Usability study techniques can help us think about the kind of environments that provide shortcuts to that production of content. UX approaches can facilitate thinking about physical and digital places that don't get in the way but that accelerate the process of scholarship, of communication, of effective policy, of education.

> The most profound technologies are those that disappear. They weave themselves into the fabric of everyday life until they are indistinguishable from it.
> (Weiser, 1991, p. 78; see also discussion in
> Dourish and Bell [2011], especially pp. 9–11)

Ethnography as a method

An effective ethnographic agenda in libraries should be about the comprehension of behavior whether it involves the library or not. Ethnographic practices, anthropological understandings of what is going on, can help situate the very idea of usability, and in particular help us realize that even notions of 'usable' are culturally constructed. In terms of usability, ethnographic techniques can help answer broader questions than whether the website is usable or intuitive. Once engaged with ethnography, we can ask: What are people doing when they talk about 'intuitive' design? Intuitive for whom? What constitutes 'intuitive'? Who defines it? What is that experience, of feeling something 'intuitive'? In a slightly different context, we can ask: What is studying? Is it the same as 'learning'? Who is in charge? Is that a meaningful question? What are the power structures we can reveal by tracing the actions and reactions of students, faculty, and staff in academic spaces? What is made, what is observable? What can we see, what needs more work before it can be shown?

What happens when we approach Google not as a competitor to the library, but as a made thing, a result of cultural processes? (Beer, 2009; Asher, Duke and Wilson, 2013). What happens when we see that students are writing research papers on subway cars using their phones? (Smale and Regalado, 2014).

Ethnographic approaches necessarily explode usability out of the library into the spaces where people are, because the things that people do in the library are only part of the wide range of things that they need to do, and are often informed by those other things (schedules, people, other commitments, etc.). This is very effectively revealed in cognitive mapping exercises (Asher and Miller, 2011, p. 14), wherein students and faculty are invited to draw their academic landscapes. In 6 minutes they produce a color-coded sketch (occasionally a list) of all of the places they inhabit or visit when doing their academic work. At this point I have collected maps from the UK and the US, and in each case participants map the library as part of a larger system (Gourlay, Lanclos and Oliver, 2015). An undergraduate map from Charlotte, North Carolina, shows the dotted lines of the movement of a student from her apartment, to her friend's house, to the fast-food restaurant (which has free 24-hour Wi-Fi) near where she works, to the university campus, and the classroom buildings where she lurks in hallways between lectures until she has time to settle into the Student Union for a break and more studying (thanks to more Wi-Fi), or the library for the same, depending on where her next class is located on campus. A map from a faculty member shows not only all of the different university libraries in the Bloomsbury area of London that he frequents, but also the chair and footstool where he sits to work at home (along with his cat), his office at the university, the nearby café where he meets with his graduate students, and the universities in the US where he does archival research. Each location mapped is visited because of a nested series of motivations, including the need for resources (information, archival materials), space (for sitting, reading), and people (meeting with professors, fellow students, colleagues); to work, to eat, to access Wi-Fi, to have a place to land between classes when the commute to the university is long and it is not easy to get home in the middle of the day.

Think about the difference between a map of a university and the kinds of subjective representations of places and connections yielded by cognitive maps. Such maps reveal all the things we cannot see if we limit our observations to institutional spaces. The mapping exercises reveal that libraries are places within a network of places, institutions embedded in larger structures. Being aware of the wider context in which libraries exist can help us realize, for example, that solutions to problems that do not originate in the library cannot be offered only by the library and hope to succeed. If there is a general shortage of study space on campus, that might be revealed in the library, but might not be solvable by the library working alone, particularly on large university campuses where it can be hard for students to easily get back to the library from their lecture hall, on their way to another lecture or tutorial. If there is a problem with printing on campus, it may be particularly visible in the library (particularly when end-of-semester papers are due), but it is seldom possible for the library working on its own to solve that problem, either. Once we see the network, it is possible for libraries to call on other parts of the network to work towards a solution. But without seeing the network, it is too easy to assume that libraries exist in isolation, and have no resources beyond themselves to address problems, or to reach for new resources for new initiatives.

Ethnographic approaches to usability studies can draw attention to the ways that people think with tools, and address the need to attend to the play of the physical and digital together. In his work on embodied cognition, anthropologist Kirsh (2001) describes situations when 'we literally think with things'. Behavior studies can capture the moment when thinking occurs with (or is stifled by) things – with places, with tools, with websites.

People can often realize the potential of certain tools and resources only after they are using them. It is hard to think about what will happen in the abstract, when it is in fact the whole experience that is relevant. Asking people to think about 'the digital' or 'technology' and asking them to describe it as separate from their everyday lived reality ignores how integrated it is into their physical relationship with the world. When I interview students about technology, they spend very little time before switching over to talking about tasks, or people, or places. It is necessary to think about digital and physical places and tools together because that is how people experience them. Counting the number of students who have mobile devices, how many times laptops circulate from the library, or the number of hits on particular web pages does not capture this holistic experience of digital tools in physical places. Qualitative methods, some of them ethnographic such as observation and participation, can yield a holistic perspective, beyond whether something is either used, or indeed 'usable'. People perceive the world as a related whole, and institutions require techniques such as those in the ethnographic toolkit to reveal these perceptions, and make them part of the information available to help inform policy decisions.

Asking questions

In his discussion of learning spaces, Bennett (2007, pp. 14–15) points to the importance of persistently asking questions, and to careful attention to the actual practices of people in spaces, regardless of the intent that went into the design of spaces. One cannot mistake the intent of the architect for the actual behaviors that then take place in the places post-construction. Studying and other academic practices are embedded in particular cultural histories. Libraries are rife with controlling processes (Nader, 1997); they are cultural institutions infused with very particular senses of what scholarship and studying looks and sounds like, what the proper material environments are for such activities, and what resources should be provided by institutions (and what should not be). Rules around noise and quiet, consumption of food and drink, occupancy of space (When is the library closed?

Does it close? Who is allowed in? Who is prevented?) are all performances of institutional control of library spaces. These rules are shot through with power: Who determines what is quiet? What is noise? Who makes the decision about who is allowed in the library?

Bennett's article treats questions as important, and does not assume they have easy answers. How might one answer them? Ethnographic techniques can be a part of the solution to that dilemma. It is important to keep asking questions, and in particular important not to presume you will always know the answer, and to involve lots of people in answering them. And keep (persistently) asking them. Questioning can be teaching as well as learning. Effective questions require knowledge beforehand. You have to know something about the situation on the ground before you start asking good questions, ones that will yield insight and paths to solutions and innovations. This is a pedagogy of questions, a way of teaching and learning by asking, by deliberately positioning oneself as not-knowing (Bruss and Macedo, 1985; Harouni, 2009, 2013; Stommel, 2014; White, 2014). An anthropological perspective is one that generates questions. And in the process of asking questions, we discover that it is more than a pedagogical practice, but an ontology – queries nested within other queries, things we do not know influenced by what we never found out.

Finding a voice in higher education depends in part on generating interesting questions. This is far more useful than telling people what they should do. An anthropological perspective is one that generates questions. Asking questions is crucial, as is accepting the fact that many of the answers we uncover are problems. Ethnographic techniques can be a part of that exploratory process, of figuring out what questions to ask, which ones might be answerable, which ones are important to follow up on. And it is in our accurate identification of problems that we can be truly useful. When people think that one sort of thing is 'wrong' their perceptions of why that situation has come to pass can be incomplete, or completely off-base. When some of the answers we provide are the outlines of problems, we are also creating space for identifying opportunities. Then we become truly worth listening to.

And the joy of it all is that we, for all the answers we offer, do not have to come up with solutions alone. That is the other part of what is at stake. Once people are listening to us, we can engage them as part of the solution, or many solutions. We no longer, in this scenario, have to be subjected to solutions imposed on us from without. We can generate solutions as a team, with our colleagues in higher education.

Anthropology as a worldview

Engaging with qualitative techniques provides chances to elicit and tell powerful stories. Quantitative techniques tend to reduce or hide complexities, and give us the impression that we can predict the future, that we can see where things will definitely go. The 'Library of the Future' has a strong pull, inspiring conferences, blogposts, articles, and even jobs with the title 'future' in them. Perhaps it seems to those talking about the future of libraries is that they are talking about the importance of libraries. The danger is that there is actually no accurate way to predict the future. Predicating library's argument for attention, resources, and influence on a nebulous future is potentially less effective than arguments grounded in what is, and the vivid potential of the current opportunities, in the present (Boellstorf, 2014).

In anthropology, there is a long tradition of historical approaches to current cultural practices, and a similar tension between the desire to know what might come next, and the need to be grounded in current practices. Matti Bunzl (2004, p. 441) argues that effective anthropological approaches constitute a 'history of the present'. Anthropologists attempt via description and interpretation to represent the result of historical processes, to describe the product of prior processes, to get a picture of where we are now.

Deeply understanding the present of libraries and higher education can help us think more clearly about how we are limiting or facilitating a wide range of possibilities, not just the ones we think the numbers might be telling us. We can point to numbers as a supplement to a particular picture of reality. The decline in print circulation is a good example – that fact needs to be informed by the larger context, which is that people are still reading, just in electronic versions. The decline in print circulation may also point to print materials (particularly bound journals and monographs) becoming something that stays in academic buildings rather than going home with users. In interviews I have conducted with students about their research habits, it becomes clear that some of them are using print resources (e.g. books or article printouts) when they want to engage deeply with the material they are reading. Students and faculty alike who are reading something new or challenging often interact with their print resources: highlighting, taking notes on the page, flipping easily back and forth between points that are related. Individuals who have long public transportation commutes take advantage of the fact that print resources do not depend on battery life or Wi-Fi connections to be read. Preferences for electronic versions of resources can stem from concerns about expense (sometimes the resource is available in the library so they do not have to purchase it themselves) and also convenience (if it's available online they might not have to enter the physical building), to name just a couple of examples. Some individuals keep many of the resources they use in electronic form so that they can work with them wherever they are, without having to carry a lot of paper with them. Some individuals want the paper with them because their access to digital devices or spaces is unreliable. The point, from a library perspective, is that there is no universal pattern around the uses of digital or analog resources, because the everyday material conditions of people's lives mean that both modes are still necessary. Institutions should therefore continue to be prepared to offer both, even as they pay attention to innovations in digital resources that close the gap between what is possible on paper and what is possible on screens.

Cognitive mapping techniques can be used to reveal a broader picture of the learning landscapes of students and faculty. Such a picture can be used to inform libraries not just of what their place is in the workflow of the university community.

Recognizing the non-library, non-institutional spaces in which people are doing academic work points to the need for policy solutions to institutional problems to go beyond local conditions. Sometimes library-located problems require larger systemic solutions. Sometimes university-evident problems require city-level solutions. Identifying the larger network allows for the opportunity to identify potential partners in working towards solutions.

This is not, therefore, simply an argument for libraries to engage with ethnography as a method, but ultimately for libraries to benefit from the perspective that comes from anthropology as a worldview. The holistic consideration of the nature of human behavior in academia, in society, can inform the whys and hows of university and library policies, spaces, workflows, and resources. Dourish and Bell (2011) call out ethnography as more than describing and defining bounded categories – it is about tracing, describing, identifying the processes, practices, and associations from which emerge the stuff of culture. Anthropology is invested in the interpretation of what is described, trying to understand the meaning of what has been uncovered in the course of practicing ethnography. Anthropological approaches to ethnography do not settle for descriptions of systems, but strive for explorations of meaning, interpretive acts that lead to insights, and frequently more questions.

Anthropological insights and student experience

When one person sees a library as a system, and the other sees it as an artifact, then there is a need to translate, to recalibrate the frames, so that a conversation, an engagement can happen, not just ineffective talking past one another. This is particularly important with regard to policy discussions. Insights derived from adopting an anthropological worldview should be just the start of a much larger agenda in libraries and higher education. Making systems and spaces navigable and legible is important if we take our mission of access seriously. Understanding why something is unnavigable or illegible in the first place takes a deeper understanding, and can lead to insights beyond design, to organization, culture, and process.

Think of the act of ethnographic description, the moment of anthropological insight, as a simultaneous act of deconstruction. It is theoretical, analytical, and transformative. Libraries need more than ethnographic methods, they need such practices to be informed by anthropological perspectives. For example, competence and incompetence are culturally constructed. Success within particular educational contexts – including universities and their libraries – derives directly from the level of participation within those contexts. Participation can mean a variety of things, and there is not necessarily one 'correct' way to participate. Universities are composed of interlocking communities of practice that students and faculty alike need to move among as they pursue their studies (Lave and Wenger, 1991). While all students are non-dominant in the hierarchy of higher education, some have more privilege than others, in terms of familiarity with higher education, as well as economically and socially. The implications for student practice, for students moving into university or library space without knowledge of practices of scholarly community are that these things can be learned, but are not 'natural' and are therefore the responsibility of educators, including library staff as well as individuals in traditional faculty roles.

Ethnographic techniques are methods that provide a way to connect the practices of students with the practices of academia (of the library, of their professors) (e.g. Bhatt, 2014). These methods can also reveal connections between the practices of faculty and those located within the library. And importantly, casting an ethnographic eye on the totality of student experience means that we can more easily reveal the locations where students cannot connect effectively to the places, resources, and practices of academia. Locating the moments where students have less access than they should to resources, less knowledge than they need to effectively use these resources, is a crucial service to the people who work at universities, and who are committed to educating citizens. Anthropological perspectives on academia provide opportunities for pause, reflection, and seeing how to emerge from that moment with new practices that are more effective at meeting needs and providing engagement.

Students socializing in the library are engaging in a form of what Lave and Wenger (1991) call 'legitimate peripheral participation' – moments where people hang back on the margins, see what is going on, or engage in a preliminary way with what they need to do. Chatting with friends in the library places students in a location where they can also witness studying all night for finals, poring over the archives in special collections, or writing a dissertation in a graduate student carrel. The practice of 'studying along' (Bennett, 2007), neither in groups nor solo, is a perfect example of an opportunity that students give themselves, in the comfortable network of their friends and classmates, to see and assimilate a variety of academic behaviors. We see revealed the importance of recognizing the socially embedded nature of studying, academic practice.

Students, much like faculty and other library users, engage in a variety of ways of defining 'quiet'. It rarely means silent, and often means still and focusing in a way that isn't entirely auditory. I have seen this in my own fieldwork in the US and the UK. Students define libraries that are unfamiliar to them as 'quiet' in large part because there are no people there who know them, and so they are relatively undisturbed (regardless of actual noise level). In other cases any noise at all being made by unknown people is cast as a disturbance, because individuals do not recognize what 'those people' are doing as studying. The social dimensions of learning, the fact that study behaviors are embedded in larger cultural contexts, in class, in race, in gender – these are all things to consider and to ask about when confronted with something like the Noise and Quiet debate in libraries.

Social and cultural contexts of learning apply to both physical and digital places. It is therefore important for us to understand the motivations not just for engagement with physical places and services, but also behind people's persistent love affairs with digital (non-library) places and resources such as Google and Wikipedia. I have, in the course of several research projects (e.g. Visitors and Residents, see Connaway, White and Lanclos, 2011; Connaway, Hood et al., 2013;

Connaway, Lanclos and Hood, 2013) interviewed more than one undergraduate who called Google a 'best friend'. Libraries don't run Google (more's the pity, financially). Our institutional lack of control over the web interfaces that our community members use the most means we need to think about usability of systems that are not local, as well as the ones that are. The usability implications include personnel and workflows – if we know the library website needs to be changed, who do we have to do it? If we do not have control over all of the web environments that patrons engage in, what are the implications? How can we make the leap from describing problems to designing solutions? The key here is that we may find answers through our investigations. But we cannot work alone towards solutions. Finding solutions has to be a collaborative endeavor.

Conclusions

Because problems do not have one particular solution, and because innovation rarely comes from homogenous environments, collaboration is the key to successful solutions to the problems and opportunities identified by ethnographic observation and description, and anthropological analysis. Multiple disciplines, multiple people should be working together within libraries, enriching the policy decisions and grounding them in a rich context of information and meaning (e.g. Delcore et al., 2009). We cannot and should never expect one person to contain all of the expertise necessary for these multidisciplinary efforts; all of these things require expertise, they are proper jobs in themselves, and they deserve the respect of full-time work.

Anthropological insights do not necessarily flow directly from the gathering of observations of UX or ethnographic data of other kinds. Training and expertise should not be taken lightly. When qualitative researchers are brought in as consultants, there is some pressure to please customers, however much we researchers might value our potential role as provocateurs. When anthropologists and other social scientists are hired full-time in libraries, we are colleagues, and our provocations, our awkward questions, our explorations of issues and patterns that are not immediately related to problems at hand are in service of the greater good. We are invested in the organization, we want our work to contribute long term, we have the time, the bandwidth, the organizational support for trying and failing and occasionally going into dark corners that people don't habitually visit.

UX, ethnographic practices, and anthropological insights should all be just the start of a much larger agenda in libraries and higher education. The act of ethnography, the interpretive lenses that anthropology can inspire, can help us fight agendas that are destructive to that educational project – being deeply embedded in the behaviors and in the lives of our students and our faculty can refute the vocational narrative of neoliberal educational policy. It is crucial that libraries contribute alternatives to notions of education that cast the role of universities as places that 'get people jobs'. The people who make up our institutions are more than a list of certifications, more than the money they might make, far more than the boxes they tick off as they work through their course modules in pursuit of their major. Those people are revealed with qualitative research. Their stories move policy makers.

We do not have to take policy makers' word for it. We do not have to take conformity to web templates lying down. We do not have to believe them when they tell us that students no longer read, or will only communicate via text, or have lost the ability to think critically. We can push back, and point out the explosion of different kinds of reading, of all the different places where communication happens, that it's our responsibility to model and teach critical thinking, not just assume that it will show up as they arrive on campus. We can leverage our grounded sense of the lives and priorities of people to make effective arguments, to drive our own agenda.

References

ACRL, 2010. *The Value of Academic Libraries: A Comprehensive Research Review and Report*. [pdf] Available at: <http://www.ala.org/acrl/sites/ala.org.acrl/files/content/issues/value/val_report.pdf> [Accessed 23 January 2015].Asher, A. D., Duke, L. M. and Wilson, S., 2013. Paths of discovery: Comparing the search effectiveness of EBSCO Discovery Service, Summon, Google Scholar, and conventional library resources. *College & Research Libraries*, 74(5), pp. 464–88.

Asher, A. D. and Miller, S., 2011. *So You Want to Do Anthropology in Your Library? Or a Practical Guide to Ethnographic Research in Academic Libraries*. [pdf] Available at: <http://www.erialproject.org/wp-content/uploads/2011/03/Toolkit-3.22.11.pdf> [Accessed 3 February 2015].

Beer, D., 2009. Power through the algorithm? Participatory web cultures and the technological unconscious. *New Media & Society*, 11(6), pp. 985–1002.

Bennett, S., 2007. First questions for designing higher education learning spaces. *The Journal of Academic Librarianship*, 33(1), pp. 14–26.

Bhatt, I., 2014. Curation as Digital Literary Practice. *Ibrar's Space*, [blog] 21 May. Available at: <http://ibrarspace.net/2014/05/21/curation-as-a-digital-literacy-practice/> [Accessed 23 January 2015].

Boellstorf, T., 2014. Trending Ethnography: Notes on Import, Prediction, and Digital Culture. *Culture Digitally* blog, [blog] 27 January. Available at: <http://culturedigitally.org/2014/01/trending-ethnography-notes-on-import-prediction-and-digital-culture/> [Accessed 23 January 2015].Bruss, N. and Macedo, D. P., 1985. Toward a pedagogy of the question: Conversations with Paulo Freire. *Journal of Education*, 167(2), pp. 7–21.

Bunzl, M., 2004. Boas, Foucault, and the 'Native Anthropologist': Notes toward a Neo-Boasian Anthropology. *American Anthropologist*, 106(3), pp. 435–42.

Clifford, J. and Marcus, G. E. eds, 1986. *Writing Culture: The Poetics and Politics of Ethnography*. Berkeley: University of California Press.

Connaway, L. S., Hood, E. M., Lanclos, D. M., White, D. and Le Cornu, A., 2013. User-centered decision making: A new model for developing academic library services and systems. *IFLA Journal*, 39(1), pp. 20–9.

Connaway, L. S., Lanclos, D. M. and Hood, E. M., 2013. 'I always stick with the first thing that comes up on Google . . .' Where People Go for Information, What They Use, and Why. *Educause Review Online* [online]. Available at: <http://www.educause.edu/ero/article/i-always-stick-first-thing-comes-google-where-people-go-information-what-they-use-and-why> [Accessed 23 January 2015].

Connaway, L. S., White, D. and Lanclos, D. M., 2011. Visitors and residents: What motivates engagement with the digital information environment? *Proceedings of the American Society for Information Science and Technology*, 48(1), pp. 1–7.

Delcore, H. D., Mullooly, J., Scroggins, M., Arnold, K., Franco, E. and Gaspar, J., 2009. *The Library Study at Fresno State*. [pdf] Available at: <http://www.csufresno.edu/anthro pology/ipa/TheLibraryStudy(DelcoreMulloolyScroggins).pdf> [Accessed 23 January 2015].

Dourish, P. and Bell, G., 2011. *Divining a Digital Future: Mess and Mythology in Ubiqui-tous Computing*. Cambridge, MA: MIT Press.

Foster, N. F. and Gibbons, S. eds, 2007. *Studying Students: The Undergraduate Research Project at the University of Rochester*. Chicago: Association of College and Research Libraries.

Gourlay, L., Lanclos, D. M. and Oliver, M., 2015. Sociomaterial texts, spaces and devices: Questioning 'digital dualism' in library and study practices. *Higher Education Quarterly*, 69(3), pp. 263–78.

Harouni, H., 2009. High school research and critical literacy: Social studies with and despite Wikipedia. *Harvard Educational Review*, 79(3), pp. 473–94.

Harouni, H., 2013. The risking of observations in the classroom: Teacher as cultural critic. *Curriculum and Teaching Dialogue*, 15(1–2), p. 57.Kim Wu, S. and Lanclos, D. M., 2011. Re-imagining the users' experience: An ethnographic approach to web usability and space design. *Reference Services Review*, 39(3), pp. 369–89.

Kirsh, D., 2001. The context of work. *Human–Computer Interaction*, 16(2–4), pp. 305–22. Lanclos, D. M., 2015. Ethnographic Techniques and New Visions for Libraries. In: B. Showers, ed. *Library Analytics and Metrics*. London: Facet. pp. 96–107.

Lave, J. and Wenger, E., 1991. *Situated Learning: Legitimate Peripheral Participation*. Cambridge: Cambridge University Press.

Nader, L., 1997. Controlling processes: Tracing the dynamic components of power. *Current Anthropology*, 38(5), pp. 711–37.

Oldenburg, R., 1989. *The Great Good Place: Café, Coffee Shops, Community Centers, Beauty Parlors, General Stores, Bars, Hangouts, and How They Get You Through the Day*. New York: Paragon House.

Potente, D. and Salvini, E., 2009. Apple, IKEA and their integrated architecture. *Bulletin of the American Society for Information Science and Technology*, 35(4), pp. 32–42.

Schoenfeld, R. C., 2014. Does Discovery Still Happen in the Library? Roles and Strategies for a Shifting Reality. *Ithaka S+R Issue Brief*, [online]. Available at: <http://sr.ithaka.org/sites/default/files/files/SR_Briefing_Discovery_20140924_0.pdf> [Accessed 23 January 2015].

Smale, M. and Regalado, M., 2014. Commuter Students Using Technology. *Educause Review Online*, [online]. Available at: <http://www.educause.edu/ero/article/commuter-students-using-technology> [Accessed 23 January 2015].

Stommel, J., 2014. Critical Digital Pedagogy: A Definition. *Hybrid Pedagogy*, [online]. Avail-able at: <http://www.hybridpedagogy.com/journal/critical-digital-pedagogy-definition/> [Accessed 23 January 2015].

Weiser, M., 1991. The computer for the 21st century. *Scientific American*, 265(3), pp. 94–104.

White, D., 2014. Wikimania. *Digital-Learning-Culture*, [blog] 21 September. Available at: <http://daveowhite.com/wikimania/> [Accessed 23 January 2015].

4 Holistic UX

Harness your library's data fetish to solve the right problems

Matt Borg and Matthew Reidsma

> Dirk Gently's Holistic Detective Agency. We solve the *whole* crime. We find the *whole* person. Phone today for the *whole* solution to your problem. (Missing cats and messy divorces a speciality.)
> —Douglas Adams, *Dirk Gently's Holistic Detective Agency*

A few years ago, the University of Michigan's Library in Ann Arbor, Michigan, photographed students holding signs they had made describing their ideal library (University of Michigan, 2012). Many of the photographs seem silly at first glance, but most asked for comfortable study spaces, free hot chocolate or coffee, or social opportunities (Figure 4.1).

As librarians, the desire to help is built into our profession. It forms part of our working life, our interactions with people, our professional training, our continuing development. It even features as part of Ranganathan's laws.

The Michigan Library's 'ideal library' photos remind us that the types of 'help' we often think of giving to our users – tutorials, better access to licensed material, more and better books, wayfinding – are only part of the picture. Many of the students' requests, from 'hammocks in the library' to 'free desserts' to 'soothing music', are all expressions of a desire to be free from worry. Our users may not understand right away that one research database is better suited for their project, but they feel strongly about the comfort of the chairs they sit in or the availability of caffeine within the library walls.

The requests of these students, far from being flippant, are just as valid as the ones we intuit from our professional expertise. In fact, we'd argue that they are more important. In order to help our patrons, we need to rely less on our 'expert intuition' and move to a model of 'expert listening'. By thoroughly listening to our patrons, we can gain a more holistic view of their needs. While we might not install hammocks in front of the new coffee bar's fireplace, we can certainly understand the anxiety our patrons feel and work to help put them at ease.

If we can use data from a number of sources and really listen to our patrons, we can better understand the *whole* of their experience. Like the eponymous detective Dirk Gently in Douglas Adams's novel, to truly help we need to see the *whole* patron. We need to solve the *whole* problem, and fully see how the patron moves through the *whole* library.

Figure 4.1 University of Michigan students' 'ideal library'
Source: Matthew Reidsma.

In this chapter we'll share our real-life examples from Sheffield Hallam University in South Yorkshire and Grand Valley State University in Michigan, in which we have tried to improve our patrons' *whole* experience.

The data has been here all along

In seventeenth-century London, data wasn't something that too many people worried about. Records were expensive to keep, and those that did exist often were in handwritten ledgers unknown to everyone but those who added the entries. However, at the beginning of the seventeenth century, officials in London began keeping records of the burials of those who had died from the plague in an attempt to better understand and prepare for outbreaks. These 'mortality rolls' were recorded weekly, and by the 1630s deaths other than those due to the plague were being recorded.

Although the data was collected to help understand and prepare for outbreaks, it doesn't appear that the parish clerks in London ever did much to fulfil this goal. But nearly 50 years after parishes began regularly reporting mortality rolls, a middle-aged haberdasher named John Graunt began analysing the data himself. His book, *Natural and Political Observations Made Upon the Bills of Mortality* (1662), would change the world forever, creating the modern fields of public health and demography.

By looking at a few decades' worth of data, Graunt produced the first 'life table', which let Londoners know their chances of surviving to different ages. In addition, he catalogued 81 causes of death in four major categories. By seeing these different causes of death all laid out, others began asking the questions of how to prevent many of these types of deaths, leading to the birth of epidemiology (Schultz, 2014).

Graunt took data collected to serve a limited purpose – understanding the plague's reach – and used it to get a bigger, more holistic picture of the public health of Londoners. Rather than make assumptions about the life expectancy of Londoners, he listened to the data. He was an *expert listener*, and his work went on to help countless people.

In libraries, we can follow Graunt's example by co-opting the data we're already collecting to get a more holistic view of our interactions with patrons. By shedding our assumptions and intuition, and letting what we hear from our patrons and the data they create guide us, we can make improvements that will help our patrons.

Chances are, you already have available in your library most of the data you need to make a better experience for your patrons. At Grand Valley and Sheffield Hallam, we have worked to bring together four different strands of data to give us our holistic view.

1. Qualitative data

To understand our patrons' needs, as well as their challenges and frustrations, we need to hear from them. Setting up interviews with patrons can be challenging (not to mention time-consuming). John Graunt couldn't have compiled all of the data he needed by himself, so he used available data that would give him enough of what he needed to get his job done. In libraries, while we might not always have the time for interviews with our patrons, we already have some ready data that will do the trick, in the form of emails, tweets, chat transcripts, and reference desk and telephone questions, that can serve as surrogate interview data.

Your library no doubt has a number of ways your patrons can connect and get help. Grand Valley has a prominent live chat button, email, and phone number posted on every web page, in every system. In addition, Springshare's LibAnalytics software is used to keep track of all questions asked at the service desk or the main library phone. Our liaison librarians also record their reference consultations and instruction sessions.

At Sheffield Hallam students and academic staff contact the library in the traditional ways, and the library records telephone, email and reference point interactions. Sheffield Hallam operates a converged service in the library – there is one contact point for information technology (IT) and library help – so there are a lot of 'calls'. The system used to track all of these contacts gives the librarians access not only to issues that are assigned to them, but also an overview of all the enquiries that are coming in.

Other communication points are available to students at Sheffield Hallam, such as the library Twitter account or through the 'Have Your Say . . .' initiative (Sheffield Hallam University, n.d.). These are also collected, curated and analysed.

Most libraries have some sort of method for keeping track of questions. Like the parish clerks, we all hope to use this data to make things better for our patrons, but it's rare that any system has yet been put in place. Fortunately, you don't need a complex tracking system to benefit from this data. You just need to set aside a little time to regularly read it all.

Reading through the email, chat, phone, desk, and reference questions that come through the library every week will give you a good understanding of what your patrons are trying to do, as well as the problems they have. (Most of what you read will be negative. You'll need a thick skin, since frustrated patrons are generally not concerned with hurting the feelings of someone who designed the system they are using.)

This does not give you the kind of targeted information you might get from crafting specific interview questions about, say, your discovery layer or your catalog's request buttons. But this disadvantage has an upside in that you'll be seeing exactly the sorts of things that your patrons are already struggling with. Of course, it's worth noting that a lot of this data will contain a heavy dose of your users' attitudes and opinions about things, which don't always correlate well to how they behave. So tempering what you learn from this qualitative data with some other data points can help you build a more holistic view of your users' experience.

2. Quantitative data

The collected qualitative data gives us a good sense of what is going wrong with our library services, but that isn't always the whole picture. By capturing quantitative data of how each of our systems is actually being used, we can better understand not only what struggles our patrons have, but also where things are working.

The easiest form of quantitative data to collect is website analytics. Google Analytics or other services, such as Reinvigorate.net, can give you a thorough understanding of where your website's visitors come from, what they do on your site (and for how long), as well as what kinds of tools they are using (computers, tablets, mobile devices, watches, etc.). Both Sheffield Hallam and Grand Valley use Google Analytics on the library website and the other tools patrons use, such as the discovery layer, interlibrary loans, the OPAC, and more.

In addition both universities have used online heat map tools to better understand visually how our patrons interact with our site (Figure 4.2). Both also use Google Analytics Event Tracking to map what elements our patrons interact with. While event tracking takes a little additional set-up, the insights gained are well worth the effort. At Grand Valley, within a few months of adding event tracking to Summon, our discovery service, we were shocked to learn that over 50% of the clicks on each page of results were on the first three items. It turns out that the folks at Serials Solutions were interested too, and they soon dropped the default number of results per page from 25 to 10, before moving to an 'infinite scroll' in version 2 of Summon.

The benefits of getting usage data out of your online systems is great, and setting the systems up requires almost no effort. But capturing quantitative data about physical services can be more challenging. At Grand Valley, our UX Manager for physical spaces has student workers do a traditional head count twice an hour in our libraries. But rather than simply recording people, they do behavioural mapping, recording sound levels, whiteboard usage, and whether folks are working primarily alone or in groups. This is a bit more time-consuming, but having this

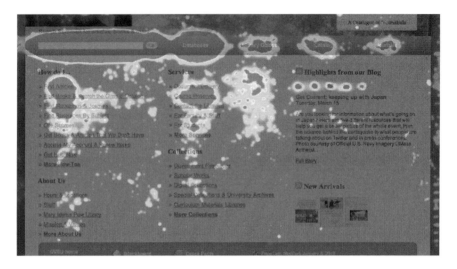

Figure 4.2 Heat map of Grand Valley website showing where users click
Source: Matthew Reidsma.

data helps to give us a more complete picture of how our patrons use not only our services but also our spaces. This also directly benefits our patrons, since we have digital kiosks throughout the library that give at-a-glance updates on available seating and rooms in the different parts of the building (see Felker, Bloom and Earley, 2014).

Sheffield Hallam have also run a number of research projects to generate similar data (explored in detail by Harrop, Turpin et al. in Chapter 14).

3. Search strings

One of the most common tasks on our library websites is searching – for books, articles, movies, and help. When we think about our search tools, it is often in a very disconnected way, since we often divide up the different tools that are appropriate for different types of results and think of them as separate experiences: the catalog, the discovery layer, the database A-Z list, the vendor database. But our users don't experience the library website that way. Where we see individual tools, our users see a holistic search platform.

This is evident when you look at some of the things that users type into the search boxes on your site. They will search for library-specific information, like hours or locations, in your discovery layer, and for PubMed keywords in your catalog. By analysing these search strings, you can add to your understanding of how your patrons expect your site to work.

Both Grand Valley and Sheffield Hallam use Summon as the discovery layer. At Sheffield Hallam, a review of the search queries showed that there were a high

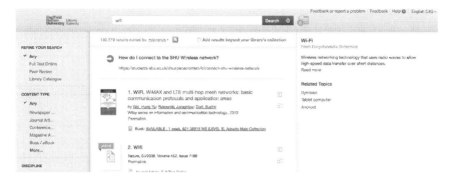

Figure 4.3 Summon Best Bet
Source: Matt Borg.

number of searches in the discovery layer for 'connect to wifi'. Summon allows for the use of keywords to trigger suggestions that are returned to the searcher at the top of the search results, so now a search for 'connect to wifi' can take the user direct to the VLE (virtual learning environment) page on how to connect to the university Wi-Fi (see Figure 4.3).

At Grand Valley, we weren't happy with how either Summon or our catalog recorded and presented search query data, so we built some custom JavaScript tools that live in each of our systems and accurately record the search terms that our patrons enter (Reidsma and Luckenbaugh, 2012, 2013). This allows us not only to get an overview of what folks are searching for, but also to do so across different systems.

4. Usability testing

While almost all libraries have access to the first three categories of user-generated data, not everyone conducts usability tests on their library tools. The perception among many librarians that do not do usability testing is that you need a lot of specialised tools, a dedicated lab, and a one-way mirror. Both Grand Valley and Sheffield Hallam have been running (almost) monthly, formal usability tests for over three years. Although these can take a little bit of planning and bribery (£5 café vouchers at Sheffield Hallam, a free t-shirt at Grand Valley), we can assure you that all you really need is a computer and a willing patron. (Technically, you don't even need these. Grand Valley regularly tests paper prototypes, and when desperate, Matthew has tested designs on his father, who calls him at least twice a week with his computer stuck in full-screen mode.)

Enough ink has been spilled about usability testing in libraries, and Matthew has already written about the how and why of usability testing at Grand Valley (Reidsma, 2011a, 2011b). But the main benefit is that you are able to watch a real live person work through common tasks, giving life to the other three types of data. At Grand Valley, one of the most important things we look for during usability testing isn't even on the screen. While running the tests, Matthew pays close attention to the emotional state and facial expressions of the patron who is completing tasks. More than what they say aloud, watching their discomfort or frustration clarifies the whole experience users go through when using our tools.

One of the most important parts of this sort of usability testing is to make sure that you are asking the participants to undertake tasks that are *meaningful* to them. Asking them to use the library website to find an archaic journal article, available in print only, on the subject of camera film sold in the US in 1983 isn't going to produce helpful results. Usability test questions and scenarios are written in partnership with liaison librarians, so we have real questions from actual assignments within the university. Library websites and discovery systems are for students, not information professionals.

Connecting the data

If you've spent a little time looking over this mound of data about your users, you have probably already found a few things that have surprised you. Maybe requesting items isn't as easy for your patrons as you thought, or maybe there is a confusing label here or there that you hadn't noticed. Looking at all of these different sources of patron-generated data helps to piece together a more holistic view of the library, and gets you out of a system-focused organisational view.

Before jumping in and changing labels or trying out a new way of requesting items, take a moment and think through everything you know about the task from a user's perspective. At Grand Valley, we like to draw out user journeys on a whiteboard or foam board so that we understand all of the steps it might take for a patron to get from point to point. For instance, you might have found a label that was stumping people at a certain point in requesting an item, but that same term may appear elsewhere: at another point along the way, in the help section of your site, or in automated emails generated by library systems. Simply changing that one label may create other problems along the way if you don't step back and take a holistic view of the patron's journey.

Of course, don't expect to get the user journey right if you're starting from how you expect your patrons to use your tools. At Sheffield Hallam, we promote Summon as the starting place for all searches. It is top and centre of the library website. We also have other rich academic sources of information that we want our students to use, and these are co-located on the library website. We included digital film and TV recordings in the Summon index, so they are searchable. We also use 'placeholder text' in the Summon search box to give an indication of what they are likely to be able to do. Initially, this just said 'Find books, articles and more . . . .'

In one of our usability tests, we asked students to find a video of the Olympic Games. The journey we had in our minds, the journey that had been shaped by our 'expert intuition', was that students would just type 'Olympic games video' or similar in the Summon search box. They would then find a load of useful results, select one from the list presented, and watch the video. They really didn't. Not at all. Out of the six users that month, none of them used the Summon box.

Instead, they tried various other sections of the website. Most of them ended up in the subject guides, where we had left the default search box in place. This is a search just of the subject guides. But the students diligently typed 'Olympic video' in the search box, only to find no relevant results. Cue frustration – from both the students and us!

The simple, quick and effective fix was to change the placeholder text to read 'Find books, articles, video and more . . . .' We ran the usability tests the following month and asked the same question to make sure that we had fixed the issue. All students that time used the Summon search to find and view their video. Win!

It's also beneficial to note exactly what you know about the problem, so that you have a baseline to measure against. For instance, if you know that 40% of your patrons aren't making it past the link resolver to get to a full-text article, you'll want to make sure to test any changes you make against that baseline so you can see if you've improved things for patrons.

Making changes

At Sheffield Hallam and Grand Valley, we used the same techniques to move beyond this point. Once we understood the patron's task holistically and had a baseline to measure from, we came up with several possible changes that might improve the user's experience. But rather than approach these as 'design solutions', we kept things flexible, and thought of them as design hypotheses. This keeps us from getting locked in to a particular solution, and instead lets us try out different solutions to find the best one for our users.

Once we've made a change, we start over again, watching our familiar data channels for information on how the change affects our patrons' experiences. Rather than a one-time task, at Grand Valley and Sheffield Hallam we are constantly engaged in this cyclical review. This helps us keep on top of how new changes are being received, as well as identifying new areas of need.

And now for the hard part

Reviewing all of this data takes a lot of time. It also takes a lot of time to digest it all and see the patterns over time. At Grand Valley, all of the raw UX data (including the different types identified here) was made available to anyone in the library through a shared Evernote notebook. Matthew also invited everyone to observe the monthly usability tests, and posted short summaries on his blog after each review (Reidsma, 2015). But processing several years' worth of usability test data, website analytics, emails, comments, reference questions, and more can be hard, even when it's the main focus of your job. So Matthew created a few tools for quickly sharing the information that folks needed to know.

First, he made an 'empathy map', for which he took quotes from 3 years of usability tests and grouped them according to what patrons said, did, thought, or

Figure 4.4 Grand Valley empathy map
Source: Matthew Reidsma.

felt during the tests (Figure 4.4). From this map he further distilled the data down to three simple personas, or archetypal patrons (Figure 4.5). The personas helped keep staff focused on the needs of actual patrons, by putting a human face on a lot of disparate data.

One of the ways this was achieved at Sheffield Hallam was to share the usability testing with all the library staff. Everyone on staff was invited to a 'Usability showcase' that included free tea and coffee. Here the anonymised videos from that month's usability testing were shown, the fixes that had been implemented were described, and there was a chance to talk to other people about real-world user cases being uncovered. Involving people in this way was hard. It wasn't just a case of sending a calendar invite – Matt and others had to go and talk to people and explain why it would be interesting and useful for them to come. Getting fellow library staff to actually see the frustrations and confusion that the library systems were generating for users enabled them to develop a level of empathy and understanding that made it much easier to embrace subtle changes to the systems.

Making it stick

Making a great user experience is a long process, and while we've shared with you techniques and tricks we've learned over the years for improving our users' experiences, it will take time to get the kinds of results we've had. That is because the

AMANDA MCGUIRE
SCIENCES UNDERGRADUATE

20 years old // Biomedical Sciences major // Grand Rapids, MI

"Full-text online is very important to me. I don't have time to request things."

NEEDS

- Concerned with the quality of her sources. Checks recency, impact factors, and reads abstracts to determine relevance.
- Only interested in sources with full-text online.
- Has a few strategies that worked in the past, and tries those for each new project. Unsure where to start research on unfamiliar topics.
- Confident she can figure things out on her own without asking for help. Prefers to use self-service help if available.
- Overwhelmed, busy, and impatient.

SERVE BY

- Make it easy to start new research, whether on a broad or narrow topic.
- Show abstracts, impact factors (citation counts, journal names, authors & affiliations) where possible in results lists.
- Offer self-service help, as well as research guidance.
- Remove barriers to doing quick research, including redundant or extra steps, page load speeds, and unfamiliar navigation patterns.

MARCIA PITTMAN
GRADUATE STUDENT

24 years old // Education - Higher Ed // Grand Rapids, MI

"I need to make sure that my research is thorough."

NEEDS

- Concerned with the quality of sources. Reads works cited lists, evaluates results based on date and relevance.
- Starts research with subject-specific databases.
- Often feels overwhelmed, but likely to ask for help or use online help tools.
- Needs access to abstracts, impact factors, and other metrics to help her quickly evaluate the quality of resources.
- Will request an article through Document Delivery that looks useful for her research if it is not available online.

SERVE BY

- Providing easy access to advanced search tools and subject-specific databases.
- Making it easy to request items that we do not have access to through MeL or Document Delivery.
- Offer self-service and in-person help, as well as research guidance.

Figure 4.5 Two sample Grand Valley personas
Source: Matthew Reidsma.

most important part of making this process work is integrating it into the culture of your library. When we write about the process, it looks like magic. But it only looks like magic if you aren't in the meetings, and you aren't writing the constant emails nudging folks along, and you aren't there for years and years repeating the same mantra over and over again. If you just read about the system and the changes that can come, you'll just see the magic.

So you'll need to dedicate some time to reviewing all of your data, and to listening to it more than you listen to your own professional intuition. You'll need to share this information with your colleagues in a variety of ways, but in the end it will pay dividends. The way that users interact with the library has changed dramatically at both Grand Valley and Sheffield Hallam from really listening to patron needs, but it has taken time.

But perhaps that is to be expected. As the magician Teller once said, 'Sometimes magic is just someone spending more time on something than anyone else might reasonably expect' (Jones, 2012).

References

Adams, D., 1987. *Dirk Gently's Holistic Detective Agency*. London: Heinemann.

Felker, K., Bloom, J. and Earley, J., 2014. *Github: gvsulib Display*. [online] Available at: <https://github.com/gvsulib/display> [Accessed 3 April 2015].

Graunt, J., 1662. *Natural and Political Observations Made upon the Bills of Mortality*. London.

Jones, C., 2012. The Honor System. *Esquire*. [online] Available at: <http://www.esquire.com/entertainment/interviews/a15810/teller-magician-interview-1012/> [Accessed 3 April 2015].

Reidsma, M., 2011a. *Why We Do Usability Testing*. [online] Available at: <http://matthew.reidsrow.com/articles/12> [Accessed 3 April 2015].

Reidsma, M., 2011b. *How We Do Usability Testing*. [online] Available at: <http://matthew.reidsrow.com/articles/13> [Accessed 3 April 2015].

Reidsma, M., 2015. *Work Notes Blog*. [blog] Available at: <http://matthew.reidsrow.com/worknotes/> [Accessed 3 April 2015].

Reidsma, M. and Luckenbaugh, A., 2012. *Github: gvsulib Summon Stats*. [online] Available at: <https://github.com/gvsulib/Summon-Stats> [Accessed 3 April 2015].

Reidsma, M. and Luckenbaugh, A., 2013. *Github: gvsulib iiistats*. [online] Available at: <https://github.com/gvsulib/iiistats> [Accessed 3 April 2015].

Schultz, K., 2014. Final forms: What death certificates can tell us, and what they can't. *New Yorker*, 90(7), pp. 32–7.

Sheffield Hallam University Libraries, n.d. . . . *Have Your Say on Library Services and Resources*. [blog] Available at: <https://blogs.shu.ac.uk/haveyoursay/> [Accessed 3 April 2015].

University of Michigan Libraries, 2012. *2012 Party for Your Mind*. [images online] Available at: <https://www.flickr.com/photos/mlibrary/sets/72157631473093536/> [Accessed 3 April 2015].

5 Applying human-centred design to the library experience

Paul-Jervis Heath

The user experience of a modern library is a complex interplay of physical environment, library services, resources and technology. Thinking like a designer and applying design methods can help libraries adapt to changing user needs and tame this complexity by focusing on solutions rather than on problems.

In his 1980 book *How Designers Think*, the architect and psychologist Bryan Lawson describes an experiment involving a group of final-year architecture students and a group of postgraduate science students. In the experiment both groups were asked to create one-layer structures using a set of red and blue blocks that maximised use of one of the colours for the perimeter. However, in the experiment there was a set of unspecified rules governing the placement and relationships of some of the blocks. These were only revealed during the course of the experiment. The two groups followed very different problem-solving strategies. The scientists started building with as many different blocks and combinations of blocks as possible in an attempt to discover all of the rules so that they could build one final, optimal model. By contrast, the architects created the best model they could. When rules were revealed that their structure contravened, they substituted just the blocks that contravened the rule and presented the next best model.

In the experiment, the scientists followed a problem-focused approach looking to analyse the situation and build a single perfect model. The architects followed a solution-focused problem-solving strategy that arrived at the solution quicker through synthesis.

This experiment illustrates the difference between an analytical problem-solving approach and one based on synthesis. Design thinking combines them both to arrive at solutions. In this chapter we will look at how design thinking and design methods can be applied to the user experience of libraries. The approach presented is based on the human-centred design methodology of my own design practice, Modern Human, but the methods, process and tools are drawn from a wide range of design disciplines.

Framing design

Before you start any design project you need to establish a brief or problem statement. To be meaningful and deliver value, your design project should be related to a real organisational goal or need. However, organisational strategies and mission statements sometimes obscure the purpose and the challenges that an organisation faces. Where this is the case, rewrite the library's goals or challenges in simple, plain English before constructing your brief.

It may seem strange to start a human-centred design project with your organisation's goals, but the human-centred design process is intended to find solutions that are a balance between desirability from a human point of view, viability from a business perspective and feasibility from a delivery perspective. Starting with your library's goals ensures that your project is relevant to the library and the stakeholders who will ultimately agree and fund new products, services and experiences.

At the outset there are many issues that may seem insurmountable. Staffing, resources or internal processes might look difficult or impossible to work with, but design thrives on externally imposed constraints. Some of the things you can't change might actually help you come up with better design solutions. It is far better to aim the design process at something ambitious at the beginning than at something safe.

The project team should return to the brief throughout the project to ensure that their work is addressing the right issues. The brief should be challenging, interesting and valuable.

The four modes of design

At Modern Human our design process has four overlapping spaces or 'modes': Immerse, Inspire, Imagine and Invent. It's tempting to think of them as steps or stages, but that's not really the true nature of the design process. Actually, we're often moving back and forth between modes as we explore the context, identify opportunities, develop ideas and experiment with those ideas.

Despite the non-linear nature of our process, each of the four modes has a clear purpose and a set of methods associated with it:

1   In the Immerse mode, we actively look for problems that need solving and opportunities for change.
2   In the Inspire mode, we turn observations into insights, creating meaning from the opportunities, needs, goals, behaviour and values we have observed. People sometimes think inspiration arrives as a flash, but it's a process of looking for meaning.
3   In the Imagine mode, we generate, develop and test ideas.
4   In the Invent mode, we develop ideas into concrete solutions – real products, services or experiences that make a meaningful difference to people.

In order to explain the human-centred design process, this chapter will work through each of these modes, suggesting methods and techniques within each.

1. Immerse

The objective of Immerse mode is to explore the problem. A successful exploration will look at the context and the people acting within it. You are looking to uncover real people's latent and currently unmet needs and then gain a deep understanding of their goals, behaviour and values.

We suggest using a mixture of design research methods to understand your users. Either shadowing or diary studies provide a good core observational method, depending on the behaviour that you are most interested in. You can augment this primary method with stakeholder workshops, contextual interviews, immersive experiences and analogous activities. Mixing multiple ethnographic research methods gives you lots of different opportunities to engage with your users and learn about their needs, behaviour, values and motivations and is most likely to lead to a rich set of insights that will form a solid foundation for your design project.

Don't forget that your preconceptions will influence the success of any design research you do. It's important to set aside your experience and try to look at the library from the perspective of a user. Adopting a fresh mindset leaves you open to imagining possible future scenarios and prevents your own preconceptions limiting the scope of your ideas.

Research methods

Shadowing

Shadowing is following people and observing their experiences, activities, behaviours and responses.

There are three ways that you can run a shadowing study:

- *Natural*: there is no interference from the design team, you just watch and note down user behaviour.
- *Controlled*: the team sets a task and observes users carrying it out.
- *Participatory*: you join in the activity being observed. It's important not to lead the participant. You have to let them set the activities and decide how they complete them but you can ask questions and ask them to explain their thought processes (designingwithpeople.org, n.d.).

At Modern Human, shadowing is one of our key design research methods because it allows you to observe real behaviour. There is often quite a difference between what people say they do and what they really do. By observing people's facial expressions and body language, and how the participant interacts with services, the environment and with other people, you gather a deep understanding of their behaviour. We suggest using the participatory protocol so that you get the chance to explore their needs, behaviour, values and motivations through discussion.

Diary studies

In a diary study, you ask participants to record their experiences, thoughts and activities over a period of time. This method is good for examining behaviour that takes place over a long period of time where it is unrealistic to shadow participants.

A diary study allows you to get as close to observing real behaviour as possible without actually being there, by providing a record of actions, intentions and thoughts over time – for example, studying for an exam.

The diary itself can be paper or electronic, but it's important to clearly set out in the diary what you want the participant to record and when. Diary studies may also involve taking photos or recording short videos to augment participants' diary entries.

Diary studies are best paired with interviews (contextual or otherwise) at the end of the study to allow you to talk through what the participant has recorded in their diary and probe at needs, behaviour, values and motivations. We will also often conduct an interview before the participant starts the diary study to get to know them and understand their preconceptions.

Contextual interviews

A contextual interview is conducted in the place in which an experience happens or an activity takes place. For example, you might interview library users while they are in the library. Contextual interviews allow you to talk to users about their needs, behaviour, values and motivations as well as seeing how they interact with their immediate surroundings. Often, the extra nuances you observe from being there provide an additional level of insight.

User journey mapping

To create a user journey map, you ask a participant to draw a timeline of their experience with a product or service. At each stage of their timeline, ask them questions to fill in the details. For example: What they were doing? What they were thinking? How they were feeling? Ask them to identify points where they encountered problems and the parts of the experience that felt best and worst.

After conducting a series of user journey mapping sessions with different people you can aggregate the findings together. This will provide your team with a set of opportunities to improve the experience. Adding quantitative data to your user journey map will support your core findings.

Immersive experiences

Rather than watching a user complete an activity, sometimes it can be valuable to step in and complete the activity yourself. It helps you to immerse yourself, builds empathy and provides a deep understanding of individual goals and tasks along the way. Doing the things your library users do in the way they do them helps you to understand their decisions, motivations, thoughts and feelings.

Capture notes immediately after rather than during the experience. Taking notes during the experience can break the illusion of really doing the activity; if possible, repeat the experience a second time shortly afterwards, taking more careful notes and casting your mind back to that initial immersion.

Analogous activities

Many useful design solutions exist outside the world of libraries. Sometimes experiencing an activity or a setting that is tangentially related to the design brief can give you a fresh perspective. Immerse yourself in these activities just as you would in an immersive experience.

To identify analogous activities it helps to think about the goals, tasks, emotions and behaviours that make up the experience you are interested in exploring. You can often then identify scenarios in other settings that have aspects in common with your brief. For example, if you were looking to understand how people navigate the physical library space, browse for resources and identify items of interest, then you might get inspiration from watching people shop in a department store. If you were wanting to know more about creating a service experience, you might get inspiration from a visit to a fancy restaurant to observe how the maître d' and front-of-house staff manage interactions.

Preparation for fieldwork

Whether you use shadowing, diary studies, contextual interviews or one of the other methods, it is important that you capture your insights as you go along. Preparing data capture sheets ahead of research enables you to quickly and easily capture key facts. Carry a hardback notebook for other observations and sketches.

Most of the equipment we take out is pretty simple, but there are a few bits of consumer technology that can help. A camera-equipped smartphone is great for capturing photos. Most will also capture the GPS location where you take photos, which can be useful for analysis later. We usually take a life-logging camera along too when we're shadowing. These discreet little cameras automatically capture a photograph every 10, 20 or 30 seconds using a fixed-focus, wide-angle lens. Various life-logging cameras are available and the software they come with can then be used to create time-lapse videos of every shadowing session. The videos are great for inspiration later and they can be used to illustrate actual user behaviour to stakeholders. Don't forget to ask permission, though, if you're photographing or videoing participants!

The right number of participants

The number of participants you'll need to involve in your research is really dependent on how diverse your user base is for the behaviour that you are interested in.

Start by forming a hypothesis about the number of different user types. Remember that you're interested in behaviour, not outward characteristics such as market segment or socioeconomic group. The groups don't have to be exactly right – it's just a hypothesis at this stage, and your research will confirm or correct it.

You'll want at least 5–8 members of each group so that you have enough points of comparison.

Identify research highlights as you go

When you're out in the field you'll capture a surprising amount of qualitative data. Allow at least 30 minutes between hour-long research sessions to process your notes and prepare for the next session. We use that time to discuss the last session and share our initial impressions with each other.

In the space between sessions we try to identify 5–10 session highlights. These tend to be memorable stories or quotes and the most interesting or surprising observations. Highlighting these now saves you time in Inspire mode.

2. Inspire

In Inspire mode the objective is to turn observations into actionable and meaningful insights and make sense of all of the things you have witnessed.

There's a myth that inspiration strikes at random. We all know the story about Archimedes in the bath or Newton and the apple tree. In my experience of leading all sorts of creative teams, you can't rely on a 'Eureka moment'. Good ideas are hard work, and inspiration strikes when you prepare yourself fully for it. Inspire mode is our way of preparing. It is analysing behaviour, looking for patterns and building models of our users and the situations they inhabit.

Your insights will form the foundation for design interventions in the Imagine and Invent spaces. The easiest way to start identifying patterns in your observations is to share stories amongst your team. As you share your research highlights you will start to identify patterns that you can turn into insights and behavioural models that will inspire new ideas.

Turn observations into insights

During your design research each member of the team will have seen, heard and learned about lots of different needs, goals, behaviours, values, decision-making strategies and motivations.

The first step is to simply share what you've learned as a team. This is an important step even if you didn't split up during research. Sharing stories will bring out the key observations you each made. Your research highlights are a good starting point for these conversations. You can start by taking it in turns to share your research highlights, but as you do this you'll find that you naturally move into more of a discussion amongst the team.

Sticky notes are an invaluable tool at this stage. Writing each interesting observation, need, value, decision-making criterion, anecdote or finding on a note and sticking it to the wall gets your combined observations out of your heads and ready for analysis. We generally start by affinity sorting, or clustering the observations around themes. We'll then give each theme a name and a sentence that summarises that theme using two additional colours of sticky notes.

It is surprising how easily you will recognise good insights as you arrive at them. They are surprising but they feel right. A good insight surfaces a deeper truth and feels important within the problem space. It provides a foundation for new ideas and concepts. Perhaps the best measure of a good insight is that it gets repeated amongst the team and stakeholders as you discuss your findings. This is a good point to look back to your original design brief and identify the insights that feel most powerful and most relevant to your brief.

Creating models

It is often desirable to encapsulate observations in models that describe overarching or archetypical user behaviour, goals, needs, decision-making criteria, values and motivations. Models are useful because they allow you to extrapolate your insights to answer questions that will arise as you design.

Experience map

An experience map represents a user experience across multiple interactions and experiences with a product, service or ecosystem (Adaptive Path, 2013).

At the centre of the experience map is a user journey map that may have been created as part of your Immerse activity. An experience map augments the user journey map with insights into users' thoughts, feelings and values. It documents the opportunities and guiding principles for future experiences.

There are several ways that you can orientate an experience map. Typically you align it to actions by using actions across time as the spine of the story. You can take an emotion-oriented approach by looking for emotional insights and drawing the emotional journey of your customers. You can also take a location-oriented approach by identifying locations where the experience takes place and organising your key insights by decision points within each physical context.

The activity that goes into creating an experience map is often as valuable as the output itself. The activity of mapping builds knowledge and consensus across teams and stakeholders and it provides an artefact that can communicate to lots of different stakeholders in an organisation.

2 × 2 matrices

Surprisingly simple models can often make complex situations clearer. A 2 × 2 matrix is a common model that maps two behaviours or attributes so that they can be compared. A 2 × 2 matrix will often highlight common needs or behaviours between user groups. They also help identify the extent to which user needs are genuinely distinct, identifying the key factors that cause them to be distinct.

The axes of a 2 × 2 matrix often suggest themselves through needs or behaviours that are mutually exclusive. For example, in a recent project designing a new loyalty scheme, we found that people either saved their loyalty points for a large reward or spent them gradually on smaller treats. For the client this dispelled the myth that members' behaviour was based on disposable income (which was actually a red herring).

In another study we found that undergraduate students were either outcome-oriented or experience-oriented, and this influenced their study objectives and behaviour. This helped us to understand students' motivations and the desirable attributes of library services.

In both of these studies we used 2×2 models to illustrate these behaviours and inspire the design process.

Timelines

Mapping goals, activities or events on a timeline highlights patterns in the sequence and can identify prerequisites or contingent strings of actions. It can also help identify the root causes of difficulties in processes when you find that people typically do things in a different order than you expected.

It can build a surprising amount of empathy to plot a timeline of a person's typical day, their work or their interactions with a product, service or ecosystem.

Relationship maps

Understanding people's relationships and social context is sometimes important to understanding their behaviour, their goals and their values. Relationship maps draw the links between individuals, teams and roles. They show who is connected with whom and how they communicate, and they describe the influences that individuals and groups have on each other.

Decision-making models

Understanding and describing how people make decisions can be fundamental to understanding how their goals and values are applied to choices they make. A decision-making model describes the factors that people use to choose between products and services or between courses of action. It also describes the activities and experiences that influence decisions and the time frame in which decisions are taken.

Having turned your observations into insights and models, it is time to apply that understanding to the next stage and start to imagine solutions to your design brief.

3. Imagine

In Imagine mode you'll generate ideas based on the things your team has witnessed and the insights and models you've identified. Up until now the focus of the process has been on observing and understanding, but this is the phase where the insights you have absorbed turn into ideas for design interventions.

Start Imagine mode by turning each of your insights into a question starting with the words 'How might we . . .' (Berger, 2012). Each question needs to be broad enough in scope to invite multiple solutions but not so broad that it leaves the ideation (idea generation) process directionless. Refine your questions by making them broader and narrower until you feel each has the right scope. For example:

> *Insight*: People keep books out on loan longer than they really need them. They return them when it is convenient to visit the library, not when they have finished using them.

> *Too broad*: How might we maximise our investment in physical resources?
> This question has too many possible solutions. Although it might be tightly related to an organisational goal, it hardly narrows the field design interventions you could make.

> *Too narrow*: How might we get people to return books sooner?
> This question is too narrow. It imposes limits on the type of solutions you could consider and maybe even addresses the wrong problem.

> *Just right*: How might we maximise the number of people who can use resources?
> This question might include ideas to encourage people to return books sooner, but it also leaves open the possibility of imagining future solutions that have nothing to do with physical books.

Select the best 3–5 questions to address in Imagine mode. Finding the right balance in your questions and choosing the right ones to focus on takes some intuition and experience. Initially go with what feels right. Choose the questions that excite you as a team and give you the possibility of generating lots of good ideas. The possibility of generating ideas is different to having lots of preconceived ideas. Sometimes it's worth avoiding questions where your team have lots of preconceived ideas of what the solution might be, unless they can put these aside.

Generate ideas alone and as a group

As you approach these questions you need to encourage a mix of both individual time and group time to generate ideas. Many teams rely on a single group brainstorm to generate ideas, which is inadequate. Group exercises are important and help groups to explore different ideas, but so is working alone.

The term 'brainstorming' was coined by Alex Osborn in his 1948 book *Your Creative Power*. Osborn was a partner in BBDO which at the time was seen as one of the most innovative advertising firms on Madison Avenue. His book captured his experience of working in the advertising world. Osborn felt that the creativity of groups was hindered because most meetings tended towards evaluating ideas. He described it as 'driving with the brakes on'. He created the brainstorming method as a way of quickly producing a large number of ideas which could be evaluated and validated later. It's worth putting brainstorming into context. Brainstorming is only one of a variety of techniques for generating ideas, and generating ideas is really only one part of the design process. There is evidence that brainstorming is not even the best choice of activity for generating ideas.

In 1958, Donald Taylor, Paul Berry and Clifford Block invited people to take part in a study of creative techniques. They placed some of their volunteers into small groups. Other volunteers were asked to work alone and pooled their ideas later. Taylor, Berry and Block asked their volunteers to spend 12 minutes generating ideas for tasks like the implications of waking up with an extra thumb, dealing with a shortage of teachers 10 years in the future, and enticing more European tourists to visit America. They found that the groups that worked alone and pooled their ideas later generated twice as many ideas as those interacting in a group.

The Taylor, Berry and Block (1958) study is often taken as a criticism of the brainstorming technique, but actually both sets of participants – those working alone and those working together – were briefed on and encouraged to use the rules of brainstorming. Their results were also far less conclusive about the quality of the ideas (Isaksen, 1998). What the Taylor, Berry and Block study does show, though, is that both working alone and working together each have a part to play in generating ideas, and so it is important to include a variety of idea generation techniques in your own Imagine mode.

Encourage dissent and critique during idea generation

In 2003, Charlan Nemeth, Bernard Personnaz, Marie Personnaz and Jack Goncalo gathered 265 participants and split them into three groups, each of which was given the same challenge. The first group was given no instructions about how to approach the challenge. The second group was given the rules of a typical brainstorm. The third group was told:

> Most research and advice suggests that the best way to come up with good solutions is to come up with many solutions. Freewheeling is welcome; don't be afraid to say anything that comes to mind. However, in addition, most studies suggest that you should debate and even criticise each other's ideas.

The results were interesting. The brainstorming group slightly outperformed the group given no instructions, but teams given the debate condition were the most creative: on average, they generated nearly 20% more ideas (Nemeth et al., 2004).

After the teams disbanded, another interesting result became apparent. Researchers asked each participant individually if they had any more ideas. The brainstormers and the people given no guidelines produced an average of three additional ideas; the debaters produced seven.

There are two important things about this study:

1   Dissent stimulates new ideas because it encourages us to engage more fully with the work of others and to reassess our viewpoints.
2   If you want to be original, then you have to get past the first layer of predictability.

Nemeth et al. also showed how crucial dissent and divergent perspectives (even incorrect ones) are to generating more original ideas. It is important that people feel completely comfortable during group ideation sessions, but questioning and critique help the group come up with more ideas.

A mix of ideation techniques

At Modern Human we use a mixture of idea generation techniques in Imagine mode. We tend to start with individual reflection on the questions and solo work. We'll then gather as a team for an idea generation activity. We find the rapid ideation game '6–8–5' works well because the structure of the game creates times for individual idea generation, discussion of those ideas and the opportunity to build on and remix other people's ideas.

Brynn Evans, Design Lead at Google, shared the technique on the *Go Gamestorm* blog (http://www.gogamestorm.com) in 2011 (Gray, 2011a). The game helps teams to explore complementary approaches rather than sticking with the first good idea they have. It encourages a team to generate lots of ideas in a short period of time. The activity can then be repeated to hone and flesh out a few of the best ideas.

Each player takes 8 sticky notes. The group sets a timer for 5 minutes. When the timekeeper says 'Go', the team has 5 minutes to silently sketch out as many ideas as they can until the timer ends. The aim is to sketch between 6 and 8 ideas – the sketches are obviously very rough at this stage. Once the 5 minutes are up, every player briefly shares their ideas with the rest of the group. Then the group plays another round.

In each subsequent round players can further develop any ideas that were presented to the group or can sketch new ideas that occurred to them since the last round. Good ways of building on ideas can be to force connections between two or more previous ideas, to blend the two previous ideas together or to blend the benefits of two or more previous ideas. Players can continue to work on separate ideas or begin working on the same idea. But the 5-minute sketching sprint should always be done silently and independently.

The 6–8–5 method is deliberately time-constrained. It helps groups generate a wide variety of ideas and also develop those ideas by exploring complementary approaches. Typically after a game, the team will discuss the various ideas and their relative merits, sometimes grouping or ranking ideas. Following this analysis we find it helps for team members to have a period of working alone to reflect on the ideas and develop some of them further.

Looking harder for ideas

Teams can struggle to leave behind the baggage of previous experience that we all carry with us. Sometimes they need a little help to explore more outlandish ideas – a deliberate nudge in the direction of originality.

Where this is the case, we take a leaf out of Luke Williams's 2010 book *Disrupt: Think the Unthinkable to Spark Transformation in Your Business* and encourage teams to search for clichés. We ask teams to examine a situation that everyone takes for granted and understand the situation quickly, informally, qualitatively and intuitively. We ask them to list 10 clichés about the current situation. For example:

- What are the clichéd product features and benefits?
- What are the cliché product attributes that are advertised?
- What are the cliché steps a customer experiences when buying and consuming the product or service?
- What are the clichés about where and when interactions take place?
- How frequently do customers purchase the product or service?
- How frequently do customers use the product or service?
- How are customers normally charged?
- How are products and services packaged together?

Once they have those clichés we then encourage them to invert, scale or deny them. Which of the clichés could be flipped in the opposite direction? For example, instead of something being expensive make it cheap, or vice versa. Which of your clichés could be scaled? Can you imagine making a factor enormously big, or infinitesimally small? Finally, which of those clichés can we deny and remove completely (Williams, 2010)?

This type of thinking tends to be a lot of fun, and an afternoon spent thinking about clichés and then subverting them can inject some fresh thinking.

Selecting the best ideas

Up until this point in the design process you have been using divergent thinking to generate many ideas and many potential solutions. At this point the design process moves to converging on concepts most likely to provide a credible and successful solution to the original design brief.

One way of identifying the best potential concepts is using a How-Now-Wow Matrix (Gray, 2011b), where you arrange the ideas according to their originality and feasibility; another way is to give participants sticky dots and ask them to vote for their preferred ideas (Gray, 2010).

There is a paradox to be aware of at this stage. Teams may think originally when generating ideas but then lose their nerve and become conservative when it comes to selecting ideas to take forward. In this situation teams end up selecting the most familiar and 'safest' ideas and undoing much of their previous hard work. It is often helpful to review the design brief and the user insight before selecting ideas to take forward.

Forming concepts

A concept is a clearly articulated central idea around which the features and benefits of a product or service combine. It is perhaps easiest to define by example. In the recent FutureLib project with the University of Cambridge (FutureLib, 2015), we came up with several concepts for augmenting library services, for example:

Spacefinder: Spacefinder is a search service that enables users to find different types of spaces in which to work and study across the University. It allows users to tag spaces for a particular activity and rate them on their suitability.

(see Chapter 8)

WhoHas?: WhoHas? is a peer-to-peer sub-lending service. It facilitates sub-lending of printed resources, turning the current 'black market' into a centrally-mediated service.

(see Chapter 9)

Each of these concepts was formed by following the design process described here.

One technique for forming concepts is to group the ideas from previous ideation activities thematically. Arrange them by the user needs they satisfy or by the user journey they take place within. In the Spacefinder example we found that one of the themes of our ideas was around finding, using and telling other people about study spaces. We grouped the ideas that concerned this theme and started to form them into a user journey that described how Spacefinder might allow a student or postdoc to find and use a space, meet their friends and then tell others about it. From here we could create a concept map, storyboards and sketches of what Spacefinder might look like and how it might work. This is the next stage for your concepts.

To create your own concept, look back at the ideas from your ideation activities. Group the ideas by themes. Once you have your themes try to summarise a product or service that addresses that group in two sentences, such as those in the previous examples.

Relate each concept back to the original design brief: for each concept also define who the primary end user is, and then describe the benefits they realise from using the concept and how your concept will deliver those benefits.

From this short burst of activity you will end up with a set of concepts. Start to validate each one by thinking about how realistic the concept might be, how likely people are to use it and how original it feels.

Refine your concepts by combining those that address similar needs for similar users; then select a shortlist of concepts that show the most promise and for each of them start to define the user experience. Think about how a user would interact with the concept and tell that story. Initially, storyboards like those used to describe film storylines work well for describing the user experience. For each step in your story or each frame in your storyboard, detail the interactions a user would have.

It is also vital to consider the context of your concept: how the user discovers the concept, the user's immediate next step after using it, and the sharing of positive (or negative) experiences. Validate your concept again by describing the immediate and long-term benefits the user receives from the concept. It's important that these benefits feel credible and realistic. Your stakeholders will have to believe in these benefits if they are to fund rollout of the product, service or experience.

Describe your concept with storyboards, sketches, mock-ups and day-in-the-life videos as well as textual descriptions to create a compelling package of material. This package represents your concepts to stakeholders and to potential users.

4. Invent

Having identified concepts while working in Imagine mode, in Invent mode you start to realise the concept then validate it and refine it with target users. The Invent mode is naturally more open-ended than the other three modes because there are different outcomes depending on your library, your concepts and your team. The core activity is to prototype at various levels of fidelity, then pilot. You may run a number of different pilots with different users, in different locations or with different iterations of your prototype.

Test and refine your prototype

The prototype for each of the concepts you selected in Imagine mode may take on a different form. In our experience, the form of the initial prototype tends to depend on the confidence of everyone in the concept, including your stakeholders. Rightly or wrongly, concepts with a high degree of confidence tend to get prototyped in higher fidelity and developed further before involving users. Concepts with a lower level of certainty tend to get prototyped and tested much earlier, at a lower level of fidelity, making the prototyping faster and cheaper.

The type of prototype you create will depend on what aspect of your concept you want to test: role prototypes explore what an artefact could do for a user; look-and-feel prototypes explore options for the concrete experience of a product; implementation prototypes answer questions about how a product might be made to work; and integration prototypes represent the complete user experience (Houde and Hill, 1997).

The testing method and protocol will also depend on what aspect you are looking to validate. There are numerous prototyping methods and prototype-testing techniques, enough to fill a chapter of their own. The interested reader could investigate scenario testing, concept probes, the Wizard of Oz technique, service walkthroughs, role play, mock environments and bodystorming.

Once you've tested a prototype, take time to debrief properly. Having seen different people and many different reactions, taking a step back allows you to develop a clear understanding of what you have found out about your concept, and gives time to understand the implications for your design and make sure you capture important insights. Reuse the analysis techniques from the Immerse mode: research highlights and affinity sorting are just as useful here as they were during your initial design research.

Decide what you're going to do about each of your findings. They may require a change to your prototype or suggest that your concept needs adapting. They may change your fundamental understanding of your users' needs, goals or behaviour. After working out how to address each of your findings you may need to modify your prototype and test an improved version. It might be more appropriate to move to the next level and start piloting.

Pilot, measure, iterate

A pilot is between making a prototype and implementing your idea. While a prototype makes an idea tangible, the pilot is a way to evolve your prototype into an experience for users. It gives you a chance to improve your idea before fully committing to it for all of your library users. Your pilot could just take a few hours or happen over a matter of weeks. The length of time will depend on the questions you want your pilot to answer.

Defining the key questions for your pilot to answer will guarantee that you learn something useful from the pilot and enable you to objectively judge whether it was a success or failure. Remember that your pilot is an experiment to learn about how users react to your concept so it does not need to be elaborate, fully developed or high fidelity.

Think about the things you want to learn in order to improve your concept, the assumptions that you have about your concept and about your users and the parts of your concept that you are most unsure of. Turn these things into questions to answer during your pilot.

Once you have your questions, plan where your pilot will take place and who will need to be involved. It's worth working with the team who will run the pilot to draw a service blueprint or flowchart of how the pilot will work. You'll also want to define both qualitative and quantitative measures for your pilot. To capture qualitative user feedback reuse some of the research techniques you employed in Immerse mode – for example, a diary study with a sample of pilot users, shadowing someone while they use your pilot or interviewing them after they have used it. You'll also want to capture some quantitative measurements. You might be interested, for example, in the number of people who use the pilot, the length of time they engage with it or the number of times they use it. Measure those statistics reliably throughout the pilot period.

Again, step back after you've piloted and assess the results. Was it a resounding success or did you learn about some things you could improve? Decide whether to try another prototype, run another pilot or graduate the concept into a full-fledged service offering.

Applying the human-centred design process

To implement your concept as a full-fledged service you'll probably need buy-in from a wider set of stakeholders. Fortunately, the human-centred design process provides evidence of user needs, tests prototypes and pilots concepts with real users. You have all of the raw material to craft a persuasive and compelling story for change. This is just one of the advantages of a human-centred design approach: the process itself builds the justification for the outcomes of the process.

Another advantage is that the process is self-correcting. If you take a wrong step at any stage, testing with real users will highlight what is wrong and suggest steps to correct it. This is true at whatever stage you might take a wrong turn. The nature of the process liberates a team to try more adventurous solutions and think further into the future.

In fact, wrong turns are almost inevitable. If you're trying new things in an environment as complicated as a library, if you're designing for real people and their changing needs, then you are likely to experiment with ideas that do not work out quite how you thought. However, with each iteration you learn something about your users' goals, needs, behaviour and values or you learn more about your own ideas and potential solutions. That new knowledge helps you to create a more successful design solution. Even an ill-conceived brief can be corrected by identifying true needs, behaviour and values during an Immerse mode in a project.

As with the adoption of any new method, there are difficulties that some teams initially experience and these can limit the value of the design solutions they ultimately deliver. The first of these is believing that users will tell you what they want. The second is a fascination with ethnographic research to such an extent that no progress is made to actually create new products, services, experiences and spaces. The third is in losing nerve and using the techniques as window dressing on what is really a traditional approach.

Users often cannot tell you their latent needs. Latent needs are by definition those that are hidden even from those with the need. The real power of design research is in uncovering unspoken needs that users are not aware of until they see a solution. That sounds counterintuitive – surely the people who use our service know what they need? – but actually most of us only really become aware of a product or service we are using when we experience a problem.

The German philosopher Heidegger described two modes of interacting with things. He described objects as 'present-at-hand' when we observe their nature and their attributes. As people, we don't know most of the things in the world as present-at-hand, most of the time. Most things present themselves to us as usable objects. Heidegger termed them 'ready-to-hand'. Heidegger reasoned that you are not consciously aware of an object that has presented itself as something usable but you are able to act through it. Heidegger also described the shifts between present-at-hand and ready-to-hand and called them 'breakdowns' (Reidsma, 2015). Asking users about their needs may be a good way of diagnosing problems with or identifying shortcomings of a product or service. They will be able to recall breakdowns they have experienced in an existing service that moved their experience from being ready-at-hand to being present-at-hand. However, as tempting as it might seem to ask people what they need, doing so will only yield small and iterative improvements. That's the failure of surveys and focus groups and why neither are mentioned or utilised in Immerse mode. If we want to design new products, services or experiences, we are usually interested in needs that the user may not have perceived yet because a solution does not exist.

The second difficulty teams experience is that they fall in love with understanding their users by conducting ethnography to the point where they forget to actually create new products, services, experiences and spaces. It is perhaps easy to see where this failure originates. Understanding users is infinitely interesting. It is also relatively safe: providing your research methodology and protocol are rigorous and your sample correct, you are almost guaranteed to deliver insights that are intuitive yet surprising and that fascinate colleagues and stakeholders. Taking the next step and designing a new product, service or experience for real people is not so safe. You may get it wrong the first time, and have to iterate and change your initial ideas and concepts. There is no formula or analysis that you can apply to your findings that will yield a successful design solution every time. Synthesis has to be employed as a problem-solving strategy. However, if you are to invent products and services that move the experience of libraries forward, the design process is necessary. Teams that are in this position are often reassured by the self-correcting nature of the process and just need a nudge to take the leap of faith to start designing.

The final difficulty that some teams experience is in engaging in process pantomime: going through the motions of the human-centred design process without adopting the design thinking that goes behind it. It is possible to apply this process as window dressing to a traditional inside-out approach of delivering new library services. It is possible to conduct design research and only confirm your preconceptions. It is possible to only generate preconceived ideas. However, it is unlikely if a team is open to fresh ideas and new ways of thinking.

The best advice for anyone wanting to apply human-centred design and design thinking to their library is to just go for it. Define a problem, pick a team and immerse yourselves through ethnographic design research, inspire the team through analysis and sense making, imagine concepts and invent solutions. Approach your library with fresh eyes and open your mind to identifying new insights, new models and developing new ideas. The process assists in delivering meaningful new products, services and experiences.

Of course, if you get stuck or you need advice getting started, there are design practices who can provide support and consultancy. This can provide rigour and experience in human-centred design. Often the value in experience is in efficiency in the process. Experienced designers are perhaps more likely to spot avenues that are worth pursuing early and focus effort on these. They are also more likely to identify where the process is working less well and being able to adapt the process and introduce alternative methods to inject new impetus.

Professional design practices can bring an outside perspective because they usually work across different sectors so can bring ideas from other worlds into the context of libraries. Innovative solutions often come from a concept that is familiar in one sector being applied in a new field.

Experts are sometimes too entrenched in their own profession. This can be true whether the sector is finance, technology, automotive, architecture or libraries. The conventional wisdom and best practice of their area can blind them to solutions that may be obvious to an outsider, or dissuade them from tackling challenges they know to be intractable and relying on solutions they are familiar with. The assumptions that come with expertise can be an impairment if you genuinely want to design products, services and experiences that are intuitive and a joy to use.

A designer coming in to a new situation has another advantage: that whilst professionals in the organisation are expected to be knowledgeable in their field, the designer's occupation and expertise are different. They can afford to play the role of the naive enquirer and ask the simple, open, naive questions that an expert perhaps could not.

Finally, a design practice brings expertise in the craft of designing products, services and experiences. Product design, service design and experience design are all distinct fields of professional practice with their own methods, tools and techniques. Experienced designers have patterns, approaches and previous experiences they bring to a design challenge.

Whilst working in partnership with a professional design practice can provide useful expertise, experience and an outside perspective, it is not necessary to be a professional designer to apply human-centred design and design thinking. Build confidence in applying the process, thinking, tools and techniques by identifying a design brief that aims to create evolutionary solutions. Evolutionary solutions are those which seek to develop new ideas for existing users or adapting existing concepts to new users. In selecting an ambitious but evolutionary brief for the first project, a team can build experience and later apply the same techniques and thinking to invent revolutionary new library experiences.

Afterword: the term 'ideation'

I've experienced some people who recoil at the neologism 'ideation'. Like most professional disciplines, design has its own lexicon and jargon. It is a portmanteau, a concatenation of the phrase 'idea generation' and is often used to shorten those two words to a single noun. Ideation actually isn't a new word. The first recorded use was in 1818 by none other than the poet, critic and philosopher Samuel Taylor Coleridge (OED, 2015). Coleridge wrote classic poems such as *The Rime of the Ancient Mariner* and *Kubla Kahn*. He's credited with coining many other words and phrases we take for granted, such as 'suspension of disbelief'.

The Scottish historian, economist, political theorist and philosopher James Mill wrote of the term 11 years later in 1829: 'As we say Sensation, we might say also, Ideation; it would be a very useful word; and there is no objection to it, except the pedantic habit of decrying a new term' (OED, 2015). You'll notice that I tend to use ideation and idea generation interchangeably but I could never bring myself to use the verb form: to ideate.

References

Adaptive Path, 2013. *Adaptive Path's Guide to Experience Mapping.* [online] Available at: <http://mappingexperiences.com> [Accessed 13 August 2013].

Berger, W., 2012. The Secret Phrase Top Innovators Use. *Harvard Business Review*, [blog] Available at: <https://hbr.org/2012/09/the-secret-phrase-top-innovato> [Accessed September 2012].

designingwithpeople.org, n.d. *Methods – Observation & Shadowing.* [online] Available at: <http://designingwithpeople.rca.ac.uk/methods/observation-shadowing> [Accessed January 2015].

FutureLib, 2015. *FutureLib.* [online] Available at: <https://futurelib.wordpress.com/> [Accessed September 2015].

Gray, D., 2010. Dot Voting. *Go Gamestorm,* [blog] 15 October. Available at: <http://gamestorming.com/core-games/dot-voting/> [Accessed June 2015].

Gray, D., 2011a. 6–8–5. *Go Gamestorm,* [blog] 17 May. Available at: <http://gamestorming.com/games-for-fresh-thinking-and-ideas/6-8-5s/> [Accessed June 2015].

Gray, D., 2011b. How-Now-Wow Matrix. *Go Gamestorm,* [blog] 5 January. Available at: <http://gamestorming.com/games-for-decision-making/how-now-wow-matrix/> [Accessed June 2015].

Houde, S. and Hill, C., 1997. *What Do Prototypes Prototype?* [online] Cupertino, CA: Apple Computer, Inc. Available at: <http://uwdata.github.io/hcid520/readings/Houde-Prototypes.pdf> [Accessed June 2015].

Isaksen, S. G., 1998. *A Review of Brainstorming Research: Six Critical Issues for Inquiry (Monograph no.302).* Buffalo, NY: Creativity Research Unit, Creative Problem Solving Group.

Lawson, B., 1980. *How Designers Think: The Design Process Demystified.* London: Architectural.

Nemeth, C., Personnaz, M., Personnaz, B. and Goncalo, J., 2004. The Liberating Role of Conflict in Group Creativity: A Cross-Cultural Study. *European Journal of Social Psychology,* 34, pp. 365–74.

OED, 2015. *Oxford English Dictionary Online.* [online] Oxford: Oxford University Press. Available at: <http://www.oed.com/> [Accessed June 2015].

Osborn, A. F., 1948. *Your Creative Power: How to Use Imagination.* New York: Scribner.

Reidsma, M., 2015. *More Than Usable: Library Services for Humans.* [online] 5 May. Available at: <http://matthew.reidsrow.com/articles/134> [Accessed June 2015].

Taylor, D. W., Berry, P. C. and Block, C. H., 1958. Does Group Participation When Using Brainstorming Facilitate or Inhibit Creative Thinking? *Administrative Science Quarterly,* 3(1), pp. 23–47.

Williams, L., 2010. *Disrupt: Think the Unthinkable to Spark Transformation in Your Business.* New York: Pearson.

6 The why, what and how of using ethnography for designing user experience in libraries (and a few pitfalls to avoid)

Leah Emary

Why ethnography is well-suited to designing user experience in libraries

If you're reading this book, it's likely that you're engaged with creating a library user experience that is usable, convenient, pleasurable and meaningful. The drive to revamp or create services is laudable, and it's tempting to begin brainstorming new services or changes to existing library spaces based on what we believe is usable, convenient, pleasurable and meaningful. Our professional understanding of what library users want from their experience, however, can differ vastly from what our users themselves want from their experience. Finding out what a user truly needs and truly wants can be deceptively difficult, as it's not a question of what we *think* our users will find usable, convenient, pleasurable or meaningful, and we also can't necessarily rely on what our users *say* they will find usable, convenient, pleasurable or meaningful. In this chapter, I argue that we *can* rely on what their actions tell us about their experience in the library, to get a truer understanding of what they want and need.

It is not as though we lack for user data in libraries. Librarians gather lots of data about users. Statistical data such as those gathered by SCONUL in the UK, ACRL in the US, and Die Deutsche Bibliotheksstatistik (DBS) in Germany are useful for tracking long-term trends and comparing institutions, but they give frustratingly little context. They leave many of us asking questions such as: A book was checked out, but did it fulfil the user's need or did they get it home and realize it was off-topic? Did they run out of time to read it? A user came in the door, but did they use the restroom and leave immediately or were they there to ask a question or spend the day wrestling with Heidegger? A user visited the website and closed the browser tab after 3 minutes. What did they plan to do or find on the site? Did they find it and leave quickly or did they get frustrated and close the browser tab?

Robust survey instruments like LibQual or a well-designed local survey that is well analyzed can tell you bits and pieces about users but you will lack a full, rich explanation. The National Student Survey (NSS) of university students in the UK is a classic example of something that is generalizable, comparable, valid and reliable. Question 16 of the NSS asks whether a library's resources and services are good enough for students' needs. It does not probe the meaning of 'good enough', how and whether a user understands the words 'library resources and services' and whether they interpret them in the same way as those analyzing the data. Quantitative data can be fine if you want to know more about a phenomenon that can be quantified, but statistics and surveys aren't very useful when dealing with concepts such as usable, pleasurable, meaningful or convenient, which are the goals of user experience.

Ethnography helps you to collect data which closes that gap. It is the classic method for understanding culture, which doesn't sound entirely practical until you consider that ethnography is a translation of a study population's language, their worldview, their culture into a product (most often a text) that makes sense to outsiders. Because a user's cultural context determines work practices and library use, ethnographic understanding provides the piece of the puzzle that we so often lack from surveys and statistics: context, understanding and insight (Greifeneder, 2012). It is a valuable tool for triangulating (checking that the results you got with other methods hold true when tested in other ways), verifying and enhancing your understanding. The goal is not to understand the magnitude and distribution of a particular phenomenon as it is in quantitative methods, but rather to gain a very deep understanding of the phenomenon in a particular setting (DeWalt and DeWalt, 2002, p. 3). As Gabridge et al. describe their approach to triangulating with ethnography:

> the survey could not provide details about how and whether these resources and services were being used. We anticipated that seeing this complete context would help highlight the service gaps that the MIT [Massachusetts Institute of Technology] Libraries needed to fill.
>
> (Gabridge, Gaskell and Stout, 2008, p. 512)

Librarians who have puzzling results or incomplete (if completely valid) results from their statistics or surveys might have a perfect area of ethnographic study.

Ethnography can also be used at another stage in user research: to inform future, more focused data collection, and to design. Because ethnography is particularly helpful for understanding and translating language, understanding users' movements and practices, it can help to design better surveys or interview schedules, and help create focus groups or experiments. In their ethnographically inspired taskscape analysis, Delcore et al. (2009) asked students to 'map' their days, drawing in their locations on printed maps at different times of the day. They discovered that many of their subjects had days that purposefully avoided the library – days that avoided the 'geographical center' of the campus because they variously needed quiet, felt unwelcome, and felt that the library wasn't a place for them because of their learning disabilities or their age. Targeting non-users can be really difficult, because they are not present in your gate count, circulation and website statistics, they don't ask questions, and they don't go to the places that you go. This background knowledge on library non-users, a tremendously difficult group to conduct library research upon, gives valuable insight for planning should researchers ever want to gather a representative sample for a survey or interview. As well as its usefulness in helping inform future research, approaching ethnographic research with a fully open mind will lead to richer data. The more open you are, the more likely it is that you will find questions, behaviors and explanations to probe that you never expected.

Though many librarians may not have the statistical skills or the training in quantitative research methods needed in order to create robust survey instruments, librarians *are* well-suited to collecting ethnographic data about their users, have the classification skills required to analyze the data, and may have the writing skills needed to write up the finished project. Librarians are both involved and detached from the user communities that they work for, which is the key element for locating and entering and beginning to understand a research field (Powdermaker, 1967; Robben and Sluka, 2012).

Delcore argues that 'in the end, to know library users accurately is to know how to reach them effectively with core library values and services' (Delcore et al., 2009). I believe that this idea can be extended to design as well: to know library users accurately is to know how to design effectively for them. To that end, this chapter describes why and when a designer who wants to create an engaging, efficient user experience in a library might like to use ethnographic methods, and what types of questions are best answered using these methods. This chapter also highlights some of the method's pitfalls and ways to avoid them. Rather than hoping (and failing) to write an exhaustive guide to ethnographic methods and research design, this chapter is meant to be a springboard and inspiration to those interested in trying the methods out, and points out relevant literature to read further. The budding librarian ethnographer is encouraged to consult the Methods Toolkit produced by the Ethnographic Research in Illinois Academic Libraries (ERIAL) research team (Asher and Miller, 2011). This toolkit is exceptionally well written and easy to understand, and points interested readers to a solid range of further reading. There are of course also many useful chapters in this very book, including Chapter 7 by ERIAL's own Andrew Asher.

What has ethnography looked like in libraries?

This section describes how ethnography and its precursors have been used in library research from the end of the nineteenth century up to the present day[1] and outlines the methods that are most relevant. There are researchers who stretch the types of data collection you can subsume under the heading of ethnography, such as role play (Delcore et al., 2009) and focus groups (Gabridge, Gaskell and Stout, 2008), or include structured (as opposed to ethnographic) interviewing. In this chapter, I focus solely on participant observation, cultural probes and thick description, and on how these techniques have been and could be used in library research.

Though the term 'ethnography' doesn't appear in the LIS literature until relatively recently, the desire to understand a user community in context and in all its complexity has a long history in libraries. In her review of ethnographic methods in LIS, Goodman points to the use of something called 'community analysis' which relies on a holistic understanding of a library's community with the goal of improving the service that a library provides (Goodman, 2011). The roots of community analysis are documented as early as 1896 with an essay advocating that librarians know their communities and understand users as individuals in order to provide better library service (Cutler, 1896). This approach was carried throughout the twentieth century. It can be argued that librarians who are interested in ethnography today should consider looking at the community assessment literature as well (McCleer, 2013). Ethnography in libraries has received a considerable boost from Foster and Gibbons's inspiring 2007 work on student work habits, *Studying Students* – it is a trend which has even been mapped – but these types of highly qualitative research studies are still a tiny proportion of the library literature (Khoo, Rozaklis and Hall, 2012).

Khoo et al.'s 2012 systematic review of ethnographic methods in LIS includes a review of useful readings for the beginner librarian ethnographer, both in LIS and in anthropology, and traces the development of the method throughout the twentieth century to the present day.

Participant observation and cultural probes in ethnographic research

In order to collect data for ethnographic research, you can conduct participant observation or you can use a cultural probe, where the study population gathers data on themselves at the request of the researcher. The researcher will be using fieldnotes and memos in an effort to write a 'thick description' (more on thick description later in this chapter) of the study population.

Participant observation

Participant observation is a combination of entering the life world of the subject, understanding its logic as the subject understands it, feeling and thinking and hearing as the subject but ultimately as an observer, or as one distinct from the group that objectifies that world (Rock, 2001). Emerson, Fretz and Shaw describe participant observation as

> establishing a place in some natural setting on a relatively long term basis in order to investigate, experience and represent the social life and social processes that occur in that setting . . . . Producing written accounts and descriptions.
>
> (2001, p. 352)

It is the ultimate form of 'being there' in the anthropologist Clifford Geertz's sense (Geertz, 1973). It is the classic method of actually collecting data on study populations in ethnography. The process of participant observation is iterative and the research goals are guided by the subject.

The phrase 'participant observation' is contradictory because as a pure participant you are too engaged to observe or reflect, while as a pure observer you are too detached to participate (Paul, 1953, as cited in DeWalt and DeWalt, 2002). The exact mixture of participation and observation will be dictated by the aims of the research and also by the individual nature of the subject community and the researcher. There may be limitations on the amount of participation that a researcher can have, given barriers constructed by differences in gender, age, ethnicity or class. In the case of a librarian ethnographer studying students at a university, the most frequent barrier will be age (you could overcome this barrier by studying mature students or by employing an undergraduate research assistant). A librarian studying a scholarly community of researchers might encounter the barrier of a lack of disciplinary knowledge. A librarian studying a public library community might encounter barriers of age, class or ethnicity.

The level of participation in participant observation can range from non-participatory observation to passive, moderate, active or complete participation. Research goals should always determine the level of participation. Practical considerations such as ethical review, employment contracts, professional duties and many other factors may well conspire, however, in taking this decision out of your hands.

Regardless of where the involvement level falls, the degree to which you participate and the degree to which you identify with the community must be clearly described in methodological notes, fieldnotes and diary entries. If you don't do this, you run the risk of ethical violations and invalid, unreliable findings. The literature on ethnographic ethics is vast, but a good starting point would be Clifford and Marcus (1986) or Murphy and Dingwall (2001).

DeWalt and DeWalt (2002) describe the key elements of participant observation as:

- Living in the context for an extended period of time
- Learning and using the local language and dialect
- Actively participating
- Using everyday conversation as an interview technique
- Informally observing during leisure (or 'hanging out')
- Recording observation in field notes.

Techniques for being a good observer include keeping in mind that you will need to describe what you have seen later and that there can never be too much detail. Naive observers tend to see more than native observers, so try to return to the field each day with fresh eyes, never taking any observation for granted. It is surprising how much you will forget. Besides DeWalt, a highly readable guide to participant observation is Crang and Cook (2007).

Cultural probe

Another data collection technique is the cultural probe, where a researcher commissions a study population to collect data on themselves. Researchers provide participants with prompts such as 'take a photo of how you like to write your essay' or 'take a photo of a place you like to concentrate' and give them tools such as one-touch cameras, blank maps of a campus or building, or postage-paid postcards with prompts written at the top. Tools can be technical, such as audio or video recorders, or as simple as large or small pieces of paper. These visual or audio artifacts are then used to jog the memories of students later in interviews or debriefing sessions and also as data for the researchers to interpret and analyze. If you had a 'students as researchers' scheme, you could also have students assist with interpreting and analyzing cultural probe data in order to reduce the aforementioned barriers to understanding. By nature, these are brief prompts, and the brevity makes barriers to participation very low. Completing the task should be easy and appealing, from the moment a participant is handed a neat package containing their prompts and tools.[2]

This method was used with great success by Foster and Gibbons (2007) when they asked students to map their movements around their university campus for 24 hours and to make photo documentaries of their study environments. They also asked students to draw and use other arts and crafts materials to design their ideal reading rooms in order to inform library space planning. Inspired by Foster and Gibbons, cultural probes are popular in library research and have been copied extensively, most notably in three large-scale ethnographic studies in the US by anthropologists at MIT (Gabridge, Gaskell and Stout, 2008) and California State University Fresno (Delcore et al., 2009), and by the ERIAL team in Illinois (Asher and Miller, various).

Because the cultural probe is usually visual, it can cut down on jargon, which leads to misinterpretation, the plague of many questionnaires, surveys and interview schedules. If a user does misunderstand the prompt and photographs or maps the 'wrong' thing, it can still give you valuable insight into how impenetrable and ambiguous library jargon can be outside of the library world. Because of the iterative nature of the method, if the prompt is misunderstood consistently, you might have a chance to clarify it on the fly. The cultural probe also gives access to places researchers might not normally be allowed, as well as allowing access to users 24 hours a day. Perhaps most importantly, it can make the data collection process fun.

Unlike participant observation, cultural probes do not have their roots in ethnographic literature. They are first described by Gaver, Dunne and Pacenti in the field of human-computer interaction (1999). These authors conceived the cultural probe because they wanted to balance between researchers' authority and the participants' voices. They wanted a tool that

> wouldn't seem irrelevant or arrogant . . . but we didn't want the groups to constrain our designs unduly by focusing on needs or desires they already understood. We wanted to lead a discussion with the groups toward unexpected ideas, but we didn't want to dominate it.
>
> (Gaver, Dunne and Pacenti, 1999, p. 22)

Interestingly, Gaver et al. differentiate cultural probes from ethnographic studies and base them on fine arts, postmodern, surrealist and situationist methods. They do this in order to be open to what they call 'unscientific' impressions, sources and inspirations in addition to the data they get from classical methods. Though the cultural probe as such is not mentioned in the ethnographic literature, a similar approach, known as 'autophotography', does have a rich literature to inform it (Worth and Adair, 1972; Ziller, 1990; Kenney, 1993; Dodman, 2003; Crang and Cook, 2007). In autophotography, 'the researcher encourages or commissions participants to take pictures of parts of their environment or activities, in order to learn more about how they understand or interpret their world and themselves within it' (Crang and Cook, 2007, pp. 111–2). How people photograph or draw their space is a rich source of social meaning.

Research design is as crucial for cultural probes or autophotographic projects as it is for any other type of user research. As Gaver et al. put it:

> we believe the cultural probes could be adapted to a wide variety of similar design projects. Just as machine-addressed letters seem more pushy than friendly, however, so might a generic approach to the probes produce materials that seem insincere, like official forms with a veneer of marketing. The real strength of the method was that we had designed and produced the materials specifically for those people and for their environments.
>
> (1999, p. 29)

Thick description

The written product resulting from ethnographic research is a thick description of the events, practices and other significant symbols, not just as you saw them happen but also the context in which they reside (Geertz, 1973). This thick description is the 'translation' of a native culture into a form that makes sense to an outsider.

To aid understanding, Geertz gives us the example of a wink, which is a physiological motion that any human can make either involuntarily or in reaction to a physical stimulus. A wink can also be a form of communication. An ethnographer observing a wink would have to figure out, given the context, whether it was a physiological reaction or a method of communication. If it were a method of communication, the ethnographer must count on being able to understand both what the person winking was hoping to communicate and whether the intended meaning was understood by the person who was winked at.

From this section it becomes clear that data gathering, analysis and writing cannot be neatly separate tasks. You will need to consider all of them at the beginning of the project and revisit them throughout. Hence the idea of thick description has been included as part of the methods section. Data gathering, analysis and writing are not separable tasks in ethnography but happen continuously, which is why thick description is both method and research output.

The ongoing evolution of ethnography in LIS

A set of core methodological commitments and common research settings has been described, suggesting that the studies reported form a coherent and emerging research genre that uses ethnographic methods to investigate libraries, their users, wider social contexts, and the relationships between these phenomena.

(Khoo, Rozaklis and Hall, 2012, p. 86)

Because most ethnographic research that is conducted in library and information is done to inform a project or for the practical purpose of gaining insight into our user population, it does tend to stray quite far from a 'pure' academic ethnography which has no other purpose other than 'another country heard from' (Geertz, 1973, p. 23). It is, rather, applied ethnography – that is, 'ethnography pursued with the purpose of uncovering, understanding and addressing social problems' (Asher and Miller, 2011). It is possible that these quick and dirty ethnographic methods are okay to use, especially those that build upon the relationships and knowledge that someone experienced in a culture may already have (a researcher studying a familiar library community has several advantages over a researcher travelling to a remote village to which they have never been before). Librarians are well-suited to doing this because we are familiar with our settings and do have allies among our study populations, and we work and live among them every day (Emary, 2015). We cut down on the more time-consuming aspects of the rapport-building inherent in classic ethnography if we put these strengths into our research design. These methods may not exactly be a classic ethnography but would rather be better subsumed under the qualitative or mixed method umbrella. You could also consider conducting what might be better called 'ethnographically inspired' research, where your interest isn't simply academic. Those interested in rapid or applied ethnography will find resources in computer science and manufacturing literature (such as Anderson, 1994; Forsythe, 1999; Handwerker, 2001; and Sperschneider and Bagger, 2003).

Though there are exceptions, such as Asher and Delcore, LIS ethnographic research is not published in traditional ethnographic literature. In addition, Goodman (2011) points out that librarians have tended to ignore the original ethnographic thinkers, instead citing research within LIS. The popular cultural probe technique's root in human-computer interaction and the arts is further evidence that a certain kind of applied ethnography for LIS purposes is developing in its own right. Because the methods are becoming more popular and established, and also lack the disciplinary influence both in publication and in their bibliographies, it is incredibly important that they be well designed.

Selecting the research question

When designing research, the first thing a researcher should do is to determine that the question is important to answer and that answering it will add to existing knowledge. This is accomplished by finding where it fits into the existing body of literature. It is of commensurate importance to match the research question to the main data collection method, making sure that the technique selected can answer the research question. Ethnography is always rooted in a time and a place, so it is best used for understanding a snapshot of current practice rather than for explaining past events, changes or future behavior.

In the case of observation, there are certain questions that are well-suited to the method, and they are ones which require description, interpretation and explanation of what is currently happening for their answer. Observation is, however, limited to things that are *observable*.

It is impossible to observe an event which took place in the past, so using participant observation and cultural probes to explain behavior which took place in the past is complicated. It is possible to gain an understanding of a cultural memory or a reconstructed life story through participant observation, conversation, artifacts of material culture and documentary analysis (Crang and Cook, 2007). Whether this type of analysis is appropriate should be driven by the research question, but its utility for user experience seems limited.

Likewise, you cannot use ethnography to predict the future because you cannot observe an event which has not yet taken place. This is deceptively complicated. Often, when we do research driven by strategic goals, we want to know what's going to happen so we can prepare for it. An understanding of current practices and cultural norms can help anticipate further actions. You can use ethnographic methods to inform future, more focused research such as the design of a Dan Ariely–style human behavior experiment (Ariely, 2009) or to generate user requirements for a library management system. It is possible to construct a strong hypothesis based on your rich understanding of culture, but you cannot rely on ethnographic data to create a model of what will happen in the future.

In the case of user experience it is useful to think about research questions which have events or practices that you might be able to observe. Events can be commonplace, routine, daily occurrences or they can be rare and special events, though the latter can be difficult by nature, because they either cannot or can only infrequently be observed. Both can be important, depending on the research question, but be especially careful about discounting the importance of commonplace events.

Research questions and approaches

This section highlights some possible questions you might like to ask about the current user experience of your library and how you might use ethnography to build a better user experience. The suggested approaches are just one of many that could be taken. Types of questions that might work best are ones that ask 'what is the nature of X in a particular setting?' and 'how does it fit?'

1   *Research question*: Users dislike the library's discovery tool and it doesn't seem to be helped by offers for additional training. You'd like to understand the nature of their discontent and what their problems are.

   Possible approach: This would be great for participant observation. Ask if you can sit with users while they search for resources. Don't limit participants to using the discovery tool, even though you'd like to! If you were interested in how users responded to and used the discovery tool, consider a so-called Think Aloud usability test, where users describe what they are doing while they search.

2 *Research question*: What kind of furniture should we buy for our reading room? What kinds of spaces do we need in our renovated library?

Possible approach: Based on the atmosphere you'd like to create in your new library space (e.g. quiet concentration, cooperative work, convivial and welcoming, relaxing), have users take photographs of their favorite places for doing that activity. If there are spaces that you know of that have the atmosphere you'd like to recreate, go there and observe. Take photos of subjects sitting when they are concentrating on understanding a complicated print book. Are there differences when they concentrate on an e-reader? How do they sit when reading a book on a desktop computer? When writing their essay or typing up research results? What do these photographs of concentrating people tell you about the way we should be designing study space? Simply counting how many people are in a particular location or engaged in a particular activity or drawing a map are good places to start.

3 *Research question*: Your library ranks consistently low on user satisfaction surveys (such as the National Student Survey), but the library's collection usage and footfall statistics have never been higher. What do users really think of the library's services and resources? What are your users' true understandings of Question 16 in that survey?

Possible approach: Identify a library research–intensive assignment such as an annotated bibliography. Ask participants to use a cultural probe such as a map or LEGO bricks to model their ongoing use of the library during their assignment. Alternatively, have students keep an audio journal as they are searching. During debrief interview sessions, try to get at the nature of the terms 'good enough' and 'library services and resources' (see the first section of this chapter for more on Question 16) to find out if the user population understands these terms in the same way that you do.

4 *Research question*: The campus wireless network needs upgrading and you need to convince management to give you major funds to do so. How do staff members use wireless in their work? What happens when it fails them?

Possible approach: Loan the target population digital cameras with precise locations and time stamps enabled. Ask them to take photos of their devices in context when the wireless network drops. This might be a tutor in a class-room attempting to connect a guest lecturer's laptop to the projector, only to discover that the wireless doesn't work. Use these photographs to gather context and understanding of how your users rely on Internet access at different locations across campus. You will be able to triangulate exact locations and times to find out where these events are taking place and whether your IT help desk is available for assistance during peak incident times.

You could also approach this with participant observation by documenting the events when they lose their wireless connection. This would be well triangulated by a paper trail.

5   *Research question*: What types of workarounds do your patrons use?[3] This 'misuse' of a service, equipment or space in the library can be a valuable example of actual user needs and gaps in the provision.

Possible approach: When you identify a workaround, try to observe it without judgment over a period of time. Try also to join in and experience what it is like to move the furniture or eat your lunch in the reading room, for example. If you notice that patrons are using the library as a safe haven because they have nowhere else to hang out during the day, abandon your desk but try to still accomplish your work.

6   *Research question*: Does the language you use on your web page make sense to your user population?

Possible approach: The approach you use here might be similar to those you used for the discovery tool research question (Question 1 in this list). Use participant observation with students as they complete a research-intensive assignment. With the help of ethnographic interviewing and observation of work practices, pay special attention to the words they use to describe their actions. Keep your ears open to familiar words used in ways that are new to you. Notice also which words are not used. It may be worth extending this to observing how tutors talk about the information search, as these are the people that they learn from. See also the approach described in Question 8 in this list.

7   *Research question*: Gabridge et al. found that undergraduates tend to stop when they find information that is 'good enough' for their assignments and that graduate students move to a feeling that they can never find anything good enough. What is going on?

Possible approach: What is good enough, and how is it determined? A hands-on portion of an information literacy session is perhaps a chance to observe undergraduate searching behavior. This might also be a place for ethnographic interviewing (for more on ethnographic interviewing see Heyl [2001] or Spradley [1979]). Find a contrasting community of graduate researchers engaged in the literature review portion of their dissertation. With the help of a primary informant, see if you can accompany this community as they write their theses. What is the nature of the feeling that they can't ever find enough? Listen carefully to how they speak about their results and also what types of judgments they can't or won't articulate.

8   *Research question*: Students listen to tutors and to each other, and rarely to librarians. You are hearing again and again from new users that a fellow student told them to come to the library to use a certain service or resource, despite the fact that you have been promoting this same resource or service on social media, on the website, in printed form, in the virtual learning environment (VLE) and in the classroom.

Possible approach: Develop rapport and a primary informant in a faculty that you are interested in. Develop a participant observation research project that asks: What does communication look like from student to student? What is the nature of the relationship between students and tutor in that discipline; does it change throughout time? Who or what is excluded from that communication and relationship, and what does that mean for the library? The location of the field might be attending lectures, completing the assignments, observing and participating in the VLE, being a part of group work and hanging out with students. Keep an eye on the written course documentation and the structure of communication between tutor and student. What is said may be as important as what is not said.

9 *Research question*: How can we integrate uploading to the institutional repository into research staff's workflow rather than creating an extra, onerous task?

Possible approach: Start by getting a holistic understanding of how they work, preferably over the course of 12 months, so as to see whether/ how practice and needs change depending on academic dates. Look at workspaces, analyzing work processes such as version control, submission to a journal, archiving and sharing practices. Again, look at workarounds and mistakes and frustrations – how can you design the institutional repository in such a way that it flows with work practice or even improves its efficiency? What do you find when you literally sit in a participant's chair? What have they printed out? Do they use a keyboard or a mouse for their work? Do they have privacy and time, or is their work environment rushed and cramped? Are there relationships and people they rely heavily upon for certain tasks? What is the language they use to talk about their research outputs? What do they value? What do they fear?

How to conduct ethnographic research in library settings: designing to maximize reliability and validity

After you have selected the question, it's crucial to design a research project that has feasible outcomes that can actually answer the question you are asking. Because ethnography casts its net so widely when looking for data and uses the researcher as the data collection instrument in many cases, it might be assumed that research design would be less important in ethnography than it would be in other areas of social science. DeWalt and others argue, however, that research design is of more central importance in ethnography than it is in other fields precisely because it is too easy to become vague and to collect irrelevant or overly biased data. Without proper design, it is not scholarly research but a collection of anecdotes, unreliable and invalid. For more on the dangers of poorly designed ethnographic research and the pitfalls and dangers to avoid, see Sandstrom and Sandstrom (1995).

Research design should optimize objectivity, which is composed of two parts:

- *Validity*: whether the description actually matches the phenomenon studied.
- *Reliability*: the likelihood that the results would be reproduced under the same conditions.

Validity is often challenged and transgressed in ethnography (Crang and Cook, 2007) because the question of whether there is an objective reality is so complex. Researchers have a responsibility to be as scientific as possible, but it's most often a case of striving to achieve rather than achieving validity. Because the researcher is the main instrument for gathering data in ethnography, a certain amount of bias is inevitable. One way to improve validity is to be as explicit as possible about your own biases in fieldnotes and in the final write-up so that others can evaluate findings in light of the bias. Triangulating data is also key for improving validity.

Reliability is also problematic in ethnography, as 'the same researcher never enters the same river twice', meaning that even the same researcher in the same location can never reproduce the same results because ethnography is rooted in a time period as much as it is rooted in a specific location (see the previous section for more on this idea). Despite this, reliability can be optimized with careful documentation of choices made, particularly with regard to how and under which circumstances data were collected. This is typically accomplished by writing detailed memos and a high level of reflexivity (Clifford and Marcus, 1986; Davies, 2008).[4]

The quality and usefulness of the research will be determined by the following factors which must be a part of the research design:

- how well the type of question can be answered with the data collection method selected;
- the selection of the research site (Are your users geographically dispersed? Can you find them all in a lab or classroom? In a virtual learning environment?);
- representativeness of the venues, activities and informants;
- strategy for recording as completely as possible;
- planning for ways in which data will be analyzed and triangulated.

Though sampling functions differently in highly qualitative methodology than it does in quantitative methodology, it is still tremendously important. The sample chosen should adequately address the question you are asking, which should not be about exact size and distribution (e.g. 'How many times does X occur?'), but rather, as was mentioned in the 'Selecting the Research Question' section, 'What is the nature of X in a particular setting?' and 'How does it fit?' Sampling can work in a variety of ways in ethnography. One could use judgment sampling, which is selecting individuals and events to study because of the characteristics that they bring to the research, or one could use convenience sampling, which could pose problems in that it seriously limits representativeness. When creating a sample, you must ask the question, 'What are the relevant sources of diversity within a group?' When looking at improving the user experience for a certain faculty, sources of diversity might include sub-discipline studied and stage in their career. Actual numbers of participants will be low compared to a survey method, because the volume of data collected on each participant will be high.

There are fabulous texts on research design, both in ethnography and for other quantitative and qualitative methods; as ever, a good place for the librarian ethnographer to begin is the ERIAL Toolkit (Asher and Miller, 2011).

Conclusions

Ethnography offers a rich and flexible method for getting to know the users whose experience we'd like to improve. With notable exceptions, libraries and librarians over-rely on surveys, questionnaires and statistics for gathering information on our users' satisfaction with our collections and services. This is also true of the LIS literature, as Khoo et al. (2012) discovered:

> a recent survey . . . of trends in information behavior research from 1999 to 2008, identified 749 articles, of which 528 were research studies; of these latter studies, seven (1.3%) were classified as 'ethnographic'. A pilot study for the present study suggested that these previously reported figures are underestimates.
>
> (p. 83)

Recent ethnographic studies in libraries have proven that results can be useful for informing how we design for users, and the tradition of using 'community assessment' to understand our users shows that documenting user culture is a long-standing interest for librarians.

There is evidence that, especially given the applied nature of the research that librarians do, 'library ethnography' is developing in its own right. This is exciting, as library and information science is a discipline where we lack our own methodology and must borrow from other disciplines, often with uneven results. This development has its perils, however, and we must be careful to maintain rigorous design in order to achieve as much objectivity and reliability as possible. Quick and dirty ethnography may well result in a 'thin description' where you focus more on the surface facts than on the context and translation crucial to thick description. One should be wary of the professional or logistical pressures which may compromise reliability and validity of the research we conduct. Finally, if we are going to base our research on second-hand understandings of ethnographic literature and publish our work outside of the ethnographic literature and conference sphere, we must make sure we do it on purpose and not because we are unaware of the disciplinary underpinnings and the method's current developments. If you are familiar with the rules by which the game is played, the LIS research will be the better for it.

Notes

1 This chapter is limited to my experiences and perceptions of academic libraries in the US, the UK and Germany, and circumstances may be different in other types of libraries and other countries. The terms 'ethnography' and 'anthropology' are used interchangeably.
2 Both Gaver and Foster have published photographs of their cultural probes' appealing packaging.
3 This example is inspired by Goodman (2011).
4 A useful tool for managing and relating memos to other data you collect is a software tool like NVivo.

References

Anderson, R. J., 1994. Representations and requirements: The value of ethnography in system design. *Human–Computer Interaction,* 9(3), pp. 151–82.

Ariely, D., 2009. *Predictably Irrational.* New York: HarperCollins.

Asher, A. D. and Miller, S., various. *ERIAL Publications.* [online] Available at: <http://www.erialproject.org/publications/> [Accessed 19 November 2014].

Asher, A. D. and Miller, S., 2011. *So You Want to Do Anthropology in Your Library? Or a Practical Guide to Ethnographic Research in Academic Libraries.* [pdf] Available at: <http://www.erialproject.org/publications/toolkit/> [Accessed 11 November 2014].

Clifford, J. and Marcus, G. E. eds, 1986. *Writing Culture: The Poetics and Politics of Ethnography.* Berkeley: University of California Press.

Crang, M. and Cook, I., 2007. *Doing Ethnographies.* London: SAGE.

Cutler, M., 1896. Two fundamentals. *The Library Journal,* 21 October, pp. 446–9.

Davies, C. A., 2008. *Reflexive Ethnography: A Guide to Researching Selves and Others.* 2nd ed. London: Routledge.

Delcore, H. D., Mullooly, J., Scroggins, M., Arnold, K., Franco, E. and Gaspar, J., 2009. *The Library Study at Fresno State.* Fresno: Institute of Public Anthropology, California State University.

DeWalt, K. M. and DeWalt, B. R., 2002. *Participant Observation: A Guide for Fieldworkers.* Walnut Creek, CA: Altamira Press.

Dodman, D. R., 2003. Shooting in the city: An autophotographic exploration of the urban environment in Kingston, Jamaica. *Area,* 35(3), pp. 293–304.

Emary, L. R., 2015. Librarians are already in the field: How and why to begin ethnographic fieldwork. *Bibliothek Forschung und Praxis,* 39(2), pp. 138–42.

Emerson, R. M., Fretz, R. I. and Shaw, L. L., 2001. Participant Observation and Fieldnotes. In: P. Atkinson, A. Coffey, S. Delamont, J. Lofland and L. Lofland, eds, *Handbook of Ethnography.* Thousand Oaks, CA: SAGE. pp. 352–68.

Forsythe, D. E., 1999. 'It's just a matter of common sense': Ethnography as invisible work. *Computer Supported Cooperative Work (CSCW),* 8(1–2), pp. 127–45.

Foster, N. F. and Gibbons, S. eds, 2007. *Studying Students: The Undergraduate Research Project at the University of Rochester.* Chicago: Association of College and Research Libraries.

Gabridge, T., Gaskell, M. and Stout, A., 2008. Information seeking through students' eyes: The MIT photo diary study. *College & Research Libraries,* 69(6), pp. 510–23.

Gaver, B., Dunne, T. and Pacenti, E., 1999. Design: Cultural probes. *Interactions,* 6(1), pp. 21–9.

Geertz, C., 1973. *The Interpretation of Cultures.* New York: Basic Books.

Goodman, V. D., 2011. Applying ethnographic research methods in library and information settings. *Libri*, 61(1), pp. 1–11.

Greifeneder, E., 2012. *Does It Matter Where We Test? Online User Studies in Digital Libraries in Natural Environments*. PhD. Institut für Bibliotheks- und Informationswissenschaft, Humboldt Universität zu Berlin.

Handwerker, W. P., 2001. *Quick Ethnography*. Lanham, MD: Rowman Altamira.

Heyl, B. S., 2001. Ethnographic Interviewing. In: P. Atkinson, A. Coffey, S. Delamont, J. Lofland and L. Lofland, eds, *Handbook of Ethnography*. Thousand Oaks, CA: SAGE. pp. 369–82.

Kenney, K., 1993. Using self-portrait photographs to understand self-concepts of Chinese and American university students. *Visual Anthropology*, 5(3–4), pp. 245–69.

Khoo, M., Rozaklis, L. and Hall, C., 2012. A survey of the use of ethnographic methods in the study of libraries and library users. *Library & Information Science Research*, 34(2), pp. 82–91.

McCleer, A., 2013. Knowing communities: A review of community assessment literature. *Public Library Quarterly*, 32(3), pp. 263–74.

Murphy, E. and Dingwall, R., 2001. The Ethics of Ethnography. In: P. Atkinson, A. Coffey, S. Delamont, J. Lofland and L. Lofland, eds, *Handbook of Ethnography*. Thousand Oaks, CA: SAGE. pp. 339–51.

Powdermaker, H., 1967. *Stranger and Friend: The Way of an Anthropologist*. London: Secker and Warburg.

Robben, A.C.G.M. and Sluka, J.A., 2012. *Ethnographic Fieldwork: An Anthropological Reader*. 2nd ed. Malden, MA: Wiley-Blackwell.

Rock, P., 2001. Symbolic Interactionism and Ethnography. In: P. Atkinson, A. Coffey, S. Delamont, J. Lofland and L. Lofland, eds, *Handbook of Ethnography*. Thousand Oaks, CA: SAGE. pp. 26–38.

Sandstrom, A. R. and Sandstrom, P. E., 1995. The use and misuse of anthropological methods in library and information science research. *Library Quarterly*, 65, pp. 161–99.

Sperschneider, W. and Bagger, K., 2003. Ethnographic fieldwork under industrial constraints: Toward design-in-context. *International Journal of Human-Computer Interaction*, 15(1), p. 41.

Spradley, J. P., 1979. *The Ethnographic Interview*. Belmont, CA: Wadsworth Group/ Thomson Learning.

Worth, S. and Adair, J., 1972. *Through Navajo Eyes*. Bloomington: Indiana University Press.

Ziller, R. C., 1990. *Photographing the Self: Methods for Observing Personal Orientations*. London: SAGE.

7 Identifying the barriers

Taskscapes and the social contexts of library UX

Andrew D. Asher

Approaching the non-user

When asked what she had heard about university library services, a graduate student in business at Northeastern Illinois University (NEIU) explained that she felt like this information had never reached her:

> Maybe it's because [I'm] older, and because [I] only go part time, but I feel like – and this is [my] first semester too – they didn't really explain to us, like, all the different options we have, and then, like, [I've] kind of bumped into some of the computer labs on [my] own and stuff like that . . . maybe because we're grad students, they don't go over that. Maybe they do, like, a training class with the younger students, but no – anything that [I've] done I've found on the internet.

Students who encounter difficulties utilizing library resources and services due to factors – such as part-time enrollment status – that are largely outside of a library's control present especially difficult design problems for the libraries trying to support them. How does a library approach and understand the user experience (UX) needs of a student who doesn't use the library? And, importantly, how does a library learn about these students in order to more effectively reach out to them and hopefully convert these non-users into patrons?

Using data collected during the Ethnographic Research in Illinois Academic Libraries (ERIAL) Project (see http://www.erialproject.org and Duke and Asher, 2012), this chapter argues that questions like these require expanding the conceptualization of UX in libraries to include not only how people interact with library tools and interfaces, but also how these systems and services are embedded within the wider social contexts of student and university life. To this end, this chapter will compare the experience of students at two universities and examine how the interrelationships between academic and non-academic tasks, occurring across varied configurations of place and time, structure and constrain students' educational practices in ways that significantly affect their use of library resources and services. Based on these empirical observations, this chapter contends that obtaining a broad and holistic appreciation of students' social and educational landscapes is essential to gaining a more comprehensive understanding of, and ultimately designing for, their library user experience.

This approach differs from the norm of many UX practitioners, who tend to emphasize in their definitions of UX a person's experience with a product or service via a particular interface (Law et al., 2009, p. 727). However, this focus risks falling into what anthropologists sometimes describe as 'the great tool-use fallacy' (Reynolds, 1993, p. 410), which 'insist[s] upon the separation between the domains of technical and social activity' (Ingold, 1993, p. 158). While many UX-focused libraries and librarians probably do consider UX to extend beyond interfaces to include face-to-face services, as librarians work to improve websites and other online tools it is often easy to lose sight of how these technologies fit (or don't fit) within the broader social contexts of their users' lives. Carefully considering the social context of UX design problems is therefore equally important and inseparable from the technical aspects of these issues; it matters very little how high quality library interfaces, tools, and services are if other social factors prevent users from ever encountering them.

For this reason, this chapter focuses on an ethnographic examination of how the social contexts of students affect their academic practices and library usage. By eschewing an examination of any particular library interface, tool, or service, this chapter presents a case study for understanding the ways students' unique social contexts have general implications for library design and provides examples demonstrating the necessity of reflecting on students' experiences holistically before considering the narrower questions of specific UX designs.

Learning about taskscapes

The ERIAL Project was a 21-month collaborative research study conducted by five Illinois universities[1] in 2008–2010 to investigate how university students conduct academic research and utilize library resources and services. The study focused on gathering first-hand accounts and observations of how undergraduate students obtained, evaluated, and managed information for their academic assignments, as well as understanding the social contexts in which this work takes place. Utilizing an ethnographic methodology that employed a variety of anthropological data collection techniques, the ERIAL Project built a rich dataset that included information provided by more than 650 students, librarians, and faculty members participating in nine research activities (see Asher, Miller and Green, 2012).

Although the ERIAL Project was not originally conceived or designed as a user experience study, its holistic and user-centered approach to understanding students' educational needs yielded detailed information about how students interacted with, or failed to interact with, library websites, tools, services, and spaces, as well as the myriad obstacles and difficulties they encountered while doing so. This approach allowed the ERIAL Project to especially examine how students' academic practices were conducted within the wider social contexts of everyday student life, and how differences in these contexts had a direct impact on students' information-gathering habits and their usage of library resources, spaces and information systems.

Table 7.1 University profiles of Illinois Wesleyan University and Northeastern Illinois University (enrollment figures as of fall 2009)

	IWU	*NEIU*
Location	Bloomington, IL	Chicago, IL
Campus environment	Residential	Commuter
Public/private	Private	Public
Type	Liberal arts	Hispanic-serving
Carnegie classification	Baccalaureate Colleges – Arts & Sciences	Master's Colleges and Universities (larger programs)
Total enrollment	2,066	11,631
Undergraduate enrollment	2,066	9,191
Graduate enrollment	0	2,440

Source: National Center for Education Statistics, http://nces.ed.gov/ipeds/datacenter/.

In order to illustrate how these contextual differences are reflected in students' user needs, I will focus my analysis in this chapter on the experiences of students from just two of the ERIAL universities: Illinois Wesleyan University (IWU), a small private liberal arts university with a residential campus located in Bloomington, a medium-sized city in central Illinois; and Northeastern Illinois University (NEIU), a medium-sized public university with a primarily commuter campus located in the urban environment of the north side of Chicago (see Table 7.1).

A brief comparison of the universities' demographic profiles strongly suggests that their student constituencies are likely to differ in their needs and experiences (see Table 7.2). For example, essentially all of IWU's students are 'traditionally' aged (i.e. under 24) and enrolled full time in their studies, while almost half of NEIU's students are over age 25, and over 40% are enrolled part time. NEIU also has a much more ethnically diverse student body than IWU (with 30% of its students identifying as Hispanic/Latino(a), NEIU is a federally designated Hispanic-serving institution), and serves a student community in greater need of financial assistance (as measured indirectly by the Pell Grant program). Based on these observations, it seems likely that these high-level differences in student population will be reflected in different types of needs for individual students.

To provide a conceptual framework for comparing students' varied experiences, I employ Delcore et al.'s application at Fresno State University of anthropologist Tim Ingold's (1993) 'taskscape' model to the analysis of the interwoven social contexts, spaces, locations, and temporal cycles within which students complete their academic work (Delcore et al., 2009, p. 14). Ingold defines a taskscape as an entire ensemble of mutually interlocking tasks, or 'an array of related activities' that 'carry forward the processes of social life' across time and space (Ingold, 1993, pp. 157–8). Spatially, taskscapes include the network of locations in which a person carries out his or her everyday activities, while temporally, taskscapes are formed by the 'complex interweaving of very many concurrent cycles' (Ingold,

Table 7.2 Demographic characteristics of Illinois Wesleyan University and Northeastern Illinois University undergraduate students as of fall 2009

	IWU	*NEIU*
Enrollment		
Full-time	99.6%	58%
Part-time	0.4%	42%
Age		
24 and under	99.6%	56%
Age 25 and over	0.4%	44%
Gender Ratio		
Male	41%	42%
Female	59%	58%
Race/Ethnicity		
Black/African American	5%	10%
Hispanic/Latino(a)	3%	30%
White/Caucasian	76%	39%
Asian	5%	10%
Unknown	7%	7%
Financial Aid		
Percent of students receiving Pell Grants (full-time, first-time students only)	16%	55%
Admissions		
Percent admitted	54%	74%
ACT Composite 75th percentile	30	21
ACT Composite 25th percentile	26	16

Source: National Center for Education Statistics, http://nces.ed.gov/ipeds/datacenter/.

1993, p. 160), such as the varying rhythms of course meetings, academic calendars, work schedules, and the obligations of friends and family life occurring across days, weeks, semesters, and years (Delcore et al., 2009, p. 14). Because of this complex web of mutually constitutive cycles and locations, Delcore et al. posit that activities like academic work cannot, and should not, be analyzed in isolation from other spheres of social life, but instead should be approached holistically and in connection with other activities (2009, p. 13). This mindset has important implications for thinking about UX in libraries: in order to provide tools and services at the right places and times we must first gain an understanding of how they fit within these complex social systems.

As a means of identifying and exploring the differences in taskscapes of students at IWU and NEIU, the ERIAL research team conducted 'mapping diaries' with

34 students, in which they were asked to map the places they went to during the course of an academic day and to briefly note what time they visited each place and their reason for going there. After the maps were complete, each student then met with one of the project's ethnographers for a debriefing interview in which their researcher walked the student through his or her day and discussed in detail the places and activities listed. The data from these debriefing interviews were analyzed in conjunction with the results from 57 more general ethnographic interviews with other students at IWU and NEIU, which provided additional information and context about the ways students approached academic research (see Asher, Miller and Green, 2012). The mapping diaries were then used to make structural comparisons of the spaces and times students engaged in particular activities. The spatial and temporal diagrams created from the student maps are too large and complex to depict here, but examples can be found on the UX in Libraries website (http://uxlib.org).

These diagrams reveal a number of similarities and differences in the ways students experienced their days. In general, students at both universities described taskscapes consisting of activities and tasks that can be roughly classified into three principal domains (academic, jobs, and family and social activities) taking place in three main locations (on campus, in off-campus residences, and at off-campus job sites). However, the experience of these taskscapes varied significantly due to the particular spatial and temporal geographies created by the ways these activities and places overlapped and intersected within an individual student's life.

Exploring student taskscapes

As is illustrated on the taskscape diagrams, the presence of a commute was one main structural difference between the taskscapes of students at NEIU and IWU, and was a difference that precipitated a great deal of the variance in students' educational experiences. NEIU students regularly reported one-way commuting times of 30–60 minutes, but the time required to travel to campus was less important than how the commute configured the cycles of students' days and separated the places and spaces that formed their taskscapes.

An NEIU graduate student in business discussed the effects of commuting: 'I mean, it's a little bit inflexible. You basically have certain things you have to do and you have to do them at exactly those times. There's no real way around it.' Other students described the commute as producing an isolating or atomizing university experience. When asked about the effects of her commute, a sophomore new to the NEIU campus explained:

> You know what, to be honest with you, it's kind of boring. I feel like I haven't met a single friend at school, because, I mean, I come usually right on time or a couple of minutes late to class and then I leave, and I think everybody else pretty much does the same thing, so it's really hard not being able to make any kind of – you know – contact with anybody . . . So, it's a little hard, and I think

it's hard to get really involved in anything on campus because . . . you're not here, [and] you don't want to be here on the days you're not here, you know?

The commute can even determine whether or not a student goes home at night. A NEIU sociology student explained:

I spend a significant amount of time at other people's houses . . . Monday and Thursday I get out of class so late that I can't even get home because my bus stops running. I guess I could . . . bike easily, but usually at ten o'clock the last thing I want to do is bike, like, two miles.

Because of the distance between their residences and campus, many NEIU students chose to use public libraries or other university libraries in neighborhoods closer to where they lived. These libraries were often places where students also had well-established relationships and habits. 'It's just [the library's] closer to me, and I just feel more comfortable [there] for some reason,' one elementary education student explained while describing why she worked at a public library. 'I've lived in that area forever. I was born there, I've always been to that library, I remember some of the librarians . . . they're not like friends or anything, but yeah, maybe that's why.' Another student differentiated between tasks she might complete at different public libraries as well as the NEIU library:

It just [depends] on . . . which public library, like in Oak Park [a western suburb of Chicago] there's one [library] with all this specific information; there's one [library] by my neighborhood, and that's for like – you know – for something really simple. Here [at NEIU] . . . if I want to stay on campus and like – [the NEIU library has] the [online] chat, so, like, you guys tell me 'oh it's here,' so, I'm like 'Yes!' I don't need to go anywhere else.

For NEIU students, home and campus were experienced as discrete places, separated by an often quite long commute. Campus was a place where students came to do particular tasks, such as attend class, study, or complete group work. Most NEIU students stayed on campus for a pre-planned and predefined period of time and then left, and the scheduling of these times was often determined in conjunction with needs dictated by schedules from other domains of activities such as work and family (more on this later).

In contrast, IWU students – none of whom reported more than a 5-minute walk to campus – had a much more fluid experience of their time spent on campus. Almost all IWU students reported spending the entire day on campus or at nearby apartments. For IWU students, 'home' and 'campus' were one and the same place – even for students who technically lived off campus. Students often spoke of the 'IWU bubble' where they spent virtually all of their time. A first-year student at IWU related how she felt about spending time on campus:

I just enjoy campus. It has everything that I need. My [dorm] room has every-thing else I need . . . I think [it's] a combination of [being] easily entertained

and being a freshman so, [I'm] still like exploring everything [on campus].
And the school [is] providing everything for me.

While the maps produced by students at both NEIU and IWU showed days
that were broken up by a schedule of classes that produced gaps to fill with other
activities, IWU's residential environment provided its students with the luxury of
long blocks of time to devote to study and coursework while on campus. NEIU
students' maps showed much more compressed periods of study time, with long
periods of time off campus punctuated by travel between locations. Both IWU
and NEIU students reported completing similar academic tasks while at home, but
because of the commute these spaces were discretely bounded for NEIU students,
while for IWU students they were experienced much more as a fluid single space.

NEIU's higher proportion of older and part-time students was also reflected in a
greater number of students who held part-time or full-time jobs, or had substantial
time demands devoted to familial obligations from children, spouses, and extended
family. The scheduling cycles and demands of these activities further delineated
NEIU students' taskscapes and limited the time available to students for academic
activities. Of the mapping diaries created by NEIU students, 70% included time
during the day for job activities, compared to only 29% of IWU students, all of
whom worked on campus (and more than half of these worked in the library itself).

A NEIU business student described the effect of her 40-hour workweek on her
study habits:

> When do I get my studying done? I don't study. I only study in study groups,
> so I usually end up taking off entire days from work because when I get home
> [from the university] – like I leave here at 8:20 [p.m.], I get home about 9:15
> and realistically me opening a book [at that time] is not happening. Besides
> that . . . pretty much I study in study groups and most of the time we have
> study groups off site and that's on Sundays . . . you know what, if I would have
> planned better with my scheduling . . . I would have fully thought through my
> schedule to say, 'Okay, it's a bad idea to spread out [my] schedule, two classes
> over four days' . . . [to] get [to campus] it's an hour, [and an] hour [and] twenty
> minutes and go home, [and] if I look at it my commute time is equal to my
> time that's in class. So, that's a wear and tear.

In addition to job schedules, family demands also routinely determined when
and where NEIU students could accomplish their academic work. When asked
about why she reported that she didn't use the library, a senior in psychology
described how the combination of her work and family obligations prevented her
from studying there: 'I have no time. I work, I have a two-and-a-half[-year-old]
boy . . . as soon as I finish whatever [on campus] I rush to work. So, I usually
study after ten or twelve [p.m.] when everybody's sleeping.' While describing her
favorite place to study, another NEIU student explained:

> in my house the dining room table is where everybody kind of gathers around.
> We eat. We study. And because I have such a big family . . . this ends up

being like my favorite place to study because I can watch my kids do their homework, and I do my homework. . . . I get up about, I want to say, about 4:30, 5:00 in the morning . . . and I study until [the] kids . . . get up . . . and ready for school.

None of the IWU students reported time devoted to family obligations, but social obligations and distractions did affect where they chose to work. For these students the university library often provided a refuge from dorm life. An IWU student related:

I usually [study] here [in the library]. 'Cause if I were even to try to study in my room, it would be impossible. There's too many distractions and too many loud noises. I live with obnoxious people on the floor. And the library is just very quiet and somewhat secluded. The people are respectful of other people; it's just a nice environment . . . this semester, I come [to the library] a lot more often. 'Cause it just gives me the opportunity to escape that on my floor. Just to escape the stress.

Taskscapes and access

Differences in NEIU and IWU students' taskscapes translate readily into significant implications on their access to library tools, resources, and services. For example, because IWU students spend almost all their time on campus, students have near-ubiquitous access both to the physical spaces and collections of the library as well as its virtual collections via the university network. Almost all of the maps produced by IWU students showed significant time spent in the university library, with many students using library spaces several times a day. From a library services standpoint, this indicates that IWU students can conceivably be reached by librarians and library programming almost any time during the day (except, perhaps, when they are in class) – including standard 9 a.m. to 5 p.m. office hours. NEIU students spent much less time physically present on campus, and while their mapping diaries also demonstrated that they do use the university library's spaces and collections, they often did so only for short, strictly allocated periods of time.

Because of this misalignment between the university schedule and the schedules of other activities in NEIU students' taskscapes, many NEIU students were unreachable during large parts of the workday, and their prime work times were often when campus and the library were not open: early in the morning or late at night. Since many NEIU students had to limit their work to specific parts of the day, or had to complete their academic tasks off campus, their access to the university library's resources could vary greatly. Likewise, because of the specific time demands of an urban geography, NEIU students often used libraries that were more convenient to their residences than the university library, but may or may not have had resources that were sufficient or appropriate for academic work. These findings echo those of Smale and Regalado (2014), who in a study of students in the urban environment at the City University of New York observed similar spatial patterns among commuter students. They concluded that 'the restrictions on access to and use of [information and communications technology] among the students we interviewed constrained the kinds of academic activities some students could engage in to specific locations and times.'

The contrasting taskscapes of NEIU and IWU students present very different UX design problems for the two university libraries. As is demonstrated by the maps and interviews presented here, many NEIU students were utilizing interfaces, tools, and services of other libraries that were entirely out of the university library's control. Additionally, many of NEIU students were effectively invisible during library hours, such as the mother who worked at 5 a.m., or the student who worked all day and arrived on campus only at night. One critical design problem for the NEIU library is therefore less about particular interfaces, tools, or services than about general outreach to these students: how can the library meet students at the times and spaces they need and at the speed they need to complete their tasks?

In comparison, IWU students, with very few exceptions, access library resources from on campus or nearby. Knowing this is the case, the IWU librarians can approach their design of library tools and services from within the context of the affordances of a residential campus and the associated luxuries of more flexible and fluid dynamics of time.

Without a doubt, these differences in students' taskscapes are also related to broader issues of class and inequality. IWU students' experience of taskscapes in which academic, work, and family and social activities align in a single place are affordances particular to IWU's residential campus and the relative wealth of the university and its students. With greater average amounts of time allocated to the demands of jobs and family, coupled with an urban environment that dictates commuting to campus, NEIU students experience much less flexibility in their taskscapes as the places where activities occur are forced to diverge. This divergence constrains their possibilities for completing academic tasks in directly observable ways, and in ways that affect and determine their ability to access the resources of the university and the university library. These constraints are almost certainly linked to many students' difficult economic realities as they juggle academic demands with providing support for themselves and their families in an expensive metropolitan area. Additional study of the impact of these class and economic structures on students' taskscapes is probably warranted, as Delcore et al. have also suggested (2009, p. 20).

By revealing the lived experience of students' taskscapes, the maps created during the ERIAL Project demonstrate the necessity of approaching UX design problems first from a holistic understanding of students' social contexts. These contexts also affect any library's tools, resources, and services generally and independently of specific interfaces. As is illustrated by the very different experiences of IWU and NEIU students, this method also underscores the importance of examining the local realities of a university campus along with how a university library fits within the complex interconnections of spaces, times, schedules, and activities that comprise students' taskscapes whenever we design and plan the systems and services we hope they interact with.

Note

1 Northeastern Illinois University (NEIU), DePaul University, Illinois Wesleyan University (IWU), the University of Illinois at Chicago (UIC), and the University of Illinois at Springfield (UIS).

References

Asher, A. D., Miller, S. and Green, D., 2012. Ethnographic Research in Illinois Academic Libraries: The ERIAL Project. In: L. M. Duke and A. D. Asher, eds, *College Libraries and Student Culture: What We Now Know*. Chicago: American Library Association. pp. 1–14.

Delcore, H. D., Mullooly, J., Scroggins, M., Arnold, K., Franco, E. and Gaspar, J., 2009. *The Library Study at Fresno State*. Fresno: Institute of Public Anthropology, California State University.

Duke, L. M. and Asher, A. D. eds, 2012. *College Libraries and Student Culture: What We Now Know*. Chicago: American Library Association.

Ingold, T., 1993. The Temporality of the Landscape. *World Archaeology*, 25(2), pp. 152–74.

Law, E.L.C., Roto, V., Hassenzahl, M., Vermeeren, A. P. and Kort, J., 2009. Understanding, scoping and defining user experience: A survey approach. In: *Proceedings of the SIGCHI Conference on Human Factors in Computing Systems*. New York: ACM. pp. 719–28.

Reynolds, P. C., 1993. The Complementation Theory of Language and Tool Use. In: K. R. Gibson and T. Ingold, eds, *Tools, Language and Cognition in Human Evolution*. Cambridge: Cambridge University Press. pp. 407–28.

Smale, M. and Regalado, M., 2014. Commuter Students Using Technology. *Educause Review Online*, [online]. Available at: <http://www.educause.edu/ero/article/commuter-students-using-technology> [Accessed 18 December 2014].

8 Illuminating study spaces at Cambridge University with spacefinder

A case study

Andy Priestner

It is not often that you attend a meeting in which different people with different agendas reach complete consensus on a way forward, but on a cold January day in Cambridge University Library's Milstein Room this is precisely what happened. The topic on the table was the relative merit of the concepts presented to us by design consultancy Modern Human, which we planned to test out in libraries across Cambridge as part of the ongoing FutureLib programme funded by the University Library (see https://futurelib.wordpress.com). The programme, which I have been managing since July 2015, is seeking to pilot new and innovative library services and products which respond to the real needs, wants and behaviours of our users, and have been derived from an ethnographic research phase. The ethnographic techniques employed during this 18-month-long phase were:

*   'guerrilla' walk-up interviews with students;
*   in-depth but unstructured interviews;
*   shadowing academics as they went about their daily lives;
*   diary studies with undergraduates so we could better understand their activities, preferences and study routines.

The research data gathered led the design consultancy to propose 12 concepts in all which could be piloted as services or products by teams of library staff who had recently been mobilised. It was precisely because each of the 12 concepts responded to a need or gap pointed up by the research that we initially struggled a little in the aforementioned meeting to reach a consensus on which concepts to take forward to test. How can you choose between concepts that have all been derived from a 'deep dive' research phase that has offered more reliable data on user need and behaviour than any previous project? Ultimately it came down to four interrelated factors: cost, maximum benefit, timescale and the ease of investigation. 'WhoHas?' (detailed in the subsequent chapter by Helen Murphy), which sought to explore the possibility of legitimising the student practice of sub-lending books to each other, won because it was a concept that we recognised would be easy to test, could be implemented quickly, and at relatively low cost. Also it responded to, and would explore, a behaviour that we were keen to learn more about. The second concept we chose, and were in unanimous agreement over, was 'Spacefinder': a new web-based service that would match user study preferences with available study spaces across the University. It would be more expensive than WhoHas? and take longer to implement, but we could all see its huge potential value to all students and libraries.

Unique terrain

Before I go into more detail about Spacefinder and the research that led to its conception, I think it is worth noting the uniqueness of our terrain. As attendees of the UX in Libraries conference will have experienced first-hand during the fieldwork project (how well I remember them scratching their heads in dismay!), Cambridge University is an uncommon place (well, there is the 'Other Place', of course, but let's not go there) with well over 100 libraries, around 500 library staff and a tripartite system that is bafflingly complex. Cambridge students are expected to navigate a landscape of libraries which incorporates their departmental library, college library and the main University Library, all of which will possess relevant and complementary resources for their studies. But of course they may go beyond that and visit other departmental libraries, especially if their research is multidisciplinary. Many students will use multiple libraries, some will use just one and others – although it always puzzles me quite how they manage it – none at all. Of course, it was the choices they make about which libraries they use, when and for what purpose, that formed some of the most interesting material to come out of the ethnography conducted during our research phase and that ultimately led to Spacefinder.

Diverse needs and preferences

Perhaps unsurprisingly, given our bewildering diversity of libraries, our research revealed that Cambridge students are not always finding the right study spaces to suit their needs and, moreover, that these needs are almost as diverse as the number of libraries. We heard from students who preferred to study in a pack, either for groupwork or what we started to call 'together alone': studying independently but alongside friends whom they could call on for either moral or practical support (a phenomenon that Turpin and Harrop et al. also describe in Chapter 14). Others preferred to work totally alone. Some of these 'loners' chose to work in crowded, quiet reading rooms in silence in order to motivate them to concentrate and put in the hours; others wanted to work in noisier, more bustling locations, stating that they are unable to work in silence. Crucially, and this will come as no surprise at all, the study spaces that users described were very often not in libraries. Some told us that they regularly worked in coffee shops, others that they only ever worked in their college room. Common rooms and areas were also uncovered as important study spaces, as were Cambridge's many attractive outdoor spaces, in summer at any rate – this *is* the UK, remember!

Our research also revealed that some students liked to work in a variety of libraries and that each space offered them different environments and were used

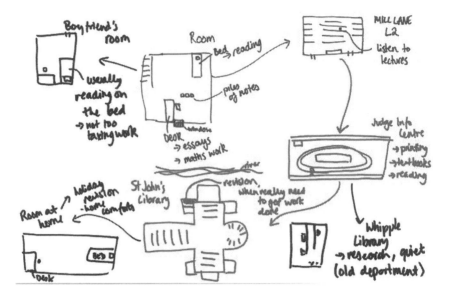

Figure 8.1 A cognitive map depicting how a Judge Business School student regularly visited multiple libraries in Cambridge for different purposes

Source: Georgina Cronin.

for different purposes. Cognitive mapping with students of Cambridge's Judge Business School (which took place when I managed Information and Library Services there) depicted how certain students used one library for books, another for quiet study and another for working with friends (see Figure 8.1). It was a discovery that was positively revelatory to me as I had always assumed that Judge students used our library as a one-stop shop for everything – an assumption that had prompted us to give very few details about other libraries and spaces elsewhere in the University. I found this pick 'n' mix approach fascinating; it opened up my eyes to a wider experience of Cambridge libraries that was going on under our very noses, that had lain hidden until we adopted ethnography to dig below the surface.

Our data also showed how users were choosing library spaces on the basis of the features available to them there. Of course the 'holy trinity' of Wi-Fi, power and phone signal were prized most highly, but other high-scoring preferences included:

- large desks where users could spread out;
- good lighting, preferably natural;
- warmth (although we quickly realised that one person's warm is another person's cold!);
- an atmosphere conducive to study (again rather subjective);
- attractive views;

- staff assistance should it be needed;
- printing, photocopying and scanning (the supplanted original 'holy trinity' of libraries);
- special equipment (particularly for science students);
- availability of PCs (we do not have a device-only culture yet);
- caffeine.

Once they had chosen their space, be it within a library or without, naturally we uncovered a large variety of activities in these places too: from writing essays, to revising, to searching the web, to manipulating data, to booking holidays and socialising with friends via Facebook.

In summary, we had uncovered a seemingly infinite number of activities in a huge variety of spaces that had been selected for an equally diverse range of reasons and preferences.

A problem of hidden abundance

Aside from these activities and preferences, we were also very aware that Cambridge has what might be usefully called 'a problem of hidden abundance'. It is a term I must attribute to Paul-Jervis Heath (see Chapter 5 in which he details the human-centred design process) who first used this highly resonant phrase during one of our Spacefinder informational roadshows. It describes the fact that we have no shortage of study spaces in our University but that we do lack a means of sharing information about them with our user population. There are so many libraries in Cambridge that are not deliberately hidden as such but are certainly difficult to find, requiring prior knowledge, a solid set of directions, or better still the company of a friend to locate. What if there was a way of showing a user exactly where these spaces were relative to their current location in the University, and which also detailed the attributes – and therefore suitability – of said study space? What if we had a space finder?

Co-design workshops

Back in April 2015, as election fever gripped the country, we set about arranging two collaborative design (co-design) workshops at which both librarians and students would be present (see Figure 8.2). The purpose of these workshops was to divine further insights into user study preferences and activities, and specifically to uncover if there were any key differences between Art, Humanities and Social Science (AHSS) students and Science, Technology and Medicine (STEM) students.

The students were incredibly enthusiastic players at these workshops, grateful to be asked their opinion and very willing to give of their time, despite the fact that their exams were coming up fast. By far the biggest barrier to student involvement was their own fear that they had nothing useful to share. However, once they understood that we just wanted to know how they chose to study, their

Figure 8.2 Librarians and students working together at a co-design workshop
Source: Modern Human.

concerns were allayed. Those who agreed to take part universally described it as a welcome respite from their exam revision and a good opportunity to clear their heads.

A significant aspect of the workshops was discovering what language students used to describe their spaces and needs. This vocabulary would later be fed in to the design process, ensuring that we used the words that they used rather than guessing at their parlance or falling back on any dreaded library jargon.

Ultimately there was very little difference between AHSS and STEM students in these workshops, although the former definitely used more descriptive and elaborate words to describe their needs than the more straight-talking and direct scientists. AHSS students did prioritise atmosphere slightly above their STEM equivalents, who placed workspace (including features and resources) and location slightly higher, but both sets broadly agreed that these three aspects were the most important components.

Designing spacefinder

It was vital that Spacefinder was very carefully designed to ensure it was laid out in such a way that students would actually use it. We knew the idea was good and that it could solve some very real problems, but we couldn't just assume it would be automatically adopted on these strengths alone. For one thing it needed to be

Figure 8.3 Modern Human's Paul-Jervis Heath and Jenny Willatt sharing the Spacefinder
prototype with students at the stall on the University's Sidgwick site

Source: Andy Priestner.

responsively designed so that it could be accessed over the web on smartphones
and tablets as easily as on a PC or Mac.

We derived further valuable insight into how to design the layout for Spacefinder by once again talking directly to students. This time we set up stalls in
two different University locations from which we shared a rough prototype of
the service on smartphones for students to interrogate and comment upon (see
Figure 8.3). Although we told them that this was a new University service which
we wanted them to test, we didn't sell the concept of Spacefinder to them as we
wanted to get their honest initial reactions to the idea without leading them at all.
In addition to observing how students chose to navigate around the prototype, we
also took notes of what they said, not only about the value of the service but also,
once again, about their use and expectations of spaces and study needs.

The student responses to Spacefinder even at this basic prototype stage were
overwhelmingly positive. Some were so enthusiastic that they already mourned the
fact that the service had not been previously available ('I'm a third year. I wish I'd
had this as a fresher!'). Some students pointed out that photographs of the study
spaces were very important ('photos would be useful so you know you're not
heading to a dank room'; 'would be good if like Airbnb it had pics of the rooms
and desks to give a sense of the space'). The fact that the service would include

common rooms and cafés was also considered a big plus ('this will remove the trial and error of trying out crap coffee spaces') and something we ourselves were very keen on given that the research had shown that many students studied outside of libraries. The only aspect which appeared to divide the students we talked to was whether the service should start with a menu. Via the menu students can discover spaces by entering their study needs and looking at matching results, while via the map they can identify spaces that are close to their current position. As these options were equally popular, we ultimately elected to offer both.

Finally, the prototype testing confirmed misgivings that we were starting to have about including a TripAdvisor-style review option for users in case this was abused. Through talking to students at the stalls we decided instead to offer the opportunity for users of Spacefinder to leave tips and tricks about the spaces to help others using the service, which we saw to be a more constructive alternative. All of this student feedback fed into a redesign of the original prototype that factored in as many of the comments as possible.

'We need your data!'

While the design consultancy busied themselves creating the final user interfaces for Spacefinder, the librarians on the project team started to describe the spaces in their libraries and in coffee shops around Cambridge so that we could start to feed some data into the service. Rather than entering information on each entire library as a single space, we categorised our libraries into different areas so they would come up as distinct spaces on the final service. Very few libraries have the same feel and layout throughout; in fact, most offer two or three very different types of spaces that students are likely to use for different purposes dependent on the sort of work in which they are engaged. A good example is the English Faculty library, which incorporates formal seating with lots of natural light downstairs; a more relaxed beanbag area upstairs; an IT lab; and another space adjacent to a special printed collection. All four areas were described and entered into Spacefinder as separate study spaces.

Once we had gathered this initial dataset it was time to go out to all the other librarians across Cambridge and encourage them to buy in to Spacefinder, ask them to describe their spaces for inclusion in the service, and seek their help in promoting it to students at the start of the academic year. Informal and interactive roadshows were the vehicle chosen to get librarians on board. These were attended by over 60 librarians in total, many of whom are responsible for running their own library within the Cambridge library system. Although some chose to opt out, mainly because they felt that their spaces were already oversubscribed and feared promoting their library more widely through Spacefinder, most happily opted in.

During July and August members of the project team were mobilised once again to test the new Spacefinder interface ahead of its pilot launch in October (see Figure 8.4).

Figure 8.4 Members of the Spacefinder project team testing the service at the English
          Faculty Library
Source: Helen Murphy.

Next steps

As I write, we are now at the stage where we are sending instructions out to participating librarians as to how to catalogue and describe their spaces, and a photog-
rapher has been hired to take professional shots of the spaces we will be featuring.
Plans are also underway to promote Spacefinder as a key library service to new
undergraduates at the Freshers' Fair at the start of our academic year, at which we
will be giving out branded compass keyrings to emphasise how the service will
help them to navigate their way to study environments which match their preferences. The next month or so will undoubtedly prove crucial to the success of the
service, but some of the hardest work is already behind us.

Conclusion

The Spacefinder experience has emphasised to me how diverse library user needs
are and how relying only on our assumptions and instincts is a very dangerous
thing to do. Only by undertaking thorough and continuous ethnographic research

can we hope to offer services and products that truly match the needs of today's users. Most of all, Spacefinder has shown me that you can think very big indeed in terms of a problem you want to solve and yet identify a relatively simple and entirely implementable solution. On the surface, Cambridge University's problems of hidden abundance of spaces and a hugely diverse range of study needs and preferences looked to be beyond our influence, but now we are well on the way to cracking them both.

Spacefinder can be accessed at https://spacefinder.lib.cam.ac.uk.

9   WhoHas?

A pilot study exploring the value of a peer-to-peer sub-lending service

Helen Murphy

Let me begin with a spoiler. This is the story of an epic fail.

In early 2015, three libraries at the University of Cambridge volunteered to participate in a pilot of a new service called WhoHas? as part of the University Library's FutureLib innovation programme. It was an idea grounded in ethnographic research carried out over several years, which had revealed a widespread culture of peer-to-peer sub-lending. As further exploration was required, a pilot was devised, scheduled, planned and carried out. We hoped for success, we hoped for a win. And then, well, it didn't work. It flunked, it flopped, it bombed altogether.

This is the story of how and why that happened, and why it was (genuinely) an incredibly positive and useful outcome.

What the research told us

Peer-to-peer sub-lending is rife among students at the University of Cambridge. At a basic level, students lend library books they've borrowed to each other; at a more sophisticated level, students collaborate and strategise over who will borrow what from where. This 'black market' for books tends to happen among students doing the same subject (though not exclusively so), and is significantly more common among groups of friends, often students at the same college. Neither of these is a particularly startling observation, but they reveal a potential inequality in terms of students' access to resources: if you're the only person in your college doing your subject (as may well be the case), then sub-lending will probably be a fairly lonely and fruitless occupation.

The research gave us some information about why sub-lending happens: usually, but not always, it's a case of demand outweighing supply, though occasionally it's purely a matter of convenience. We discovered that the majority of these conversations were taking place on Facebook, specifically within private, invitation-only groups set up by the students themselves. While negotiations varied, from students entrusting colleagues with borrowed books and their due dates to requests to work alongside their friends and share all their resources, they tended to begin with the same question: 'Who has . . .?'

(Do you see what we did there?)

Why a pilot?

The research had shown us that sub-lending was happening, but we wanted to investigate how (and whether) libraries could intervene. Our assumption was that libraries could legitimise sub-lending, and that this would be useful, both for the students and for the libraries. We thought we might be able to mediate it so students didn't end up responsible for their friends' library books (and library fines!). We thought we might be able to expand it so that the playing field was levelled, so that the ability to benefit from sub-lending wasn't dependent on one's college or how numerous, generous and organised one's friends were. We never thought sub-lending was a negative activity; our assumption was that we could facilitate it, and make it fairer and better. We needed a pilot to validate all of these assumptions.

The project team

The team was made up of representatives from Cambridge University's Wolfson College Library, Medical Library and English Faculty Library, and we were led in our endeavours by the human-centred design consultancy Modern Human. It's safe to say that these three libraries are different from one another, which was exceptionally useful. Not only did it considerably broaden the expertise of the project team, but it ensured that the pilot was balanced, realistic and flexible, and that the 'service' was designed with a variety of different user needs in mind.

The pilot itself

It became apparent fairly immediately that our current LMS would rule out 'official' peer-to-peer circulation; we needed a workaround and so we decided to join the students on Facebook. It represented a familiar, non-threatening setting, and had the added benefit of cheapness – limiting any financial investment was obviously a bonus. We decided that each library involved would set up its own Who-Has? Facebook group and invite students to join. Students could ask their peers for books, organise swaps, and – here's the crucial bit – when a swap had happened, both parties would confirm it on the Facebook group and library staff would manually switch the book from one student's record to the other's. It would be fairly similar to what was already happening, with the main difference being the library getting involved at the end.

In addition, though, we needed more qualitative information about sub-lending. A term-long diary study of students from the three participating libraries was planned, to coincide with the pilot. This was run using an app called DScout, which prompted students to answer questions about their sub-lending activities. It was preceded by a kick-off meeting and finished with an exit interview.

Planning for the pilot took place over several weeks via a series of meetings and using several hundred sticky notes. We began by designing a service blueprint – a series of situations which would lead to a student using WhoHas? and how they would navigate it. We discussed recruitment, promotion and – though this now seems like rain on your wedding day – how we'd measure success or failure. The crucial thing about the pilot, though, was that it was never, ever going to be a 'miniature' version of whatever it might eventually turn into. For the real thing, for example, we wouldn't have touched Facebook with a bargepole. This was driven home for me by a few heated and largely inconclusive discussions about how to make a service like WhoHas? fit with existing practices, such as a recall or holds system. We racked our brains and came up with zero solutions. We even struggled with finding workarounds, and in the end decided to cross these bridges when we came to them. So the pilot would always be imperfect and – slight leap of faith aside – that was OK. (In case you're wondering, these unsolvable problems weren't responsible for its failure.)

How it failed

In the beginning, things looked promising. Without too much effort, or too great a push, students chose to join the groups we'd established in high numbers. At the English Faculty Library, for example, over a third of those we'd invited joined straight away. It seemed to confirm that we had a good idea. There was a brief and retrospectively highly ironic panic that we might be overrun with what we'd termed 'transactions': students requesting a book swap, hopefully with a positive result.

And then, nothing. We had a tumbleweed moment, and then another, and then seven weeks more. Of course the project team rallied and tried to encourage students to take part – we considered posting a fake transaction, for example, done by library staff. But by the end of the 8-week pilot, there had been three 'failed' transactions (i.e. someone asking for a book and receiving no response) and one 'successful' transaction. Across three groups. In 8 weeks. With 174 participants in total. Let me repeat: one successful transaction.

It hadn't worked. More to the point, it really, *really* hadn't worked.

Why it failed

The post-mortem began and plenty of reasons for failure were identified. At least some of them we'd considered and dismissed in advance. Its length, at 8 weeks, was short, and certainly not long enough to bed in a new service. Its relative complexity might have been an issue – a successful WhoHas? transaction required a fairly complicated set of processes. Its timing was troublesome, as we'd held it in 'exam' term, which usually tends to see slight drops in loans. So it's true that we didn't have the optimum set of circumstances to run the pilot. The likelihood is we probably never would have.

In fact, what helped us to understand better why the pilot flopped was the diary study alongside it. While the numbers of transactions in the WhoHas? Facebook groups were abysmal, the diary study told an entirely different story. There, among 10 participants, there were 22 successful transactions. This strongly inferred that the lack of activity in the Facebook groups wasn't representative of the reality of sub-lending going on. It wasn't that students weren't sub-lending – it's that they weren't using the groups to do it. Unpacking (via the exit interviews) why they were ignoring the groups altogether showed us that the pilot probably never would have worked. Here are some of their reasons:

1   *The timing, again.*

The students raised it too, so perhaps we should have waited for what we thought was a 'better' time. They said exam term wasn't particularly representative: 'most textbook reading is done during previous terms' (a law student), and 'we've only really needed one book' (an English student). (All student quotes in this case study are taken from the WhoHas? pilot study findings, 2015.)

2   *They prefer to ask their friends for favours.*

They didn't need to use the groups because they have friends they can ask for books, and they can contact them outside of the Facebook group: 'I have a wide network of people I can borrow from if I need anything' (an English student). And yes, that doesn't particularly help those who don't have a large college group, but also . . .

3   *They don't like asking people they don't know for favours.*

So those who don't have a large college group probably wouldn't feel comfortable asking for books either. They don't like to admit that they need help, especially from strangers. And the groups don't help with that because . . .

4   *It's all too public.*

One of the medical students said he 'wouldn't want to be the first or only one'. The necessary public environment of a service like this, which limits their anonymity, was another problem.

5   *Ultimately, though, their other strategies are working fine.*

The medical students hadn't used the groups because they have their own methods of obtaining and circulating the texts they need, and the systems they've developed are more convenient for them. The WhoHas? groups weren't a radical new solution, but an alternative and more problematic solution.

The value of failing

If I'm giving the impression that the project team was thrilled by the pilot failing, I apologise. I might even be implying that its failure was something we all found immediately easy to accept – not true either. A roaring success, which coated us all in glory, and revolutionised library services globally would, of course, have been marginally preferable. All credit to the project team for making sure no one took it personally or felt embarrassed, and delivering enough distance to be able to stay light-hearted.

Failing was, in fact, an exceptionally positive outcome. We learned more about sub-lending and why it goes on. We learned about the problem that necessitates sub-lending and the reasons why it's such an attractive solution to that problem. We found out, for example, that students consider e-books as the copy of last resort (they've pipped reference books to the position, apparently), and how highly they rate convenience both in terms of resource format and borrowing habits.

For me, the most fascinating thing we discovered was that for some students there's an emotional barrier when using library services. Sometimes it's about asking for help ('my librarian's already done so much for me this year. I don't want to give her any more trouble by asking for another favour' [an English student]) or using library services like recalling books ('if the book has been taken out then that person obviously needs it, so I'm not going to recall it' [a law student]). That's a really valuable bit of information, and a lens through which we can evaluate other library services.

The pilot flunked: this is unavoidable. We didn't validate the assumptions we set out with. We didn't even prove beyond a doubt that they were nonsense. But our conclusions took us way beyond these assumptions. Of course all of these things require further exploration; no one ever said UX had an endpoint. We've learned what the next questions could be. We've discovered other directions in which to take our UX approach. This is because of the ethnographic methods we employed throughout the entire process, from the initial research into sub-lending through to the completion and evaluation of FutureLib's WhoHas? pilot. We now have more evidence and more information and, success or failure, that's where the value of the pilot lies.

Reference

Priestner, A. and Modern Human, 2015. *WhoHas?: Findings of a pilot study exploring the value of a peer-to-peer sub-lending service for users of Cambridge University libraries.* Available at: <futurelib.wordpress.com>.

10 User experience beyond ramps

The invisible problem and the special case

Penny Andrews

UX is for everyone, not just those who are deemed to be the majority group. Everyone is entitled to a good user experience, and no user is 'lesser' than another. To adapt Ranganathan (1931): libraries are for use, libraries are for all and we should save the time of the user. Every user.

Many users' experience of libraries is negatively affected by library anxiety and hidden disabilities – problems of which most of the people around them are unaware. This chapter outlines the problems and provides recommendations to address these issues. I am both disabled and have experienced library anxiety, and I take a practical as well as theoretical approach, employing autoethnographic techniques to explore the issues. Autoethnography describes and systematically analyses the researcher's personal experience in order to gain understanding of cultural, social and political experiences (Ellis et al., 2010). While this chapter is predominantly about academic libraries in the UK, many of the UX problems and solutions described here are more widely applicable in other situations. Case studies are used to provide examples of ways in which libraries can work for or against users in this context.

Library anxiety and accessibility

Library anxiety is the name given to the phenomenon of users feeling apprehensive or uncomfortable when using a library (Jiao and Onwuegbuzie, 1999). Users with an existing mental health condition may experience library anxiety, but it also affects large numbers of people who are not otherwise anxious and is sometimes described as a form of 'phobia'. It is one of the key reasons for students avoiding the university library for as long as possible, unrelated to understandable barriers like location and fines, so it is something everyone should want to understand.

Library anxiety can be caused by:

- The size of the library
- Lack of knowledge of where to find things
- Not knowing where to begin
- Not knowing what to do in the library (Mellon, 1986).

In addition to these factors, perfectionism over the 'perfect' search process, leading to procrastination and anxiety around the library building and library websites, can be a real problem for postgraduates wanting to use the library (Jiao and Onwuegbuzie, 1998).

Library anxiety can be reduced by:

• Getting to know a librarian, through sessions concentrating on building that relationship rather than instruction
• Feeling that librarians really want to help
• Making library staff visible in the library (Mellon, 1986).

Accessibility is not just about disability. It is about making a building, product, device or service available to and usable by as many people as possible.

Many of the problems faced by users who find libraries to be inaccessible relate to the problems faced by users with library anxiety. Where to go, what to do, where to start and the barriers to answering these questions are common to a lot of people. More importantly, if a user feels that their needs are not met by the library or they do not know for sure what will happen, whether that is due to disability or misunderstanding, they will experience library anxiety and not want to go to the library or use its services.

Hidden disabilities

Hidden disabilities are disabilities and chronic mental and physical health conditions that are not immediately apparent to other people. You cannot tell from looking at me that I have autism and cerebral palsy, unless you are familiar with these conditions. Libraries know they must cater for users with visual impairments, d/Deaf[1] users and users in wheelchairs. However, most people with mobility impairments do not use a wheelchair or mobility aid. While dyslexia is increasingly accepted and understood by a mainstream audience, many other conditions such as autism, rheumatoid arthritis, fibromyalgia and ME are not. People with hidden disabilities deal daily with the assumption that they are not disabled, and the effects of stereotyping and misinformation. People with mental health conditions are also more likely to receive this kind of treatment.

Many of these disabilities seriously affect user experience in libraries and little provision is made for these groups. Autistic people commonly have problems with sensory integration (Griswold et al., 2002). They can be over- or under-sensitive to sensory stimuli such as lights, colours, sounds, smells, touch and taste and have difficulty in filtering desirable from undesirable input. For example, flickering lights can be unbearable, bright colours can confuse vision, and it can be difficult to hear what someone is saying if there is any noise in the background. This means that autistic people can become easily overwhelmed, which can lead to meltdown – where their minds and bodies can no longer cope with the situation, and they experience severe emotional and physical distress. These problems can also occur for people with mental health conditions, neurological disabilities, visual or hearing impairments and so on.

So modern academic libraries, with their busy study areas, overhead lighting, coffee shops and bright furniture and carpets can be a nightmare for some. These modernisations were mostly carried out with the aim of attracting young students, but can exclude a lot of people. This means that the affected users will avoid the library where possible, just like the anxious users. It is rare for building design to consider the sensory impact of aesthetic choices on disabled users in any real depth.

Disclosure

Please note that many disabled students will not disclose their condition. This does not just mean that they do not disclose to their friends or lecturers, but also they do not wish to tell the university itself, for a number of reasons, including not identifying as disabled, having a poor experience with disability support in the past and feeling either that they would be ineligible for support or do not need it. Relying on the numbers of students registered with Disability Services is a poor measure of disability within a university.

Clashing priorities

It is inevitable that improving a space for one group will disadvantage another. For example, visually impaired users with some vision often prefer brighter lighting and bolder colours and patterns, whereas autistic users can find bright light painful and prefer ambient light from lamps and softer colours. The key is to try to balance the needs of both by engaging in consultation with those affected and trying to find a mutually agreeable solution, rather than throwing hands up in despair or privileging one group over the other as more deserving.

Beyond ramps

The usual approach to accessibility for businesses and organisations is to meet legal requirements by providing lifts, ramps and (potentially) facilities for users with visual and hearing impairments. Understanding of disability beyond this is poor, and often even these basic provisions go wrong, such as ramps that are at too steep an angle for wheelchair users to access. Meeting legal obligations is not enough. There is not space here to go into the social and medical models of disability, and why the latter is problematic, but the Scope charity's website (Scope, 2014) has good explanations of the social model.

Traditionally, support for students with disabilities in the UK has been provided by Disabled Students Allowance (DSA), which pays for equipment, resources and non-medical helpers to adapt the student to university. The largest group of students claiming DSA is students with dyslexia, followed by other specific learning difficulties such as autistic spectrum conditions, ADHD and dyspraxia. Changes to the system mean that the university is now responsible under the Equality Act for funding and providing this support, instead of DSA. This is a difficult transition period for disabled students. However, it is also an opportunity for the university and the library to meet their obligations beyond building regulations and the law, to make their buildings and practices inclusive and accessible instead of expecting the students to adapt.

A short tale of two libraries

An autoethnographic approach was taken, as it was my wildly different reactions to these two library spaces that in many ways led to the writing of this chapter. Please note these are honest reactions to the libraries as a disabled user and not an attempt at objective observation.

Case study 1

I walk up to the library. I already have a headache from the violent hue of the building in the sunlight. The turnstiles are very close to the doors; I can see them from the glass. I have no time to gather myself when I get in, I have to scramble for my student card and take a couple of attempts with my shaky hands to swipe my way to entry. As soon as I get through, I am faced with a sensory assault. I can smell the café, which is serving food and coffee. I can smell the toilets, which are disgusting. I can hear a thick wall of noise that buzzes around my head and makes me feel woozy. The lights are harsh. In front of me is a staircase, which I usually prefer to the lifts because I get anxious that the lifts will break down. Before I can walk any further, I am distracted by some sort of abstract painting or design in lurid colours that makes my eyes wobble. I make it to the stairs. They are very narrow and I struggle to get past people up to the top.

I reach the floor I need. I can't work out where I am meant to go to find books or anything else; it's like a confusing maze and the signs are not very clear. I try to find the toilets to gather myself. The doors are heavy. I feel physically sick and have a headache. I need to leave as soon as possible. When I leave the toilets, there is more noise and more smells and more bright lights. The website says the building is fully accessible. I just feel like I never want to go back. It takes me over an hour to recover when I get out.

Case study 2

I enter the building. There is a quiet area with tables and chairs after the building doors but before the library doors. All the doors are glass and I can see what is happening. There are several choices of door – one that opens with a button, one that is a revolving door and 'normal' push/pull doors. I like this because revolving doors make me anxious and if the normal door is too heavy, I can use the button door. Plus if there are a lot of people, I can choose the least busy door.

I go through the library door and again there is some space before the turnstiles. The barriers are open, as the library is available to the public for most of the day without needing to sign in or swipe. This saves me the fumble for my card, but there is plenty of room if I do need to swipe.

The ground floor is in calm colours. There are big signs everywhere telling me what things are and where to go. I can see the stairs ahead of me through a glass door and they are wide. There is a sign for the lifts behind them and the toilets are at the back. I can't smell anything or hear much apart from low-level chatter.

I go upstairs and every floor has the same clear layout and simple signs. There are also unambiguous floor plans available on a display on every floor and as a leaflet in an obvious place. I do not get lost. There are signs explaining where books are. The toilets are near where the lifts and stairs come out. On one floor there is a room just for disabled students. Where there are computer rooms, there is a sign saying what software is on the computers. All the computers in the library have assistive software. I don't have to go to a special room.

One floor has brightly coloured carpets on part of the floor, in a pattern that makes my head hurt. I avoid that area. All other colours are used for colour coding or are much calmer shades. I feel comfortable here.

Comments

Case Study 1 is not the worst library ever. It is constantly packed with users who can cope with its idiosyncrasies. However, as the main library for the institution and home to most of the available study spaces, and as a model for other buildings at the university and elsewhere, it fails because it is an actively horrible and/or inaccessible place for many students.

Case Study 2 is not the best library ever. However, it is built around the idea of including everyone, rather than appealing to a particular group, and its management is much more open to changes that are user-centred.

The 'special case'

It is difficult as a member of library staff dealing with many queries and complaints to realise that most users will not speak up and will either have to absorb the additional cognitive load of 'coping' with problems or engage in avoidance tactics at their own expense. Those who do complain or ask for help dread becoming the 'special case', where something may be fixed for them (often in a way that does not achieve real equality) but the overall problem is not tackled and things are not changed for the next person. Usually getting the special case requires research, support from others and a 'fight' that demands highly developed self-advocacy skills – something that is rarely taught in learning environments or explicitly supported by libraries.

I have experienced many special case situations as a disabled library user, who also experiences library anxiety and social anxiety. The library described in Case Study 1 has rooms where non-library lectures and seminars can take place, which is not uncommon for university libraries. While generally and understandably avoiding this library site as a student, as others were available, several lectures for one of my modules were booked into one of these lecture rooms. Explaining the problems with accessing these lectures to the lecturer led to an awkward meeting with the manager of that site and a diversity manager, where eventually it was agreed that a side entrance intended for deliveries, which opened close to the lifts and stairs that led to the lecture rooms, could be used as a quieter alternative. My student card would be updated to allow swipe access.

This side door was incredibly heavy and I was not allowed to ask friends to enter the building with me to make opening and closing this door easier, as this entrance did not have a turnstile, and I was only permitted to use this entrance during staffed hours for security reasons, even though the building was open 24 hours a day. Additionally, no changes were made to website text or information made available to disability advisors and lecturers, so this only solved the problem of access (in a fairly poor and less than equitable way) for me and not for anyone else with similar problems. No assurance has been made that the problems with the entrance to this building will not be replicated in future library and study space building projects.

Even simple tasks like reserving a book can be difficult. If the book is not in stock, and the user placing the reservation is only able to get to the library on an irregular basis, the item may well become available and the reservation period expire before the user is able to collect it. Library staff may well be happy to extend the reservation period if the user emails or telephones the library, and will indeed do this on a regular basis. However, many users will not contact the library, as this just adds to the transactional costs of being a 'non-standard' user, and the work of processing the reservation will be wasted as well as the inconvenience worsening the user's perception of the borrowing experience.

If it is possible to extend lending and reservation periods automatically for users who do not live near campus or who have other barriers to accessing the library, do this. If your system does not allow this, speak to your vendor.

Fix for one, fix for many

If a user alerts you to a problem that you can fix or know you need to fix, make the solution available to everybody and tell everybody that it exists. Either the issue was a problem for a lot of people, in which case the solution becomes the new norm and it is a good job you fixed it, or it was a problem for a smaller group who will be grateful not to go through the same process as the first user. The library will not suddenly be inundated with inconvenient requests or 'too many' people using the alternative provision you have highlighted – and if they are, something is already wrong with your building and/or service provision.

The special case harms everybody's experience of the library. The first user to raise the issue will probably not get an entirely satisfactory solution. Library staff will have to repeat the extra/alternative process instead of it becoming part of the library workflow, creating extra work. And future users with a similar problem will either have to start the process again themselves, 'cope' without a solution (adversely affecting perceptions of the library and their ability to do their work) or avoid the library altogether.

Real inclusion and a better user experience for all

Understanding user experience principles and employing ethnographic approaches to find out about our libraries lets us see beyond all doubt that users of even the most specialist library are a heterogeneous bunch. No, we cannot think of everything and no, people do not always know what they want and need. However, that does not mean we can continue to design services for one majority group (e.g. '18–25-year-old students') and treat other groups such as disabled users, part-time students, older users, non-native English speakers and so on as add-ons – the 'non-traditional students' or the 'socially excluded'.

Imagine you are a mature, international research student with a chronic health condition who commutes from a city an hour or two away. The university library does not know what to do with (or how to support) someone who experiences a number of hardships at the same time. It is designed for the young, non-disabled undergraduate student living locally and speaking English as a first language. Everything else is an add-on or extra – the Distance Learning department (which does not really apply to the commuting student), Disability services, International Student services, services for postgraduate students and researchers, initiatives aimed at part-time students or students who are parents and so on. All of these services tend to be poorly integrated with each other and into the whole.

Real inclusion is not about separation and othering of any user. Huzar (2014) discusses the library as a radically inclusive space. He argues that targeted initiatives aimed at marginalised groups make libraries less inclusive, as they feel they have done their part or ticked that box for inclusion, and yet those who do not meet the criteria for the initiative are excluded and the concept of a place that assumes equality for all its users is eroded. Part of the reason why public libraries are so attractive to minority groups is that they do not try to police communities in the same way as services aimed solely at those groups, and have to include everyone by default. There is no single assumption of what the 'general public' means. This should be the same for every library and its community.

Often if you solve a problem for non-traditional or minority users, you have solved a problem for many users. Lots of things we provide or fail to change as librarians, deliberately or inadvertently, users can just about 'cope' with, except for the users with conditions and disabilities that mean that they cannot. For example: non-ideal lighting, heavy doors, noise where there should be none, smells, inconsistencies in processes and layouts, chairs too uncomfortable for anyone to sit on for a long time, awkward positioning of facilities. Why do we accept this, even when we know (1) some people cannot deal with it at all and (2) nobody *likes* it?

We need to get better at enabling independence for all our users, in this self-service, 24/7 culture. Providing a mobility-impaired user with someone who can carry their books for a few hours a week does not solve the issue that the books are too heavy for most people to pick up and use comfortably and no e-book was available, or that there is often no way for students to move several books around the library themselves without discomfort or pain. We need to be better at challenging vendors to provide us with formats that work for our users, as well as business models that work for our budgets, and we need to get better at challenging our idea of what users should be able to put up with before they complain.

Positive actions

1) The quiet entrance

Physically getting in to the library comes with many potential barriers (see Case Study 1). Make it easier for users by making sure at least one entrance to the library is 'quiet'. No toilets or café, no group study or seating area near the doors, no bright colours, artwork or startling lights. It is helpful to provide something of a buffer zone before entering the library, so people can gather their thoughts before being faced with turnstiles and counters. If at all possible, users should be able to see lifts and stairs from the entrance and access them with no barriers or diversions once they have entered the library (see point 2).

2) Paths, consistency and codes

Desire paths (or lines) are the journeys people take through a built environment in order to get to their destination or achieve a task as quickly as possible and with minimal effort, even if this is not the way the environment was designed. You can see 'alternative footpaths' everywhere, where walkers take shortcuts across the grass instead of the winding, paved route.

Good user experience design looks at the paths currently taken by users, and examines how the potentially shortest route is currently blocked or could be compromised by furniture or shelving or other barriers. The designer then aims to remove them in order to make the space more effective for the users, even if the original idea was to make users take a longer route to 'discover' other features – the latter tack being one often taken by supermarkets to encourage impulse purchasing behaviour.

The need for unimpeded pathways goes double for anxious and disabled users, who have enough barriers in their way already. It is especially important that the quickest route is also wide enough to allow easy access by users of wheelchairs and mobility aids – and of course this will also help parents with buggies, users with big bags and so on.

Other helpful practices include:

- Promoting your facilities and services – do not make it hard for people to find out what is going on and how you can help (see point 6).
- Making help obvious – where is the help desk or counter? If there are several, is it really clear which one somebody should use?
- Very clear signage, including the use of unambiguous pictograms to explain food and drink policies (Belger and Chelin, 2013).

- Consistencies of layout – do not change the layout of a space regularly, and replicate layout of rooms, equipment, facilities and so on where possible on different floors.
- Locating toilets sensitively – plumbing is an issue, but putting toilets right at the entrance causes problems with noise and smell. Equally, placing them too far away makes it difficult for users needing to access them in a hurry.
- Understanding routines and sensitively managing expectations – if a student with anxiety or an autistic spectrum disorder likes to regularly use a pod or a particular study room, problems will ensue if it is suddenly unavailable.
- Zones and flooring – use changes of flooring colour, pattern or material to indicate a change of use or specific facilities (e.g. a printer area or silent study), rather than purely because it is aesthetically pleasing. Visually impaired users with some vision use these signals to navigate, and it is confusing if they are used for other reasons.
- Coding zones of the library and book sequences by colour (Lanfear, 2008). This helps dyslexic and visually impaired users to navigate. Where possible, also use unambiguous patterns with the colours to avoid issues of colour blindness and ambiguity.

3) Choices

Offer disabled users in particular a real choice of study space. Some universities have individual or group quiet study rooms for the exclusive use of disabled users. This works against the idea of avoiding segregation, but for some disabilities existing choices of spaces and rules do not really work well. A study of a sample group of libraries in England and Wales reported that individual bookable study rooms would be very popular with dyslexic students (Belger and Chelin, 2013). Bodaghi and Zainab (2013) found that carrels set aside for visually impaired users led to a greater sense of belonging and security, which is particularly important for groups who are vulnerable and feel marginalised. Additionally, autistic users describe their difficulty with the volume levels in group study areas (Martin et al., 2008), and yet silent study areas are too quiet and the pressure to refrain from any noise is uncomfortable (Madriaga and Goodley, 2010).

It is not possible for most academic libraries to widely offer single-user study rooms and most require more than one user's student number in order to book a group study room – which are in high demand for most of the year for planning group work. However, many students with autism and other disabilities would prefer to work alone or with a companion in not-quite-silence, and these policies work against their needs, so a pragmatic solution like study rooms for students declaring a disability is required, or a disability resource area (Lanfear, 2008). Please note that many students with disabilities do not disclose their disability to their peers, and therefore booking and access systems must be sensitive and discreet.

4) Get out of the silo

When planning changes to library spaces and services, do not just talk to experts within the library and the Estates department, but also outside it. For example, speak to disability advisors, the local disability assessment centres, the International Students office, the Art and Design department and Equality and Diversity staff groups. Build a good business case for changes that are related to accessibility but are not legal requirements.

Please note that it is not a good idea to carry out all your consultations with users and non-users of the library in the library building itself. This excludes anyone who currently has problems accessing the library, or has anxiety relating to the library as it stands, from taking part.

5) Skills

We can only solve the problems we know about, and we only hear from users brave enough to articulate their problems well and advocate for their needs. Universities should be encouraged to teach self-advocacy skills for learning and living. Remember from earlier in this chapter the issues around library anxiety and information literacy teaching and the struggles of some groups to participate in sessions. Learners with strong self-advocacy skills have better outcomes academically, socially and economically. Provide resources and sessions on this topic. (Do not call it self-advocacy! Integrate it into other sessions.)

6) Better information

Do not claim that your library building is 'fully accessible'. Many libraries and public buildings include language of this type in their communications, but it is not the case or indeed possible, and it shuts down conversation with those who disagree because their needs are not being met. The Library of Birmingham's visitor guide says the library was designed to be 'accessible to all'. However, despite the presence of lifts and wheelchair accessible toilets, visitors blogging and tweeting about the library describe getting lost and confused, even when following this guide. This is due to routes designed to encourage 'discovery and serendipity' (Gambles in Prospero, 2013). These routes are prized over convenience and accessibility. Additionally, this library made some opaque choices over the naming of areas, failing to make explicit which collections were held under these names in the visitor guide. In the rush to create a unique user experience, the basic functionality of the library can be compromised and users alienated.

A better approach is to communicate well what the library does (and in some cases does not) have, in terms of facilities and services. Display this information in an easy to read way, with pictures if possible, in a basic manner outside the entrance as well as in full on the website and in leaflets, so people can make their own decisions. Make this section of the website obvious from the front page, rather than buried in a special section, as the information provided is not just applicable to those who identify as disabled or outside of the 'norm'. Each item could then link to more detail where relevant, but at least people with multiple needs and concerns then only have one place to check.

Presentation of the information is key: group the information in ways that make sense and use web design features such as the ability to expand or collapse threads under headings instead of chunking the content into separate pages. Try to use headings that describe what the information is about rather than who it is supposedly for. Examples could be:

Getting around

- We have an alternative quieter entrance (insert location) that you may prefer to use.
- Follow the star path on every floor to get straight to the lecture/computer rooms without travelling through busy or noisy areas.
- We have two lifts on each floor, each of which is wheelchair accessible. The call buttons are accessible from a seated position.
- Most public areas of the library are wheelchair accessible. At the moment areas X and Y are more difficult to access, particularly in larger vehicles such as powered chairs and mobility scooters – please let us know at the desk if we can help you.
- Registered assistance dogs are welcome in the library, but no other pets or animals can be admitted.
- All our permanent signage has tactile text and Braille elements. We keep printed posters to a minimum, as they are not often accessible to visually impaired library users.
- The green baskets on wheels are there to help you carry books around the library. The red and blue trolleys are for staff, so please let us know if you can't find a basket rather than use those. ☺

Being understood

- The counter on the ground floor has a hearing loop. Please switch your hearing aid to the T setting, if available, and press the bell by the loop sign for assistance.
- Some library staff can communicate via British Sign Language (BSL) and they wear a blue 'ear' badge on their lanyards.
- The self-service machines can be accessed from a wheelchair and can be navigated via audio or on-screen options.

Facilities

- All desks on the second and third floors have individual reading lights. The light on these floors is softer than on the first floor, which has mostly overhead fluorescent lighting.
- There is assistive software (specify) on all computers and a small number of height-adjustable desks on every floor.

- There is a small prayer and meditation room on the third floor that is available to all library users, including non-religious people.
- We have male (3 cubicles, 4 urinals), female (5 cubicles), wheelchair accessible (1 cubicle), and gender-neutral (2 cubicles) toilets on each floor of the library. Other toilets are available in X location(s) nearby.
- Children under 14 can enter the library if an adult accompanies them at all times. We have no special facilities for childcare, buggy storage, baby changing or heating milk or food.

Final thoughts

Even just knowing what is and is not there can reduce anxiety for many library users and visitors. Offer 'low barrier' ways – incurring minimal transactional costs for the user – to contact the library that recognise the difficulties users with anxiety or additional needs may well have in contacting you and the inconvenience it causes them. Users with problems or concerns who cannot 'just give us a call!' on the telephone or drop in to speak to staff can lose out in terms of response times via email or other means.

However, if you make it as easy as possible for everyone to use the library equally without having to contact you (thanks to considerate provision of information and services), and you make it as easy as possible for users to contact you when they *do* have to and with a guaranteed timely response, library anxiety for all groups and individuals will be reduced.

Note

1 Small 'd' deaf indicates a person who views their hearing loss as a medical problem and wishes to identify with hearing people, whereas big 'D' Deaf people identify as culturally Deaf and part of the Deaf community.

References

Belger, J. and Chelin, J., 2013. The inclusive library: An investigation into provision for students with dyslexia within a sample group of academic libraries in England and Wales. *Library and Information Research*, 37(115), pp. 7–32. Available at: <http://eprints.uwe.ac.uk/21845/> [Accessed 28 November 2014].

Bodaghi, N. B. and Zainab, A. N., 2013. My carrel, my second home: Inclusion and the sense of belonging among visually impaired students in an academic library. *Malaysian Journal of Library & Information Science*, 18(1), pp. 39–54. Available at: <http://ejum.fsktm.um.edu.my/article/1337.pdf> [Accessed 28 November 2014].

Ellis, C., Adams, T. E. and Bochner, A. P., 2010. Autoethnography: An overview. *Forum Qualitative Sozialforschung/Forum: Qualitative Social Research*, 12(1), pp. 345–57. Available at: <http://www.qualitative-research.net/index.php/fqs/article/view/1589/3095> [Accessed 24 August 2015].

Griswold, D. E., Barnhill, G. P., Myles, B. S., Hagiwara, T. and Simpson, R. L., 2002. Asperger syndrome and academic achievement. *Focus on Autism and Other Developmental Disabilities*, 17(2), pp. 94–102. Available at: <http://foa.sagepub.com/cgi/doi/10.1177/10883576020170020401> [Accessed 30 November 2014].

Huzar, T., 2014. Neoliberalism, Democracy and the Library as a Radically Inclusive Space. In: *IFLA WLIC 2014*. Lyon: IFLA. pp. 1–9. Available at: <http://library.ifla.org/id/eprint/835> [Accessed 28 November 2014].

Jiao, Q. and Onwuegbuzie, A., 1998. Perfectionism and library anxiety among graduate students. *Journal of Academic Librarianship*, 24(5), pp. 365–71. Available at: <http://www.sciencedirect.com/science/article/pii/S0099133398900738> [Accessed 28 November 2014].

Jiao, Q. and Onwuegbuzie, A., 1999. Is library anxiety important? *Library Review*, 48(6), pp. 278–82. Available at: <http://www.emeraldinsight.com/journals.htm?articleid=859567&show=abstract> [Accessed 30 November 2014].

Lanfear, L., 2008. Enhancing the first-year experience: Ten ways to involve library services. *Assessment, Teaching and Learning Journal (Leeds Met)*, 4, pp. 31–4. Available at: <http://eprints.leedsbeckett.ac.uk/1121/1/Enhancing%20the%20first-year%20experience.pdf> [Accessed 28 November 2014].

Madriaga, M. and Goodley, D., 2010. Moving beyond the minimum: Socially just pedagogies and Asperger's syndrome in UK higher education. *International Journal of Inclusive Education*, 14(2), pp. 115–31. Available at: <http://www.tandfonline.com/doi/abs/10.1080/13603110802504168> [Accessed 28 November 2014].

Martin, N., Beardon, L. and Hodge, N., 2008. Towards an inclusive environment for university students who have Asperger syndrome (AS). *Journal of Inclusive Practice in Further and Higher Education*, 1, pp. 3–14. Available at: <http://www.lancaster.ac.uk/fass/events/disabilityconference_archive/2008/papers/martin2008.pdf> [Accessed 28 November 2014].

Mellon, C.A., 1986. Library anxiety: A grounded theory and its development. *College & Research Libraries*, 47(2), pp. 160–5. Available at: <http://crl.acrl.org/cgi/doi/10.5860/crl_47_02_160> [Accessed 28 November 2014].

Prospero, 2013. Library of Birmingham: It's not all about the books. *Economist Prospero blog*, [blog] 6 September. Available at: <http://www.economist.com/blogs/prospero/2013/09/library-birmingham> [Accessed 28 November 2014].

Ranganathan, S.R., 1931. *The five laws of library science*. Madras: Madras Library Association. Available at: <http://babel.hathitrust.org/cgi/pt?id=uc1.$b99721;view=1up;seq=19> [Accessed 12 December 2014].

Scope, 2014. What is the social model of disability? *Scope*. Available at: <http://www.scope.org.uk/about-us/our-brand/social-model-of-disability> [Accessed 28 November 2014].

11 Changing the dialogue

The story of the award-winning Alan Gilbert learning commons

Rosie Jones and Nicola Grayson

Through the creation of the award-winning Alan Gilbert Learning Commons (AGLC), the University of Manchester Library has changed its dialogue with students. This has transformed the relationship into a partnership with both parties taking an active responsibility for learning. This chapter will trace the journey of the AGLC against the context of traditional library models of interaction with students. It will illustrate the process through which students became critical to the building's success, resulting in a model that is aspired to by future developments at the University of Manchester and beyond. This model not only requires observation from within learning spaces in regard to how students are using them, but it also necessitates an ongoing dialogue that enables students to participate in the co-creation of such spaces from the earliest stages. We will show how the student voice resonates throughout the AGLC itself and is prevalent in all services operating within; it is at the forefront of everything we do. We will demonstrate that a partnership with students is vital to the successful development of new learning spaces, as only by nurturing a collective responsibility for learning can a space be dynamic in both a holistic and practical way.

Framing the problem

Traditionally students experienced academic library spaces as guests, having to respect the 'rules' of the house. These rules were not set by or for them and often created barriers as they sought to fulfil their academic requirements. Traditional models for informing spaces and the services within them were designed to accommodate the systems and preferences of librarians and other key stakeholders. This meant that the nature of services, policies, space design and assistance were dictated by the 'owner' of the house: the librarian. As a result, prescriptive measures were taken which meant minimal consultation in line with assumed needs that were *projected onto* the students. Whilst spaces designed in accordance with such models are fit for some purposes, the landscape of the academic library has changed, and thereby also the model of interaction between students and service providers has evolved considerably.

In relation to reference services, the traditional library models (of the pre-1980s) are based on a set of core values or key elements which evolved with the changing values of the community that the library serves. Tyckoson (2001) cites these values as including accuracy, thoroughness, timeliness, authority, instruction, access, individualisation and knowledge. After 1980 the approach to reference services began to go through changes, for example, the Rethinking Reference project (Rettig, 1992), the Brandeis model of tiered reference service (Massey-Burzio, 1992) and the online call centre model (Coffman, 1999). Each was heralded as innovative in a way that made librarians feel nervous about changes to their role, suspicious of new roles, and worried about the future (in terms of how it could impact on their definitive core values). The role of the library in relation to the community it serves was to provide requested, relevant information and to organise available resources. Tyckoson notes: 'As faithful servants of the community, librarians took on the new responsibility of helping users find what they needed. This is what we now call reference service' (Tyckoson, 2001, p. 185).

Visitors to the library were often referred to as patrons and viewed as guests. As such, they were treated as if they needed to be told the rules by which library resources were organised and to be taught how to use and search the collections. The librarian took on the role of question-answerer: the expert on finding information and advising readers of how to further their knowledge and interests. The inherent values of the reference service therefore now concerned information literacy, accuracy, thoroughness, timeliness, authority, advice, knowledge and the promotion of the library within and to the community it serves. Remarkably, even as early as 1876, Green observed that 'one of the best means of making a library popular is to mingle freely with its users and help them in every way' (Green, 1876). In a positive sense, the librarian made each patron feel that they were working to serve them individually, and no matter what your class, background or education, the library was a place where people were treated equally. In a contrasting (negative) sense, this positioned the librarian as the keeper of knowledge in respect to the way library collections were organised and could be searched: the librarian set and followed rules that patrons were often unaware of. The librarians' specialist knowledge therefore created a divisive hierarchy. However, with the advent of new technologies and a rise in public education the terms of the interaction began to level and change, though some core values of early reference services remain constant.

The most commonly recognised models of reference service concern the 'conservative' or 'minimum' model and the 'liberal' or 'maximum' model:

> With the liberal, or maximum model, the librarian's responsibility centres on delivering an answer in response to a user's inquiry. The librarian does not attempt to educate the user in the process; rather, he or she puts all effort into finding accurate and credible information. Conversely, the ultimate goal for the conservative, or minimal, model is to train users to make use of the library independently, as the process of finding information is valued above the information itself.
>
> (Agosto et al., 2011, p. 237)

With the minimum model, the emphasis is on the process of instruction and the patron is encouraged to be independent. With the maximum model, the librarian answers questions with authority in a timely, accurate way and the patron is dependent upon them for the answers to their queries. Most academic libraries now use a combination of the two approaches; for example, the research student often learns the processes necessary to search through collections and the 'subject' librarian would traditionally act as an expert for students and academic staff to consult.

The impact of technology on the reference service effected great changes which called for new models of approach. There were worries amongst the library community that their role would become redundant as a new type of service was necessary to serve a changing (and sometimes not even physically present) community. Some of the models that Tyckoson sets out retain the traditional values; for example, the traditional reference model, the teaching-library model, the tiered reference service and the virtual reference service (Tyckoson, 2001). The traditional reference model is a maximum model where the librarian answers questions for patrons. The teaching-library model is a minimum model where the librarian provides instruction in relation to the research process, usually to groups of patrons, before they embark on research. The tiered reference model (or Brandeis model) involves different staff answering different types of queries: support staff and student members of staff answer some simple quick questions while reference librarians answer more detailed and complex questions. The virtual reference service (earlier referred to as the call centre model) is usually an online service which uses email, chat, or a call centre to answer queries in a timely manner. Some libraries have adopted this approach as it is very cost-effective and can even be provided 24/7; however, Tyckoson notes that satisfaction rates of patrons using this type of reference service are usually much lower.

In all of these models, the services took place in pre-existing spaces that were either built with the reference service models in mind, or they could accommodate these types of interactions. Tyckoson argues that the traditional reference service remains the predominant model in libraries today, but with the changing learning landscape (due to new technology and a rise in use of the Internet in respect to collections) new learning facilities are being built. These study environments no longer need to feature the same reference service facilities (though some values remain inherent); the AGLC symbolises a shift from the librarian as the owner of the house to the students themselves as the ones who need to shape and inform the learning spaces and services that are in place for them.

The 'information commons'[1] is heralded as a new, dynamic model of reference service:

> On one level the phrase describes an 'exclusively online environment in which the widest possible variety of digital services can be accessed via a single interface,' while concurrently denoting 'a new type of physical facility . . . designed to organise workspace and service delivery around the integrated digital environment' (Beagle, 1999). This model reflects the way in which

academic libraries are responding to the demands for technology, combining information resources and reference assistance, and creating collaborative workspaces for acquiring and shaping knowledge.

(Agosto et al., 2011, p. 237)

With the increase in tuition fees, students became viewed as 'customers' and libraries took steps to rethink their relationship with 'paying' students. At the University of Manchester, specialist library assistants became customer service supervisors, and students were treated as consumers who could expect an excellent service in response to the 'product' of education. However, evidence is emerging that students recognise that they do not have much power as consumers; in this role they can only comment and give feedback in response to what has already been delivered to them. At the University of Manchester Library the vocabulary used to refer to students has therefore changed significantly: they have moved from being 'patrons' to 'customers', and now they play a more collaborative role as 'partners'. We realised that if students are to contribute to helping institutions find solutions to the problems that they care about and are directly affected by, the relation between students and service providers must be reconfigured.

Students gain more power in systems of partnership which value their understanding and experiences; they can work together with service providers using a model that is flexible, holistic, inclusive and open to change. In these respects we can ensure that the model used in the design, development and delivery of our learning spaces continues to remain relevant (National Union of Students [NUS], 2013). Inclusion, participation and the opportunity to co-create their own spaces and services all amount to a more positive student experience, and although this is difficult to measure in respect to general consensus, it is clearly evident in projects such as this one where students have been given such opportunities and can directly express the impact this has had on them (e.g. through testimonials).

Initiating a dialogue

The collaborative relationship used in the development of University of Manchester Library spaces treats students as partners; they are no longer guests, or customers, but are active in the ongoing co-creation of their study spaces and services. The use of participatory design methods increased as the project progressed so that the partnership evolved and students were engaged as consultants and stakeholders. Participatory design ethnography has also been used in the US in the creation of new learning spaces (e.g. Purdue University's Active Learning Center, a project led by anthropologist Nancy Fried Foster).

The journey towards the opening of the AGLC in October 2012 inspired the initiation of a new dialogue with students and was part of a wider university initiative to engage, listen to and act in response to the student voice. Designed by students for students, the AGLC was the University's first building project to properly embed the student voice in its governance. Student involvement in every decision, from grand concept through technology choices, furniture design, interior colour, opening hours, right down to the selection of the coffee, gave strength and credibility to this important partnership.

Typically the student consultation started as an information gathering exercise and fell within the traditional models of interaction in libraries: treating students as guests. For example, the feedback from students was viewed from a customer service perspective as they raised issues that we (as *owners* of the service) sought to address. As such, the initial driving forces behind the creation of the AGLC as a project were drawn out of common complaints received from feedback mechanisms across the library sites. The key issues that students raised were:

- Longer opening hours
- More space
- An increase in study rooms
- More power and data.

The University of Manchester's existing library and learning spaces could not satisfy these demands, and this motivated the creation of a new type of learning space.

In 2008 the University's approach started to diverge from a model of interaction where students were treated as visitors or guests when staff were asked to consider spaces from the student's point of view. A learning space survey was sent to the Heads of School and they were asked the following questions:

1   What types of learning spaces do you presently offer in buildings that are managed by your school?
2   What sorts of learning spaces do you feel your students may be limited by within the present availability and configuration of space in your school?
3   What sorts of space are you presently not able to offer (or offer enough of), for example, spaces for group work or particular kinds of technology to enhance learning?
4   Which elements of your present learning spaces work best for students?

The final question initiated a change in approach as it encouraged consideration from a user perspective.

This survey still took a prescriptive approach to the students' needs and relied on the opinion of the Heads of School as key stakeholders. However, there was a shift in value with respect to a need to improve the student experience, and the results gained demonstrated that more social and group meeting spaces were wanted across the schools. The survey also revealed a requirement for PCs and access to new technology as well as 24/7 bookable learning spaces. This gave a baseline indication of what was needed in the AGLC space, and working within the traditional approach could have signalled the end of the consultation process. However, further consultation was then carried out to gain actual student input which first supplemented and then replaced any presumed requirements.

A social learning space survey was addressed to the whole student body in 2009 to gather student insight into their use of learning spaces. It centred around their use of technology, what they viewed as important in such spaces, group study rooms, and how they preferred to access help. Over 2,000 responses were received, and this survey not only gave invaluable data which informed early AGLC designs, but it also involved students in the brainstorming and research stages of the project. The survey marked the start of the partnership as the library invited students to embark on this exciting new journey with them. Of the 2,000 respondents, 68% were already using our existing study spaces. We therefore had a balance of input based on what worked already (and what didn't), and we had the opportunity to identify what was preventing other students from utilising existing spaces. The survey gave us data that enabled us to see that there was a high demand for group study rooms (as 41% of students were already using them) and physical PCs (as 66% used the computer clusters), so it was vital that these aspects were included in the new space.

The student input gained from this survey challenged many presumptions about a Learning Commons space that had been made even at this early stage. For example, the library and the Heads of School had assumed that most students would use laptops instead of desktop PCs, therefore initial designs reflected low numbers of desktop PCs in the space.[2] However, when the students themselves were consulted about this, 45% said they did not bring a laptop in with them to study, so we had to rethink. In addition, technology-rich spaces were seen as a priority for the Heads of School (in the previous survey), but the students themselves made comments such as: 'No fancy stuff, don't waste money.' This low-technology requirement was confirmed when technology-rich group rooms were presented to students. In early designs these spaces included advanced kit such as interactive work surfaces, but the students in no uncertain terms steered us away from this approach, claiming all they needed was a whiteboard, a table and chairs, and a screen. They wanted equipment that they could use easily and that required little technical support and instruction from staff. Students told us what was important to them in a study space: reliable Wi-Fi, silent study spaces, PC provision, desk space, comfortable seating and food-friendly areas. With the traditional reference model of a library space this consultation would not be deemed necessary and therefore would not have occurred. As a result, anything not fit for purpose would only have been identified after launch, when problems were demonstrated in customer behaviours through low usage and pointed out in negative feedback.

By 2010 students had started to take on the role of important partners in the key stages of the development process. Representatives from the Students' Union were embedded in the governance of the AGLC project and were given a voice as part of the Project Committee and Implementation Group. The Students' Union representatives participated in and informed key decisions in relation to design and policies, right through to how the learning space would be staffed. At times the dialogue on the committees was robust and challenging, but the representatives could demonstrate the validity of their opinions with reference to feedback gathered from other students (often from social media groups). The student representatives gave input that at times stood in direct contrast with the assumptions being made by the committee. This meant that decisions had to be rethought in order to ensure that students would get exactly what they required of the space, not just what we thought they needed. An example of how policy had to be completely rethought for the AGLC can be found in relation to food and drink.

The food and drink policy is now the most relaxed the library service has ever had, as students can eat cold food and take drinks (with lids) into all areas of the space. The student representatives helped us to see the way students work from their perspective; they encouraged us to value their ways of working on an equal footing to our own. Students were clear about their needs so that we understood how they would be working in and using the space. Just as we would expect to eat or drink at our desks (especially at times of high pressure), so too did our students. We therefore decided to break the old rules of the house – which prohibited food and drink within a library space – and embrace a much more relaxed policy that allowed cold food and drink throughout the building. In fact this has actually been one of our most successful policies in the AGLC. The Students' Union representatives agreed to fully support the library should this new policy become problematic and need amendment or withdrawal; there were worries that we would end up with a huge litter problem and damages, but this has in fact become easier to handle. Students tell a member of staff if they spill something (they no longer need to hide it), and we pushed for the most robust cleaning model on campus so that litter when left is obvious rather than concealed. This policy serves as a clear example of how years of behavioural observation were confirmed by the initiation of a dialogue that did not seek to change or challenge student behaviour, but to negotiate terms that both parties could work with. As a result, a depth of understanding – as to why students behaved in this way and needed to work like this – was achieved that traditional library models of interaction would not have reached.

In the summer of 2011 students got to test the AGLC ideas when a pilot space was set up in the Joule Library (part of our North Campus). Traditionally a pilot would have been used merely as an opportunity to introduce students to what we (as experts) had in store for them in their new learning space, but this one had a different objective. Ordinarily students (as customers) would only get the chance to feedback on furniture, space and technology *after* these things had been chosen and implemented (e.g. by demonstrating their dissatisfaction). However, the pilot space was used as an opportunity to see how concepts would work in reality and to test out furniture (tables and chairs of different heights and designs) in a practical way. Staff were not only able to observe how the space was used by students; these observations prompted useful dialogue that enabled us to gauge what students valued about their study environment. The pilot space proved a good opportunity to collect some qualitative feedback responses that went beyond the set questions in the social learning space survey of 2009 and once again enabled deeper insight into our students' study needs and preferences. It also enabled us to take some initial ideas to a wider demographic of the student body (beyond that of the student representatives) and to present students with different types of study space (individual spaces, group spaces and also a group room) and different PC setups before deciding definitively on these for the AGLC itself.

By working with students as partners we learned how the space would work in a practical way and we were able to make vital changes to the main AGLC project. Feedback was obtained through focus groups, informal chats with those using the space, and further supplemented by responses gathered by customer service staff. Making changes at this stage – before furniture and equipment was purchased on a wider scale – proved extremely cost-effective and helped us to ensure that the space was as fit for purpose as we could make it before opening. On the basis of feedback we rethought a number of decisions around furniture, technology and accessibility. The pilot space showed us that in the group room setup the input leads were not conveniently placed for the students and the height of the whiteboards was not accessible. These and other comments gathered in respect to the pilot group room helped to shape the design, technology and appearance of the bookable group study rooms that we now have in the AGLC. Feedback from the pilot space even informed a decision to provide privacy screening on the glass for the group rooms in the AGLC. Student feedback prompted the decision to remove the arms on PC chairs, informed the choice of a 'freemote' PC setup (which is clutter free and made desk space more flexible), and allowed for a robust testing of many products.[3] The response to the pilot space informed many of the choices made for the AGLC and ensured that practicality and student needs took priority over what was pleasing aesthetically.

In December 2011 a student consultation group was set up with Students as Partners, which consisted of a series of discussions targeting key stages and areas in the development.[4] During consultations students voiced their opinions about what they knew about the concept of a Learning Commons. They were asked to consider what it could mean for their own individual and group learning methods, how it could impact on and affect their personal development and what content would be useful on our interactive screens. We held further consultations in 2012 where students were asked to explore specific ideas such as the provision of skills sessions and the development of an innovation area. They were also asked to think about a prospective role for student members of staff (who were then called Learning Advisors but later became the Student Team) and worked to generate an appropriate job description for this role. In recognition of their valuable input, student consultants were given an exclusive 'hard hat tour' of the space prior to the official opening of the AGLC. As they walked round the building they were surprised and pleased by how much their suggestions had been acted upon and were delighted with how the concepts they helped to generate had become a reality: 'My voice has been heard and hopefully inspired other students to share their own!' (Linguistics and English Language student and participant in the 2011–2012 consultations).

In early 2012, to provide inspiration for everybody studying and working in the AGLC, students were invited to draw or capture an image that stood out as representative of Manchester students and the Manchester experience. As students were instrumental in the planning and consultation stages it was natural that their creativity should appear on the very walls of the building designed to inspire them, and this is a key element that makes the AGLC unique. The art competition received 450 stunning entries from all disciplines; submissions included drawings, photographs and poetry, all of which are unique to the University and to Manchester. Sixty-five bespoke pieces of student artwork feature in the AGLC; they are printed onto the walls, doors, and glass panelling of the learning spaces for everyone to see. Students were extremely proud that their work had been selected and often brought friends and family to see it in the building. These artworks inspire others, and the images in the building are frequently used in social media posts about the space, but it is the opportunity that students were given to participate actively in the design of the space that affirms it as theirs. This contributes to a more positive student experience as a result of this ongoing dialogue with the library service, where their views are respected, valued, listened to and learned from.

A selection of students who were involved in committees and consultations or who successfully submitted artworks were invited to the building's grand opening. This again broke with tradition, as such an occasion usually involves mainly VIP guests. The building also remained open to students for study throughout the launch event, showing how the student experience is valued and lies at the heart of every decision surrounding the AGLC. As part of this event, tours were taken round the building and the student artists stood near their artwork to explain their creations. The Students' Union General Secretary, who had been heavily involved in the project, also shared the stage to give a speech with the University Librarian; this act once again demonstrates the value that both sides saw in the partnership that had been cultivated throughout the project. A specially commissioned book was produced for the event, a copy was presented to each guest and the pages were dominated by the students' impressive artworks.

Feedback from early tours was really positive, with many comments about the space and design, and an eagerness from students to spend time studying in the Learning Commons. Numerous responses displayed a pride in the building and recognition of the University's investment in the student experience: 'Very good, very impressed, can see where my £9,000 went' (quote from a student on prelaunch tour).

The comments we now receive (mainly through social media) continue to be favourable, although there are suggestions for improvements. Changes have already been made in response to these, including replacing a number of coffee tables with desk-height tables, reducing lift announcement noises and introducing a 'Text Me' scheme. We also monitor behaviour and rather than dealing with 'bad' behaviour by reinforcing the rules, if students act a certain way we try to help them achieve their needs and keep the dialogue open. For example, students using a particular piece of furniture were repeatedly pulling up part of the floor to plug into sockets below – traditionally, having observed this we would have stopped such behaviour, but instead we installed extra power sockets into the furniture itself to address the students' need to use it this way. We also received feedback that the hand dryers in the toilets were too loud (and this was disruptive to the students), and so in response we have replaced them with quieter models; this shows the students that we are willing to listen and respond to their concerns.

The approach to the co-creation of the AGLC has changed the dialogue with our students; feedback is given rather than complaints and as such the space and the services are constantly evolving. From the initial day of opening, even as equipment was being plugged in, students were settled in the space with their feet up on furniture (without their shoes on). They are comfortable in the space they co-created, they recognise that it is here for them and they are eager to remain valued consultants who continue to be part of the journey; we know this as they respond very quickly when asked for comment.

Business as usual

The AGLC is the UK's first 'bookless' library (1st library to have no books, 2012), therefore the services that take place within diverge greatly from some of the traditional reference models mentioned earlier. Some key aspects remain, as front-line customer service staff assist students by answering questions and instruct them on how to use library resources (they also operate a Library Chat service and answer email and telephone queries). However, the main difference lies in the fact that there is no physical collection, we have a Learning Development Team that teaches academic skills and showcases new technology to the students, and our customer service staff also deal with a high number of estates issues (as the AGLC is a new building). Customer service staff log maintenance requests and chase works that needs to be done whilst ensuring there is minimal disruption to the students. Their roles differ from those of front-line staff in a traditional library model as they play an intrinsic part in organising maintenance, tracing and initiating the development of new services and ensuring the ongoing evolution of the project.

To give you an idea of how the AGLC runs its services we will give a brief overview of the different departments operating within. Each of these departments has a connection to the student voice embedded within them as this forms a key part of our 'business as usual' operations. There are three main departments within the overall team: Customer Services, IT Support and the Learning Development Team. Each one maintains a dialogue with the students that goes beyond a simple 'you said, we did' approach and takes the form of an ongoing conversation as student feedback is acted upon, responded to and continues to influence the services. Students are engaged in an ongoing dialogue that does not concern reactive, prescriptive interaction but emphasises collective responsibility more along the lines of 'you said, we think, what should we do together?' The services within the space are designed using a holistic model which treats feedback as a key indicator in relation to the needs of the community (of students) that it serves, so that the services and space can evolve accordingly.

Some examples of how students have informed customer service policies can be found in respect to food and drink (as already discussed), opening hours, and how they express different needs during exam time. During this time students asked for extra desk-height furniture, they requested silent zones and they wanted extra study spaces. These changes are now put into place for each exam period. Students also influenced policy to initiate a Text Me service so that they can contact a member of staff (anonymously if they wish) to make noise complaints, give feedback or ask questions. Our Customer Service team have developed a mapping programme so that they can monitor how students are using furniture and the spaces to ensure these are configured in the way that is most useful to them. Student feedback is reacted to in a positive way; we ask *why* they are behaving in this way? Is there a need that's not being met? What are they trying to tell us?

In the AGLC we have a physical IT support desk integrated with Customer Services and, in direct response to student feedback, the hours of this support were extended from 9 a.m.–5 p.m. throughout the week to 9 a.m.–9 p.m. every weekday and 9 a.m.–5 p.m. at weekends. We learned that more students were bringing in devices to help them study and use the space. In response to this there was demand for a new type of IT support. Central IT services therefore used what we had learned about the needs of students (by working in partnership with them) to develop a pilot project concerning a Personal Device Support Desk. This desk is currently managed by a graduate intern, and student members of staff are employed to advise fellow students on software provided by the University and to give them guidance on how to fix problems with their personal devices. The desk currently has a 98% resolution rate for the problems they encounter, and due to the success of the pilot project this service is being extended.

The Learning Development Team deliver and manage the Open Training Programme which forms a significant part of the University of Manchester's library skills programme: My Learning Essentials (MLE). The Open Training Programme combines one-to-one support with workshops and online resources, and MLE recently won the Blackboard Catalyst Award for blended learning. Many partners work together to deliver workshops, for example, the Careers Service, the Counselling Service, the University Language Centre, Manchester Business School and the Cultural Institutions (including Manchester Museum and the Whitworth Art Gallery). As the AGLC is located at the heart of the campus, it serves as a convenient and accessible centralised location from which to offer such support to our students. The objective behind the programme is to creatively engage students and ensure a positive learning experience using methods which foster a growth mindset in relation to learning (Dweck, 2008). In contrast to the type of instruction traditionally offered (e.g. in the minimum model), the Open Training Programme utilises a workshop format to emphasise active learning and the technique of facilitation which reinforces the status of the students as independent learners. As a consequence of these methods, the librarian is removed from the status of 'expert', and responsibility for learning and searching for answers remains in the hands of the students themselves. During the workshops the facilitator works with the students (and gets them to work with each other) to emphasise collaboration and encourage them to make progress rather than to strive for perfection. In summary, the methodology behind the training necessitates a workshop format (to encourage engagement and activity), sessions must be open to all students from any discipline and of any status, and sessions must be skills based (so that students can immediately put into practice what they have learned). All workshops must also be open to feedback, as it is not only important for students to feel that their feedback is useful for effecting change, but that it gives them the chance to inform and co-create future sessions (Hattie and Timperley, 2007). The methodology behind the programme is designed to encourage learners to construct their own learning experience, and it is underpinned by research (funded by the HEA and the NTF) into 'HEARing student voices' conducted by Jennie Blake et al. The study indicated a need to ask not 'What do students need?' but 'How can we get students involved as co-creators?' How can we make sure students are proactively looking for support before they reach a crisis point? The objectives behind the resources on offer in the programme are therefore to assist students so that they can support themselves (Blake et al., 2010, 2011). In many ways the programme sits so well in the AGLC as it promotes the same values and methods with respect to treating students as partners and requires the same dialogue to ensure that student needs are being met.

The Learning Development Team mark a new addition to the traditional models of reference service as, in addition to traditional library teaching models (which centred around bibliographic instruction or information literacy), this team also deliver academic skills support and give students the opportunity to interact with and learn about new technology. The student voice is embedded within the Open Training Programme, as students can give feedback in response to training that has been delivered and they can submit ideas and requests for training that is not currently part of the programme. In this way they shape their own learning experience, and the team are proud to have a really quick turnaround when it comes to producing new workshops – an important attribute, as it means that any student who requests training is also able to attend it. Examples of such sessions include 'Critical Reading', 'Reflect on Your Performance' and 'Understanding British Culture', and workshops which help students to 'Manage Exam Stress' and 'Present With Confidence'. If students need support with developing or improving upon particular academic, well-being, career or information literacy skills, the mechanisms are in place for them to raise this concern and inform us so that the programme can facilitate their progress. Our students have the power to dictate, mould and shape the support that is on offer to them, and the high number of attendees is a testament to the success of both the programme and its methodology. We are currently at the end of year 2 with the Open Training Programme, and the number of attendees at workshops has increased by 61% compared to year 1 (from 2,424 to 3,899). Exemplary student feedback is used to promote the programme on the digital signage around the AGLC, to demonstrate the way it impacts on the students and their experience.

Our AV and New Technologies Coordinator is also part of the Learning Development Team and runs Digilab in a joint venture with Digital Technology Services (this serves as another example of a role that sits outside of those in the traditional reference models of service). Digilab is a regularly scheduled event that gives students the opportunity to interact with new technology in a pressure-free, relaxed environment. Students can suggest technologies to be tested and can pilot their own technological developments (e.g. apps, electronic devices or websites). At Digilab events, members of the Student Team are on hand to help demonstrate the technology to their peers, and the emphasis is not on teaching but on experimentation and exploration. Examples of the technology Digilab has tested out include Oculus Rift (virtual reality) environments, Google Glass, and 3D printing. The events provide students with the opportunity to participate in and influence decisions concerning the types of technology that the University should buy (and what it should/could be used for). Digilab also gives University staff the opportunity to test out different or competing brands of technology, as well as things they have designed themselves (e.g. a careers management database) so that they may gather valuable student feedback.

In addition to these departments our Student Team are student members of staff who rove around the building – they collect data in relation to how the space is used and help with the evaluation of services from a Customer Service, IT and Learning Development perspective. The Student Team promote MLE, they help to inform the workshops and they provide an invaluable link to the student community. The team are paid members of staff who work two 4-hour shifts a week, though we are flexible with them around exam time. We are currently working with our second generation of staff, and the first generation have helped to train these by sharing what they have learned in relation to the departments within the building and their role in relation to each area. The students have gained a wide range of valuable skills, such as customer service experience, project management skills, presentation skills, data collection and analysis experience, political networking skills and an insight into pedagogy, research methods and evaluation.

In summary, the student voice is embedded as part of business as usual in all aspects of the teams that work within the AGLC, which ensures that they continue to evolve with the changing needs of the community. The statement made by Green in 1876 retains its relevance: in the AGLC the space is popular amongst students as we have sought to break down the traditional barriers between staff and students. As a result, both are 'owners of the space' and the services within.

Future shaping

Allowing students to be co-creators of a library space has been a radical change for library staff. When recruiting staff to work in the AGLC it became apparent that there was a real fear of the unknown on the part of potential applicants and amongst those who had already been recruited. Although certain functions could be predicted, the main requirement for obtaining a post in the AGLC was an ability to respond to changing student needs and to identify opportunities to continually improve the student experience. As the library service moved forward into new territory, staff had the opportunity to shape their own job roles (to an extent), however not everyone was comfortable with this. It soon became clear that recruiting people who embraced this creative approach was crucial to the success of the building and its services. Our new staff developed their job roles with energy and enthusiasm; this is now viewed as a real plus point for the building and is something that the library is keen to capture elsewhere. The team are dynamic, proactive and experimental in their approach to working in the space and students really appreciate their responsiveness.

The innovative approach taken in the creation of the AGLC was recognised as we won the *Guardian* Higher Education Facilities Award in 2014 (see Guardian University Awards 2014 Ideas Bank, 2014). This award uniquely concentrates on the impact of a facility rather than the aesthetics of a building. Many buildings win awards for design rather than functionality, but what we have captured in the AGLC exceeds its presence and appearance as a physical building; we sought to engage students by embedding learning within the very heart of the space. Fresh, dynamic library roles have been created and we have engaged in new types of ongoing dialogue with the students; both of these advancements inform the evolving library landscape. The AGLC journey has taught us that it is really important for clients to assert the importance of functionality to their design teams when engaged in such a project. We continually had to ensure that the focus always valued the student experience over visual appeal (although ideally you *can* have both).

The journey for the University of Manchester Library does not end here: the new dialogue created during the AGLC project continues to be developed. This process marked the start of a journey, but our partnership with students continues to inform both the AGLC and University-wide developments:

> Close student partnerships continue to be central to the further enrichment of the AGLC, as we consider future needs and evaluate the building's success. We now need to fully understand how the building and its services are used – we will then contribute our experience to other new and ambitious university plans.
>
> (Jan Wilkinson, Guardian University Awards 2014 Ideas Bank, 2014)

Following on from the success of the AGLC in terms of its consultations and student participation, students are now part of the journey to redevelop our Main Library building. In 2013 they took part in a consultation for a new project to redesign the Main Library. Students were challenged to consider what a world-class research library should look like and how it should relate to other facilities. The partnership with students will continue throughout this project and we will build upon the best practices learned from the AGLC development to co-create this space and enhance the student experience for the future.

The AGLC project has uniquely informed other University of Manchester estates projects and, as part of the 'Manchester 2020 Vision', the University will invest £1 billion over the next 10 years to create a world-class campus for our staff and students. Other library and learning spaces are being developed across campus and the AGLC has enabled us to share a model of best practices in relation to treating such projects as an opportunity to co-create spaces with our students so that we can pool our perspectives. The library will utilise the AGLC as a space to trial potential concepts and ideas to the wider student body to assist with and input into these new developments. A desire to share good practice has gone beyond internal audiences, as the AGLC has been visited by over 100 other higher education institutions:

> A HUGE thank you . . . it was so inspiring and I feel very excited for our similar project . . . I really appreciated all the nuggets of info and advice that you shared.
>
> (quote from a visiting university staff member)

We will continue to try and share our experiences and knowledge through journal articles and conference presentations within the UK and abroad, but if we could give one invaluable piece of advice from what we have learned, it is this: we genuinely believe that the success of the AGLC is due to the way we changed our dialogue to engage students as partners throughout the whole process. They helped us co-create this space, and together we continue to take a collective responsibility for improvements by learning from one another and keeping the dialogue between us current and open.

Notes

1 Information commons is an early iteration of Learning Commons though the latter differs in respect of its physicality: its presence, make-up and design.
2 Often a question of the ratio of desktop PCs to laptop spaces is still asked when tours are delivered on the AGLC. Currently we are of the belief that there is no formula for calculating this in the space. We feel the AGLC would still be heavily used if desktop PC numbers were doubled and equally so if they were reduced by half. We would advise that flexibility of space is key, and that the more spaces that can be used for either function, the better.
3 The arms on PC chairs were being damaged by the desks and students did not think they were necessary. Student feedback caused us to disregard certain pieces of furniture (e.g. pinch stools that were aesthetically appealing from a design perspective, but the students told us they were not fit for purpose). Some furniture also failed after high usage despite assurances from suppliers.
4 Students as Partners (SaP) is a programme of work managed by the Teaching and Learning Support Office in liaison with the Faculties at the University of Manchester – see: http://www.tlso.manchester.ac.uk/students-as-partners/

References

Agosto, D. E., Rozaklis, L., MacDonald, C. and Abels, E. G., 2011. A model of the reference and information service process. *Reference & User Services Quarterly*, 50(3), pp. 235–44.

Beagle, D., 1999. Conceptualizing an information commons. *Journal of Academic Librarianship*, 25(2), pp. 82–9.

Blake, J., Clift-Martin, P., Walmsley, L. and Wass, V., 2010. Self Portraits and Perpetual Motion: The Student Experience of Informed Choice and Feedback. *ELSIN Conference*. Portugal.

Blake, J., Clift-Martin, P., Walmsley, L. and Wass, V., 2011. HEARing Student Voices: NTFS Final Report. *HEA Funded NTFS Research Project*. University of Manchester.

Coffman, S., 1999. Reference as others do it. *American Libraries*, 30, pp. 54–6.

Dweck, C. S., 2008. *Mindset: The new psychology of success*. New York: Ballantine.

1st library to have no books, 2012. *Sun*, 20 September, p. 29.

Green, S. W., 1876. Personal relations between librarians and readers. *American Library Journal*, 1(2–3), pp. 74–81.

Guardian University Awards 2014 Ideas Bank: Winner: University of Manchester, 2014. *Guardian*, [Online] 27 February. Available at: <http://www.theguardian.com/higher-education-network/2014/feb/18/winner-university-of-manchester-facilities-project> [Accessed 26 March 2015].

Hattie, J. and Timperley, H., 2007. The power of feedback. *Review of Educational Research,* 77(1), pp. 81–112.

Massey-Burzio, V., 1992. Reference encounters of a different kind: A symposium. *Journal of Academic Librarianship*, 18(5), pp. 276–80.

National Union of Students UK, 2013. *NUS Partnerships*. [video online] Available at: <https://youtu.be/Ls7FFB7Bkl0> [Accessed 26 March 2015].

Rettig, J., 1992. Rethinking reference and adult services. *RQ,* 31(4), pp. 463–6.

Tyckoson, D., 2001. What is the best model of reference service? *Library Trends*, 50(2), pp. 183–96.

University of Manchester. 2015. *Teaching and Learning Support Office: Students as Partners*. [online] Available at: <http://www.tlso.manchester.ac.uk/students-as-partners/> [Accessed 26 March 2015].

12 UX and a small academic library

Margaret Westbury

This is not a story of how a UX mindset brought radical change to my library, but how over a few months it was a quiet yet persistent voice of empathy with my users, which resulted in keeping some old policies and starting some new ones that made my library a much friendlier place. Again, we are not talking radical change, but proof that a UX mindset, coupled with ethnographic methods, can generally sharpen the discussion about – and provide solid justification for – putting people first in your library.

Background

I run a small college library at the University of Cambridge. College libraries – 31 in total – play an important role in the ecosystem of libraries across the University. The college library is often the first library that new students visit and their subsequent 'home' library for the duration of their degree. Cambridge college libraries offer interdisciplinary collections that cater to the reading lists of taught courses and tend to have excellent spaces for studying. Most offer basic induction and searching classes, and as such are quite important for acclimating students to the culture of doing research at the university level.

The students at Cambridge tend to be high academic achievers, and perhaps because of this – for better or worse – I and the administration of my college tend to carry around certain assumptions about our students, some of which are so commonplace they become remarkably ingrained. One that I often hear is that 'students these days come to university with multiple mobile computing devices' such as laptops, tablets, mobile phones and so forth. Many do, but do all? Realistically, probably not. Yet it is so compelling, and it so feeds our ideas – or fantasies – of living in a technologically advanced world, that we rarely unpack it. I am just as much to blame as others. I regularly like to talk about how wired and technologically savvy my users are. The big question is, what are the implications if we start to design library services underpinned by assumptions like these?

This is where a UX mindset becomes very important, because it helps cut through these comfortable assumptions and stereotypes to reveal the complicated lives, experiences and desires of individual real people. For example, when important people at my college recently asked if we really needed a room in the

Figure 12.1 The Wolfson College computer room
Source: Margaret Westbury.

library with 15 big desktop computers because 'students these days' all come to university with multiple mobile computing devices, my first thought was, 'That room really *is* anachronistic – let's do away with it and replace it with something whizzy and future-proofed.' You see, the computer room arguably is a bit odd (see Figure 12.1).

It is a meeting room with various old tables for the computers, bad lighting and flooring, wires spilling out the back of the computers and monitors – not exactly a showpiece of modern library space. But thankfully – and in part because of the UX mindset I had recently started adopting – I slowed down and said that it might be interesting if we took the time to *ask why* students used that particular computer room. Because use it they do: it almost always has people in it and is very often over half full.

Asking why

So, I very quickly threw together a print survey and left it round the computer room for the period of a week; during this time, I also informally spoke with students working in the computer room. The survey and interview questions asked: 'What are you doing in the computer room today?' 'Why did you choose to work here?' 'If you could change anything about the room what would it be?' Between the 30 survey responses I received, and the 20 people I chatted with, it was a good rate of return, certainly enough to see some trends. The results were very interesting and, to many people at my college, including myself, quite surprising and illuminating.

It turns out that some common reasons students worked in the computer room were as follows:

- They needed to be out of their rooms, working in a space with other people.
- The monitors in the computer room were bigger and more comfortable to look at than their laptops.
- The computers have software already loaded (such as SPSS – a statistical package) which they cannot afford themselves.
- The computers have direct access to big printers (no need to configure your laptop for wireless printing).
- Their laptop had crashed and they could not afford a new one at the moment.

Interestingly, many of their reasons were shaped in opposition to – or at least in relation to – the existence of mobile technologies. And there *clearly* were compelling reasons to continue to provide access to big, old-school computers. The survey was so interesting to me and the administration of my college that I believe it *saved* the computer room. Without the evidence – the voices of the students themselves – it is likely that the computer room would have been repurposed to something perhaps less valued by the college community.

The mini-interviews in themselves were intriguing, but I felt they were the tip of the iceberg in terms of what could be learned. My sense was that despite the fact students used the computer room for different, though somewhat related reasons, the interesting underlying differences about *why* they chose that spot couldn't be illuminated through a simple survey and set of short interviews.

Cognitive mapping

At the end of the short interviews, I asked if the students would be interested in doing a longer 10-minute follow-up interview with me, and about a third said 'Yes'. I felt strongly that there was likely more to be said about their use of the computer room than my simple survey could derive. I had always been intrigued by the method of cognitive mapping as a quick, efficient way of describing students' 'learning landscapes' (i.e. all the places where they did their academic work and why) and wanted to know what combination of factors contributed to making such decisions. My recent reading about UX and digital literacies, and everything that I had ever studied about anthropology, led me to think that the answers were going to be interestingly and deliciously complicated – and all different.

I was not disappointed. I used a structured 6-minute exercise in which I asked students to draw a map of all the places where they did their academic work, switching pen colour every two minutes, starting with the red pen, so as to easily be able to see the most important places first (the assumption being that the first thing students draw would be the most important to them). I also followed up the exercise with a short interview where the students labelled the map and discussed the various points on it. The maps were beautiful and illuminating and clearly showed that even if students were using the same space, their reasons for doing so, how they felt about the space and how they made it uniquely *their* place was based on a combination of many factors including discipline, degree, nature of work undertaken, maturity, age, preferences, availability of electrical outlets, proximity to amenities such as water and toilets, proximity to friends and/or other people, availability of comfortable seating and/or natural light, noise level and – very intriguingly to me – memories and/or associations with a space.

The college common room

To tease out just one example from these maps, let us focus on a popular common room in my college which looks like a nice, welcoming living room (see Figure 12.2).

Who wouldn't want to work there? However, students tend to feel passionately one way or another about the worthiness of the space. In fact, it is far more politically fraught than you might think. Figure 12.3 shows two maps, both of which have indicated that this room is a place where they often do work (the room is marked 'KSJ' or 'Karen Spärk Jones Room' on the maps).

The first student loves this room because she can sit comfortably with her laptop near a window, drink coffee and be around other people. The second student finds the room quite stressful: there are tensions for him about whether he can talk in the room or not (technically you *may*, but in practice it is often so quiet that one feels uncomfortable doing so). He also feels stressed by the coffee machine, because it is not clear how it works and you have to purchase coffee for it elsewhere in college. Another student I spoke with will not work in there *at all* because she

Figure 12.2 The Karen Spärk Jones Room
Source: Margaret Westbury.

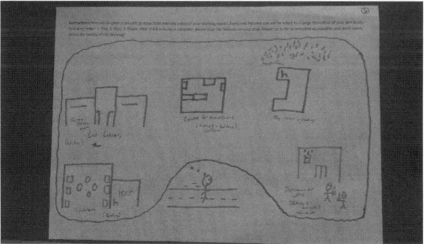

Figure 12.3 Two student cognitive maps depicting their 'learning landscapes'
Source: Margaret Westbury.

associates the space with her interview day at the college when it was used as a waiting room, and yet another student loves the place because a few years ago he used to socialise often there with friends. Two further students I interviewed both find the furniture in the room incredibly uncomfortable: tables too low, backs of sofas too hard and so forth.

Without taking the time to talk to students and really probe why and for what reasons they made a choice about workspaces, none of the problems, tensions and politics of this room would have been discerned. Indeed, until then, I had always showcased this room as an example of the sort of space that we needed more of around college.

In just 10 of these mapping surveys, the amount of data that I got was so rich it was stunning. These were interviews with students who were all relatively heavy users of the library's computer room, and yet what they were doing in there and what they subsequently did elsewhere – where and why – were very different and complicated.

Quick wins

So, how did this research lead to library policy changes? Directly stemming from this research, I changed the policy in my library to allow food and drinks. It met with some raised eyebrows from the administration of my college, but my interviews with students showed undeniably that they valued comfort in their study spaces – that they would actively choose one space over another because of its food and drink amenities.

The other policy I changed was the loan-and-renewal policy. I dramatically increased how many books students could borrow at one time as well as the number of times that books could be renewed. After listening to students discuss in the interviews how they juggled short loan periods and dealt with punitive emails about returning books, the old circulation policies seemed stingy. Students still *do* need to return their books of course, but I am now just a little less concerned if they want to keep them for extended periods.

Several months later, with the change of policies in place, my library has not become a mess of spilled food and drink, nor have we been overrun with vermin eating leftover crumbs. And books continue to be returned to the library regularly. With very minimal impact to the daily routine of the library, I gained a huge amount of goodwill throughout my college as heading a department that really cares about students' needs.

The UX mindset

As I do my daily rounds in the library and observe students working, it is easy to fall back on assumptions about how they work and what their needs are. I like to note how students creatively use the study spaces, as I tend to be relaxed about them leaving their belongings overnight on desks. Figure 12.4 shows three typical ways that students use the study spaces.

Students have colonised these spaces, making them mini-offices and storage places, and it is quite easy to label the usage with any number of simplistic stereotypes (like *colonisation*, actually). But it is important for me as a librarian to realise that this usage is actually quite complicated and hardly neutral: it is a combination of needs-meeting, performance for self and other students, and negotiation with limitations (perceived or real) of the space. Each student makes the space his or her place in different ways, for highly personal reasons. As I interact with students and design library services, I must keep this complexity in mind (i.e. have the UX

Figure 12.4 Three examples of study space use in Wolfson College Library
Source: Margaret Westbury.

mindset), for otherwise I am likely to wind up creating policies that are not flexible enough to meet a wide variety of their needs.

In the end, the small-scale studies I did illuminated a complicated set of behaviours and will forever change how I think about the students who use my library. With no money and very little time, I successfully used some ethnographic techniques to sharpen the discussion about students' technology, resource use and study-space needs at my college. Such techniques revealed a host of previously unconsidered issues and heightened awareness of many aspects of the library service I run that could and should be changed.

And, as an added benefit, without even realising I was doing it, I got people in my college excited about UX. I sneaked the approach and methods into my normal responsibilities and very easily proved their value. That these small victories can bring about rather nice improvements in the experience of users means that they are definitely worth trying.

The bottom line is that most librarians are not their end users, and therefore our assumptions about our users' desires and goals, what tasks they would like to achieve and whether their needs are met by using our services will often be incorrect. If our mission is to help our users be as productive as possible then we need to fully understand what drives and motivates them, and UX methods are truly excellent for that.

13 Understanding our students and ourselves

Transformative library instruction through an ethnographic lens

Michael Courtney and Carrie Donovan

There is a story that was oft told by S. R. Ranganathan, long considered the father of library science and quite possibly its greatest (and most earnest) champion of the role that librarians play in the educational process. Having never had access to a library during his formative years of schooling, he recollected that most students of his generation had never heard of nor could even comprehend the word 'library', never mind appreciate the underlying role of a library. Seldom having had exposure to a dictionary (although his teacher would occasionally use one), young Ranganathan learned not through inquiry but through the recitation of rote statements, such as 'Birmingham is noted for hardware, Reading is noted for biscuits, and Sheffield is noted for cutlery' (1961, p. 19). Yet, he had the benefit of two teachers: one a Sanskrit instructor throughout his primary schooling; the other a teacher who also was a tenant in Ranganathan's home. Both took great delight in answering the endless questions the young boy posed, and while much of their shared knowledge came from a lifetime of understanding, they instilled a fundamental structure of critical inquiry that was to last him the rest of his life and, arguably, alter his attitudes and approach to the transformative power of education.

Librarians' success as educators, too, depends primarily on the ability to align our work with institutional priorities and to understand the processes, feelings, and behaviors that our learners undergo as they experience the transformative effects of education. While information professionals are involved in designing, implementing, and assessing instructional initiatives in a variety of ways, the driving force of many of these approaches is a learner-centered philosophy that acknowledges the holistic engagement of students as critical to their success. In order to better understand how students access, use, and evaluate information to achieve learning goals, librarians can apply the principles of ethnography to investigate students' understanding of and experience with the processes of information seeking and use.

The application of ethnographic methods to library instructional programs can provide opportunities for students to develop their own self-awareness and advance their thought processes. In addition, these methods have the potential to increase understanding of these processes on the part of librarians who can, in turn, influence the design of library spaces, the delivery of instructional programs, and the role of librarians in students' lives. Based on our own experience of using ethnographic methods to illuminate student beliefs, behaviors, and attitudes, throughout this chapter we will describe the effective application of ethnographic methods to library instruction and how such approaches can be built into one's instructional repertoire at the course, curricular, or programmatic level. The power of qualitative data for aligning teaching with the student experience and explaining the value of the library as an important context for student learning, including librarians' roles as change agents within that context, will be the guiding framework for this chapter.

Setting the stage

In order to design library instruction that is relevant to individuals and institutions, librarians must fully understand their communities of learners, including their prior knowledge and capacity for achievement. Some educators look to characteristics and skills across generations of learners in order to comprehend the preferences, patterns, and performance of students, while others depend upon educational standards to guide their integration of specific learning outcomes into existing curricula. These broad approaches can be helpful in establishing a framework from which to start, but should not be the sole means for developing and sustaining learner-focused instructional initiatives over time. While librarians at Indiana University had a general idea of our students' research awareness and information-seeking savvy, we did not have a full understanding of the ways they conceptualize and engage with information systems in order to achieve their academic goals. By applying ethnography, the qualitative method of observing and recording the everyday practices of a cultural group in order to better understand their lives (Duke and Asher, 2012, pp. 3–4), librarians have the opportunity to understand research behaviors from the point of view of students at their own institutions. Inspired by the Ethnographic Research in Illinois Academic Libraries (ERIAL) Project (see http://www.erialproject.org), librarians at Indiana University engaged in a year-long ethnographic study using interview and observation techniques to explore the research processes of students in a first-year survey course and an upper-division course in an undergraduate disciplinary major.

The experience of conducting research through an ethnographic lens created opportunities for us to think, and act, like anthropologists in other aspects of our professional practice as well. In doing so, it became obvious how well the ways of thinking and knowing, framed by this social science, can apply to librarianship. For example, librarians provide many of our services and enact our professional activities in the same environments in which we have the opportunity to observe our students' learning, researching, and studying. By participating in this study, we have adapted new ways of 'seeing' our students' research behaviors in our everyday work as it occurs in library classrooms, throughout the library, and when we review the transcripts and queries captured through our research consultation services. Such opportunities for observation, both physically and virtually, allow us to make data-informed choices when we talk with faculty about their students' research practices and how these should inform the design of assignments and the integration of library instruction, especially for students who are new to the knowledge practices of their chosen major or discipline.

We know that one of the ways in which students make sense of new information has to do with their prior knowledge (Heath and Heath, 2008, pp. 54–5); this is why we use metaphors and analogies to explain the intricacies of the research process. For knowledge to take hold in the memory, it must latch onto some existing mental framework or schema. For students who are new to the college and university experience, their prior knowledge of the research process may revolve around a familiar search engine or online resource, but the depth of inquiry required for many advanced research projects will not be something that is yet part of their mental model. Similarly, students are less and less likely to know of the important role a librarian can play in their academic lives and in their learning, as evidenced by the decline in visits to our libraries' reference and information services desks. Based on data from Head and Eisenberg's Project Information Literacy survey (2010, p. 16), which indicates that librarians are nearly last in the list of people students ask when they have a research question or problem, it is apparent that the place of librarians in the prior experience of college students is not what it once was. This is no surprise when we consider the lack of funding for libraries in primary and secondary schools, resulting in a diminished role for librarians in the daily lives of students during their formative years. Through our own observations, we have recognized that students are comfortable approaching their peers to request help or to ask for information in the library. Accordingly, we employ students at public service desks in library spaces that are commonly used by undergraduates, and have questioned the relevance of naming our online reference service 'Ask a Librarian'.

Without much prior knowledge of the layout of libraries and library collections, both physically and online, and the resulting confusion as to how to seek information and get help with the research process, many learners suffer from library anxiety. Already vulnerable in an unfamiliar space and tasked with research requirements for which they have little or no prior knowledge, many students regress to using information sources and research practices that are familiar to them, whether or not they are appropriate for their research needs. The confidence with online sources exhibited by novice researchers does not always translate to the effective use of information resources and advanced research strategies. Because of this disconnect, students can miss the opportunity to experience the research process as a chance to elevate their thinking and challenge their own deeply held beliefs. The anxiety around the research process can transfer to students' feelings about the library, library staff, and library resources as well.

With the proliferation of user studies, focus groups, and surveys, it is evident that libraries of all kinds are increasingly paying attention to the experiences, preferences, and needs of our various and diverse audiences. Maintaining an awareness of current trends in higher education, pedagogy, and usability is important for librarians in order to understand the broad range of possible inquiry methods that may influence the design of library spaces and instructional programs. Among these many opportunities for studying our learners, ethnographic methods can provide relevant and specific knowledge of students' research behaviors and attitudes within the local context of our own institutions. These methods are directly aligned with the learner-centered professional philosophy that drives many librarians and provides for them a foundation upon which to build programs, services, and partnerships. Librarians who are mindful of general standards, current trends, and intersecting priorities without letting them dictate their mission and vision can succeed in demonstrating their relevance and value to their local campus community.

Learner-centered instruction through an ethnographic lens

With so many questions plaguing academic libraries (e.g. How are library collections and spaces used? How do faculty engage in research? What sort of support and services do graduate students require for their research?), a holistic ethnographic study could easily begin to seem like a panacea to the issues that we face. However, an authentic ethnographic approach demands that our research questions, data collection, and resulting actions maintain the interests and practices of our users as the central focus. For this reason, we chose to center our particular ethnographic investigation on the ways in which course assignments influence student research behavior, specifically the description and structure of the assignment. By illuminating student research behaviors, we hoped to discover good practices for assignment design that balance faculty expectations with students' sense of ownership, responsibility, and self-efficacy in the research process. The lessons learned through this study have informed our instructional techniques, especially as they relate to our consultations with faculty on the design and timing of research-based assignments across a variety of disciplines. For example, we know that scaffolding research assignments or creating multiple mini-assignments that lead students through the steps in the research process is helpful, as long as students understand the connection and meaning behind each individual step so that the mini-assignments seem worthwhile.

Eschewing the traditional method of teaching and moving beyond the pitfalls of the unidirectional 'empty bucket' approach (Bateman, 1991, p. 27) – in which students are regarded as empty vessels waiting to be filled – instead incorporating inquiry into teaching, has empowered us to imagine new ways to inspire learners. By inviting students to take more responsibility for their own learning, we welcome them as partners in the educational experience and acknowledge that they will make valid contributions. Such empowerment and inspiration have proven to be integral components of the teaching and learning process and, in turn, have helped shape our ethnographic approach. We seek to find context in how our learners engage in the research process and, perhaps, our quest aligns with the very ethnographic process that seeks a multitude of explanations at each stage. Much like the undergraduate research projects we chose to observe and analyze, the ethnographic approach proved both opportune and pertinent in illuminating the complexities of the students' own methodologies and experiences in and out of the classroom. While we had basic assumptions about student research behavior, we were frequently reminded that the student experience is in constant flux. For example, some students had a foundation of research based on our locally licensed databases and would begin their investigation with the libraries' website, but others relied on sources used in high school or those recommended by friends as a starting point for research.

By observing our learners through an ethnographic lens, we began to view them in deeper and more meaningful ways. This, in turn, has reminded us of the complexities of the learning process – though commonalities exist, learners employ a wide array of approaches to performing research, and while librarians may hold a library-centric philosophy to learning, our students seemingly view the library as only one component of a much larger system of support in the academic process, each integral in its own way.

Understanding these complexities, both of the learning process and the learners themselves, will help you develop a research question as a basis for inquiry. This, perhaps, may prove to be the most difficult hurdle to overcome and presents librarians not classically trained as anthropologists/ethnographers with a rather thorny problem – what do you want to know? While we benefited from the professional advice of an anthropologist on our research team, we encountered some difficulty in scaling down a rather broad and ambitious desire to know everything about our learners. Instead, we focused somewhat more realistically on identifying specific characteristics and approaches to the research process that would enable us to better understand our learners' research needs as well as their understanding of the research process. This, we hoped, would better position us to improve not simply basic library research-support services, but our approach to the teaching and learning process (empowering our instructional selves and, in turn, inspiring our learners). Not unlike the 'Rochester method' (Gibbons, 2012), which seeks greater understanding of the larger institutional setting in which a library is positioned to identify opportunities and challenges between library services and user needs, we sought to identify both gaps in our support of the research process as well as opportunities inherent in our own (unique) community of learners and how we might capitalize on this newly gained knowledge in an instructional sense.

Applying ethnography in a library instructional context

Ethnographic methods yield qualitative data that allow the tracking of attitudes and emotions, in addition to behavior and cognition. This makes ethnography an especially useful approach for illuminating complex processes, such as research and inquiry. Having the experience of designing and implementing an ethnographic study at Indiana University, we realized that the practices we employed to gather and analyze student data and the insights we gained were relevant to the design, delivery, and assessment of our instructional programs more broadly. Not only did we learn how our students acted, thought, and felt as they were seeking information and using it to create new knowledge, but we understood how to observe and appreciate our students from a variety of perspectives in order to expand our own thinking. Qualitative assessment is not only a useful means of gaining insights into students' innermost thoughts and emotions related to the research process, but it can also be helpful in illuminating problems and challenging issues faced by academic libraries regarding student learning. How and when is direct contact with librarians essential for student success? What is more influential in students' research practices: their own prior experience or the directions provided by their instructors? With limited staff and resources, how should librarians design information literacy initiatives to meet the diverse learning needs of student researchers? The more knowledge we gained about our students through ethnography, the clearer it became that centering the design and delivery of library instructional programs around these learners and their needs would help to address some of the difficulties we face in integrating information literacy into student learning across our campus.

What we learn from ethnography is that a multifaceted approach is often the best way to achieve your goals. Indeed, the process of triangulation requires an ethnographer to gather evidence and data using a variety of methods, thereby giving multiple perspectives on a single question, experience, or activity. When translated to the context of implementing information literacy programs for an entire campus, this process can be manifest in the effective design and assessment of learning. Triangulating the design of student learning experiences could result in various opportunities for students to experience information literacy education within and beyond the context of the curriculum. Learning could happen in living spaces, social spaces, and public places as well as in the classroom. It could happen as a result of active, engaged collaboration or individual, contemplative thinking. Similarly, the assessment of such learning could happen in traditional formats through course assignments and grades, as well as through self-paced or community-based activities (such as sets of prepared questions that afford students the ability to respond at their own pace, or reflective exercises). Assessment would be considered formative (or 'in-process') if it were used to improve instructional practice and student learning, while summative (or final) assessment would be a means of looking back at student progress over time.

There are myriad ways to apply ethnographic methods to the traditional one-shot instruction session, as a pedagogical practice or as a learning assessment. Research process interviewing is one possibility for illuminating the underlying strategies for information seeking and the potential challenges the researcher may expect to face when enacting their research plan. In this scenario, one student would talk through their strategy for research, while demonstrating their own information-seeking and evaluation processes in real time. Acting as their partner in this exercise, a classmate would ask questions in order to prompt the researcher toward the next step. There are many benefits for creating openness around a process that is usually solitary, including the verbalization of a research strategy as a means of better understanding it. Another positive outcome is the opportunity for the student to fail and try again in the safe environment that a library classroom affords. While this approach can be challenging to novice researchers who may not immediately appreciate the learning that can result from such failure, the experience of engaging in such a deeply reflective experience is usually rewarding enough to make up for it.

One of the most common ethnographic research methods is observation. Although librarians are observing student behaviors constantly in the library classroom, shifting the focus of this activity toward student-to-student observation is an interesting way to take a learner-centered angle on this proven method of inquiry. By observing another student, each participant is empowered to influence the thinking of another through peer instruction on the research process, whether they have more knowledge than their partner or not. Sharing one's thought process with someone requires one to reconsider the process, to practice it, and to verbalize it. These activities alone can serve as a learning opportunity. In addition, students who are observing a partner in one or more aspects of their research process will think about their own approach to information seeking and evaluation as compared to the actions of another. They may also be able to offer feedback, insights, or suggestions to the student that would not have occurred to them otherwise. Naysayers of this approach will argue that students who are being observed will purposefully use more advanced strategies than they normally would in order to please or impress the observer, thereby rendering the observed behavior less than authentic. Although that is possible, our response would be that any observer should keep such pitfalls in mind, and we would prefer to be open to observing slightly skewed information rather than to miss this opportunity to gain valuable insights into student research behaviors at all.

Another ethnographic method that can be applied in the library classroom is cognitive mapping. As a student talks through their research process, whether before, during, or afterwards, they can create a visual representation of key moments of strategy and decision with paper and pen. This reflective act can illuminate for a student their own ways of thinking, as well as assist them in identifying areas of challenge or any questions they may have. The cognitive map is an artifact of learning that illustrates thought processes that would otherwise be hidden to the instructor and to the student. This kind of deep thinking about one's own approach to information seeking, a form of metacognition, is inherent in the reflection inspired by research process interviewing, student-to-student observation, and cognitive mapping. Each of these three strategies could be applied in the library classroom to illustrate students' research processes to the librarian and to increase the students' awareness and understanding of their own thought processes in order to improve their research.

Through the application of ethnographic principles, we can take a programmatic view or a student-specific view of the impact of our information literacy programs. One of the most difficult aspects of doing so is the gathering, tracking, and understanding of qualitative data obtained as formative or summative assessments. Such results may come in the form of written feedback, self-reflection, or visual representations and it is helpful to have themes by which to categorize and rank the qualitative information. Librarians at Indiana University have identified *Inquiry, Evaluation, Knowledge Creation*, and *Conversation* as the cornerstones of information literacy learning outcomes for our particular audience of learners. By thinking of these as themes that guide our instructional programs and determine their impact, we can also use them to organize and make sense of the qualitative data we gather through broad-scale information literacy initiatives or through the one-on-one instruction we provide.

Results: communication and action

As with any mindfully designed endeavor that seeks to contextualize and more fully understand the learning process, it would be difficult to predict the frequently circuitous routes that are forged, as well as the divergence (and convergence) of assumptions previously made and conclusions quantitatively drawn as a result. Throughout the course of our own ethnographic study, we as librarian-researchers employed methodologies that we have shown can be readily used in the classroom in an instructional context. We would be remiss, however, to ignore some of the larger aspects of our new understanding of our own community of learners as it relates to our immediate colleagues and administrators as well as the much larger community beyond. In much the same fashion that we had to decide *what* we wanted to know through ethnographic methods, we also must ask ourselves *how* we intend to best capitalize on this newfound knowledge. As you engage in the application of ethnographic methods in the library classroom, so too must you consider how you might best communicate your new understanding of your community of learners to others and what impact it might have in both your local environment as well as the community at large.

Teaching through an ethnographic lens will empower the learning process in exponential ways. You will gain a deeper understanding of the uniqueness of your learners, which will in turn allow for more focused and specific approaches to information literacy instruction. What you discover about your learning community can be communicated to your peer colleagues to improve and empower their own teaching activities. Ideally, a combined effort of understanding your local community of learners will only serve to improve the library's approach (as a whole) to information literacy and research support. Sharing this knowledge with other librarians at your institution can take many forms – informally via peer-to-peer conversation or more formally in the manner of workshops, presentations, and other programming methods. Simply retaining your newfound understanding of your learners to inform your own instruction is just one step of the process and we encourage you to empower your peers in both the understanding *and* the process. Our own desire for engaging in ethnographic research was not simply to gain new understanding of our learners to improve our teaching; rather, we endeavored to improve upon our library instruction programmatically, with a hope (over time) to make our practices have higher value and more meaningful impact across our learning community. This, of course, is not a solo effort: to be successful requires a combined effort across your library.

As mentioned previously, what you discover about your learners using an ethnographic lens will also serve to inform other library services and spaces. Communicating your findings to your administrators, whether gained from a one-shot instruction session or through a larger ethnographic study, is essential to enact greater change across the organization. It may not always seem apparent how your findings might affect greater library services as a whole, but you should always consider that all parts of the puzzle can help inform how the library engages with both the teaching and learning communities across the institution. Ethnographic methods used in the library classroom can help shape the teaching and learning process at the curricular and programmatic level, which in turn will have an even greater impact on library value and lifelong learning. Inasmuch as it can be difficult to exact change in the classroom in even the best librarian-faculty/instructor partnerships, there is the potential to have a stronger impact by demonstrating to your faculty partners, with clearly identifiable, qualitative information about your community of learners, what you now know about those learners. This has the potential to better position librarians as agents of change across the curriculum.

Enacting professional change

Academic libraries have marked their success in the past by calculating numbers of patron visits and quantities of collections, as well as the innovative services provided. Academic libraries, professional associations, and other influences external to our campuses often define the benchmarks for achievement in these areas. However, as the ubiquity of information access continues to transform how individuals engage with knowledge and as the role of libraries in this process evolves, our focus should shift more toward internal influences as we reconsider and recreate our professional identity and purpose. By using our ethnographic lens, we can see that no matter how large the collection or innovative the service, a library that is not built upon the needs of our learners will not achieve its full potential.

Instead of comparing ourselves with our peers among academic libraries and measuring our value solely against generalized guidelines for quantity and broad standards of proficiency, we should work hard to know our communities and situate ourselves within a local context. While overarching professional standards can serve as signposts for understanding the landscape of student learning and librarians' potential contribution to higher education, it is the application of such standards to our own unique institutional contexts that give them sense and meaning. While refocusing our energies on the ever-changing variable of our students' behavior would be the most challenging and unpredictable professional challenge we could undertake, it may also be the most rewarding.

The nature of the research and learning processes of our students could, when observed and known, inform the re-envisioning of the role of libraries within a particular educational environment. Situating ourselves more purposefully within the local campus context in order to define the library as an integral part of student learning in higher education will not only require the adoption of new philosophies on the part of librarians, but also the energizing of ourselves as agents of change in support of learner-centered services, environments, and experiences. While difficult, this role makes more sense for librarians than perhaps for any other professional on a college campus. In our positions, we see across disciplinary boundaries and levels of learning in ways that other faculty and staff do not. This perspective allows us to experience a greater depth of understanding and awareness of students' mindsets, attitudes, and approaches to learning that should be the driving force for the design and delivery of higher education. As each institution will have a unique audience of learners based on its educational vision, librarians who cultivate a professional philosophy that is focused on the practices and needs of these learners will not only become more integral to their academic experience but to the mission of the institution overall.

References

Bateman, W., 1991. *Open to Question: The Art of Teaching and Learning Through Inquiry.* San Francisco: Jossey-Bass.

Duke, L. and Asher, A., 2012. *College Libraries and Student Culture: What We Now Know.* Chicago: ALA Editions.

Gibbons, S., 2012. Techniques to understand the changing needs of library users. *IFLA Journal*, 39(2), pp. 162–7.

Head, A. and Eisenberg, M., 2010. *Truth Be Told: How College Students Evaluate and Use Information in the Digital Age.* [pdf] Available at: <http://projectinfolit.org/images/pdfs/pil_fall2010_survey_fullreport1.pdf>.

Heath, C. and Heath, D., 2008. *Made to Stick: Why Some Ideas Survive and Others Die.* New York: Random House.

Ranganathan, S.R., 1961. *Reference Service*. London: Asia House.

14   What makes an informal learning space?

A case study from Sheffield Hallam University

Bea Turpin, Deborah Harrop, Edward Oyston, Maurice Teasdale, David Jenkin and John McNamara

This case study will explore what makes an informal learning space. To do this we will consider the evidence-based practice at Sheffield Hallam University and the 5-year redevelopment project which transformed learning centre spaces. Redevelopment projects are expensive, long-term investments, and you need to maximise the chance of meeting current and future student needs and expectations. The research underpinning this case study explored learner preferences within informal learning spaces. In the course of this chapter we will focus on the following aspects: (1) the development of a robust research methodology and the creation of a typology of learning space preference attributes; and (2) the translation and implementation of research outcomes into practical design solutions which support the preferences of learners and enhance the user experience.

There is no universally agreed definition of informal learning spaces, so we elected to define them as 'non-discipline specific spaces frequented by both staff and students for self-directed learning activities'. These spaces can be within and outside library spaces.

Sheffield Hallam University is based across two campuses. The larger campus is located in the heart of Sheffield city centre, and the smaller campus is in the leafy suburbs and is predominately a one-faculty campus. Both campuses offer near equitable provision in terms of the types of informal learning spaces provided, including learning centres, open access PC laboratories, catering outlets, cafés, atrium spaces and hallway spaces. The architecture differs significantly between the campuses, and both present benefits and challenges in equal measure.

All of the different types of on-campus informal learning spaces were part of our research which commenced in late 2008 and, due to its scale, continued in tandem with the early phases of the redevelopment project.

Research methodology

The catalyst for this robust, evidence-based research stemmed from a Learning Centre department working group which looked at how the learning centres were being used by students. This group comprised staff from the Learning Centre department, wider support services, including IT, and representation from the Students' Union. Investigation was also undertaken by way of visits to other higher education institutions and feedback obtained from an ongoing learner engagement strategy. In addition, the appointed architects, Alexi Marmot Associates (AMA), had prior experience in learning spaces research (AMA Alexi Marmot Associates in association with Haa Design, 2006; JISC, 2006), and so this was utilised and considered a meaningful factor when awarding the redevelopment contracts.

Data collection

The aim of our research was to investigate what makes successful higher education informal learning spaces. Our objectives are summarised as follows:

> to determine learners' behaviours, attitudes and preferences in relation to where, what, when, how and why they use informal learning spaces; and to enable evidence-based decisions in the redevelopment of the learning centres and contribute to informal learning space design internally and externally.

The research used mixed mode methods, was longitudinal and broken down into two distinct phases. In brief, Phase I included all Sheffield Hallam University learning centre spaces, while Phase II looked at a stratified random sample of non-learning centre, informal spaces. Both phases used identical methods and were piloted.

The quantitative data, collected in the form of non-participant observational sweeps, with predefined criteria recorded using a 'five-bar gate' tally, sought to establish who, what, where and when, in relation to learners' behaviours and activities in informal learning spaces. In Phase I, the observational sweeps were undertaken on three different dates during a 4-month period. Phase II was undertaken 1 year later and one date was selected. On each date, the sweeps were carried out at four intervals throughout the day. The dates for the observational sweeps were randomly selected within the 4-month period, which was chosen to cover peak assignment hand-in dates and examination periods.

This research was followed up with qualitative data collection exercises which included coordinate mapping (learners drawing on a map where they had been or planned to go that day) or photographic mapping (learners taking photographs of preferred spaces based on a list of questions). Both exercises concluded with a 5- to 10-minute semi-structured interview which was recorded. The qualitative research focused on why learners exhibited and held particular informal learning space behaviours and attitudes, and in doing so sought to 'illuminate the people behind the numbers and put faces on the statistics' (Patton, 2002, p. 10). Phase I generated 80 interviews (20 interviews per qualitative exercise at each campus). Phase II generated 160 interviews (20 interviews per qualitative exercise, repeated twice at each campus). Combined, this generated 240 interviews.

Data collection was undertaken by ourselves and other colleagues from Sheffield Hallam University. (Some examples of the data collection templates used can be found on the UX in Libraries website – see http://uxlib.org.)

In addition, we undertook a broad literature search to try to identify possible theoretical frameworks which underpin informal learning space design and evaluation.

Data analysis

The quantitative data was transposed into Microsoft Excel and used to calculate the maximum and mean usage of spaces and aspects such as percentage occupancy; percentage of learners working in pairs; percentage working in groups; and size of group. The results were also used to create a series of colour-coded maps. The qualitative data was coded using a thematic, emergent coding scheme, as described by Robson (2011, pp. 474–6). From the data, there surfaced a number of themes which were important to our learners and therefore our spaces. Using this data, we generated a typology (a system of classification) of learning space preference attributes. The typology comprises nine attributes which are not hierarchical. The typology is designed to inform evaluation and decision-making activities relating to informal learning space design in higher education. These attributes, and a brief description of each, are as follows:

- Destination – where learners go to study;
- Identity – the ethos of a space and how a learner feels it should be used;
- Conversation – spaces for collaboration and interpersonal communication;
- Community – support and a sense of common purpose which can be found in shared learning spaces;
- Retreat – privacy and sound levels;
- Timely – just in time and on demand, planned study, short and long stay;
- Human factors – ergonomics of study spaces and their physical attributes;
- Resources – access, what and how resources are used;
- Refreshments – food and drink.

For further details about the typology, see Harrop and Turpin (2013).

Rationale for methodology

Our decision to use quantitative non-participant observational sweeps was informed by Roberts and Weaver's (2007) research which evaluated the Learning Gateway at the University of Cumbria by exploring the interactions between learners and their environments, and which sought to capture learners' current and future learning preferences.

The coordinate and photographic mapping exercises were designed to elucidate why learners exhibited and held particular informal learning space behaviours and attitudes, but were intended to be complementary and yield different types of responses. Our evaluation of Phase I revealed the qualitative 'why' aspect to be the most complex question, and prompted us to repeat the qualitative exercises twice in Phase II. This adaptive approach is referred to by Robson (2002, p. 87) as a 'flexible element' in a research strategy.

The use of semi-structured interviews in both qualitative exercises was purposeful as we felt that this approach enabled participants to have more latitude in response, whilst at the same time retaining focus.

The photographic mapping exercise was adapted from a study undertaken by Nancy Fried Foster and Susan Gibbons at the University of Rochester in the US (2007). In particular we selected it because Briden's (2007) evaluation revealed anecdotal evidence that the approach increased participation as learners found the method more engaging. However, Briden also identified the time lapse between learners taking photographs and the follow-up interview as problematic. Consequently, at Sheffield Hallam University, photographs and interviews followed on immediately from one another and we accompanied the learner throughout the data collection exercise. This approach had the added advantage of ensuring learners did not take photographs of other learners without their permission. Overall, the photographic mapping succeeded in providing a type of visual sociology as it enabled participants to 'move from the concrete (represented by the literal objects in the image) to the socially abstract (what the objects in the photo mean to the individual being interviewed)' (Harper, 1984, p. 21).

The same study at the University of Rochester also used a near identical 'mapping exercise' (Clark, 2007), where learners were given maps of the campus and asked to record where they went on one given weekday. This information was then supplemented by interviews. To maximise the reliability of responses, learners were only asked to comment on their movements on the day of the research. The strategy was amended at Sheffield Hallam University to reduce the quantity of descriptive data and shift the focus towards why learners were exhibiting particular behaviours and attitudes.

Presenting the findings from our research was challenging, as was working within time frames that allowed them to be easily fed into the redevelopment of the learning centres. Of particular use was a 2008 study by Sheffield Hallam University to evaluate a newly built learning centre space on level 4 of the Adsetts Learning Centre, using what were called 'research diaries'. A key lesson from the authors' evaluation of their own research was that the use of verbatim student comments provided a 'powerful contribution to ongoing institutional initiatives' (Aspden and Thorpe, 2009, p. 1). In the context of our research, photographs and maps could easily be shared with colleagues to offer a visual snapshot of learners' behaviours and attitudes. The option to readily integrate this information, alongside verbatim student comments, was pivotal to our decision to use the typology described earlier.

Using a typology to present the findings enabled a collection of attributes to be associated with learners' informal learning space preferences. It also allowed in-depth analysis and discussion of each attribute whilst still responding to the research aim as a whole. Presently, we have identified one example (Beagle, 2004) of research on informal learning spaces where a typology is used as a means to distinguish a learning commons from an information commons. Walton (2006) and Watson (2007) use similar approaches, although their findings are organised into themes.

Once we had decided on our research methods, a research protocol was submitted to the Learning Centre department working group which looks at how the learning centres are being used by students. Ethical approval was not required as our research did not collect information of a personal or sensitive nature. Digital signage and posters were displayed to make learners aware of the quantitative data collection, and participants in the qualitative exercises were asked to complete a consent form. All data collected was anonymised, and personal information from the consent forms was kept confidential and separated from the research data.

Critique of methodology

The decision to use three data collection methods, with each having large sample sizes, maximised opportunity for data triangulation and sought to achieve reliability and validity. A consequence of this was the challenging quantity of data gathered from the research. The volume of work could have been mitigated through extension of our research team; however there was concern that a larger team may not be as effectual and the same depth of understanding of the data may not have resulted.

The five-bar gate tally, which was used as the instrument for the quantitative data collection, was problematic because we were unable to tie spaces to the specific activities being undertaken at them. The research did not collect data during overnight periods, so if learners' preferences varied pre-10 a.m. and post-7 p.m. sweeps and they did not report these preferences in the qualitative data collection exercises, then this information would not have been recorded. During data collection exercises, we felt we were readily identified by learners as staff from the Learning Centre department. This was despite not needing to interact with participants during the quantitative data collection and not identifying ourselves or making participants aware of the context of the study until the qualitative exercises had been completed. During the coordinate mapping exercise, the learner was accompanied throughout the data collection exercise and the data was entered onto the maps on the learner's behalf, as the maps were internal documents and not felt to be user friendly. It would have been possible to reduce the risk of the 'Hawthorne effect' (Payne and Payne, 2004, p. 108) – individuals modifying or improving an aspect of their behaviour in response to their awareness of being observed – by recruiting a data collection team not containing Sheffield Hallam University staff. However, this would not have been financially viable. We also felt that involvement in data collection made staff feel closer to the project and more able to assimilate the findings.

As a case study, the findings are generalisable to learners at Sheffield Hallam University during the time frames of the data collection. Whilst it is impossible to assert that our findings are generalisable, or externally valid, outside of the context of Sheffield Hallam University, our research adopts Denscombe's (2003, p. 43) stance that 'the extent to which findings from the case study can be generalised to other examples in the class depends on how far the case study is similar to others of its type.' In this respect, generalisability could have been attained, as research published about other higher education institutions' informal learning spaces cite elements comparable to our findings (e.g. Herbert, 1998; Elliot Burns, 2005; Walton, 2006; Foster and Gibbons, 2007; Watson, 2007; Bryant, Matthews and Walton, 2009; Dugdale, 2009; Lippman, 2010; Matthews, Andrews and Adams, 2011). Bassey (1981, p. 85) suggests 'relatability', as opposed to generalisability, is of greater merit when reflecting on the research design and methods involved in a case study. He goes on to say it is more important that an individual is able to relate to an external case study and interpret the findings for their own decision-making purposes, rather than simply using research able to claim generalisability. Advocating Bassey's stance, our research at Sheffield Hallam University is valuable and is intended to strengthen dialogue with others involved in educational and learning spaces research; but the applicability of the findings should be interpreted at a localised level. Bassey concludes that any findings with relatability extend the boundaries of knowledge and are therefore valid for educational research.

The learning centres redevelopment project

The project scope

The learning centres at Sheffield Hallam University provide access to physical and electronic library resources, learning spaces for a range of study activities, IT facilities and support for both library and IT services. Both locations include café facilities, and food and drink are allowed throughout the buildings. All learning centre physical spaces were in the scope of the redevelopment except where stated later.

The award-winning, purpose-built Adsetts Learning Centre is a seven-storey building located in the city centre. It provides six levels of open-plan learning spaces and a central atrium running through the middle of the building. The entrance is on Level 4. Levels 2 through to 6 house the main printed library stock, student learning spaces and support services. These were the areas in the scope of the redevelopment project. Level 1 (comprising the stack), the Level 4 café area and Level 7 (staff spaces) were not included.

The Collegiate Learning Centre is a smaller two-storey building, offering a series of interconnected spaces which pull together new buildings and repurposed environments. Both of the levels were part of the redevelopment project. The staff workspaces were excluded.

The project also involved the reorganisation of printed materials and redevelopment of the help desks.

The project brief

The original learning centre model developed at Sheffield Hallam University was driven by an educational philosophy which recognised that students learn best when they are actively engaged in learning and that they are more likely to succeed when they have the maximum number of choices as to how they engage in learning. The breadth of opportunities provided for individual and collaborative learning and the integrated approach to services and resource provision were what made these learning centres distinctive when they were introduced in 1996. Their approach was sector-leading and had largely stood the test of time since then, but the purpose of the redevelopment project was to refresh and update the concept, to accommodate evolving learning styles and preferences, as well as developments in information provision, within refurbished and reconfigured buildings. Furthermore, as the number of formal and informal learning spaces across campus was increasing, there was a recognition that the distinctive role of learning centres needed to fit into a broader, coherent learning landscape. Above all, the project aimed to ensure that the learning centres stayed true to the original brief described by Bulpitt (1996) of creating a building that conveys the excitement of learning and discovery to students.

As this project was a refurbishment of existing buildings, working sympathetically within the current architectural designs was essential, although there was some scope to make limited structural changes. The project also provided an opportunity to maintain and improve the environmental control systems.

The project: a phased approach

The redevelopment was carried out over 4 years. The majority of the building work took place in the quieter summer months, whereas the planning and design work was undertaken during term time. Work started in 2010 with the conversion of a relatively small area that was previously a staff workspace in the Adsetts Learning Centre into new learning spaces for students. This work also provided the opportunity to introduce a new automated book return facility and a redesigned and extended help desk. The project was completed in 2013 with the opening of the newly redeveloped spaces at the Collegiate Learning Centre. The phases of the project are shown in Figure 14.1.

The phased approach enabled the learning centre services and materials to remain available throughout the project. Additional funding and resources were required to move materials from areas being developed to open areas and to provide alternative facilities when these were required. As far as possible, work was undertaken outside of opening hours or at quiet times to mitigate disturbance. This was feasible at this time because opening hours were more restricted during vacations. Today the learning centres are open 24 hours a day, 365 days a year.

Having several phases proved to be fortuitous in providing opportunities to learn from and build on the ideas implemented previously and to develop the project in a dynamic way. It also enabled a deeper understanding of the results of the research and allowed time for refinement and reflection.

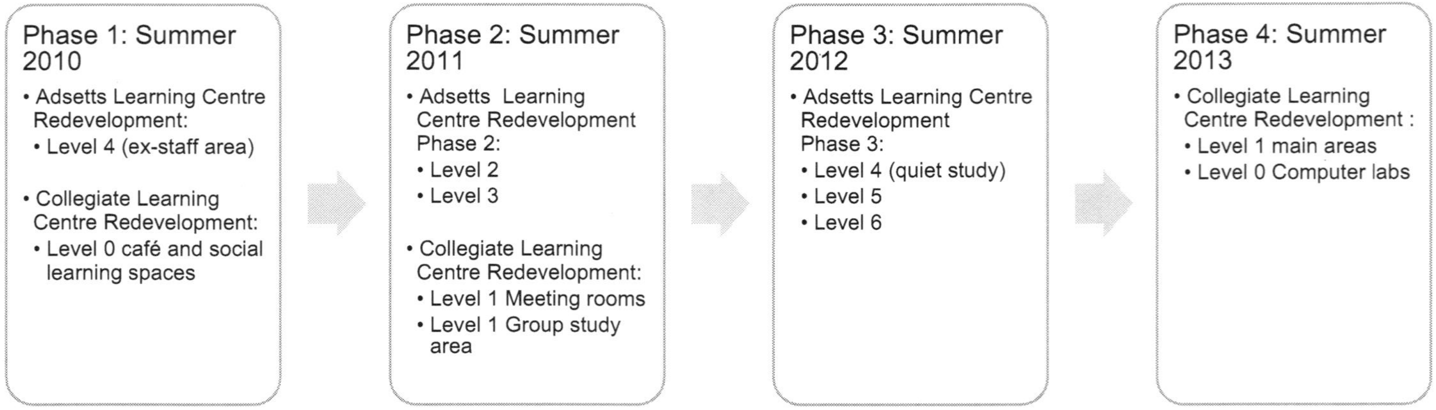

Phase 1: Summer 2010
- Adsetts Learning Centre Redevelopment:
  - Level 4 (ex-staff area)

- Collegiate Learning Centre Redevelopment:
  - Level 0 café and social learning spaces

Phase 2: Summer 2011
- Adsetts Learning Centre Redevelopment Phase 2:
  - Level 2
  - Level 3

- Collegiate Learning Centre Redevelopment:
  - Level 1 Meeting rooms
  - Level 1 Group study area

Phase 3: Summer 2012
- Adsetts Learning Centre Redevelopment Phase 3:
  - Level 4 (quiet study)
  - Level 5
  - Level 6

Phase 4: Summer 2013
- Collegiate Learning Centre Redevelopment :
  - Level 1 main areas
  - Level 0 Computer labs

Figure 14.1 Phases of learning centre redevelopment

Translating learners' needs into design

The challenge at Sheffield Hallam University was to weave the findings from the learning spaces research into the Learning Centres Redevelopment Project, along with the knowledge, experience and expertise of staff from AMA, the Learning Centre department and the Estates department.

The designs for the learning centres evolved using a collaborative and dynamic process and allowed many facets to be considered. There were two key areas to consider: first, how to make the overall environment of the existing learning centre buildings better suited to the students' learning experience; and second, how to use the learning spaces research and experience of those involved in the redevelopment project to devise new layouts and spaces within these buildings.

Improving the overall environment

At both learning centres, the approach was to return to the original building concept and to make more of the design features of the spaces. For example, in the Adsetts Learning Centre, opening up the atrium allowed daylight to penetrate further into the floors, while keeping enclosed rooms to the edges kept the central areas free from restricted views. Improved circulation routes and aspects across the levels resulted in the building being more navigable and welcoming, and was a return to a clear planning arrangement associated with the original intent of the Adsetts Learning Centre.

Improving the quality of light was a prime consideration as the design process developed. A simple but important change was to paint the learning centre ceilings white and install new low-energy light fittings to realise the full height and scale of the spaces, giving the feeling of bigger, simpler and more pleasant environments. This was supported by new controls for the lighting and the environmental systems.

Although there was much debate about how big the printed collections might be in the future; currently access to the books remains important, so we decided to locate the collections in the same place on each floor. This ensured easy access and localised study facilities. The floor loading was already sufficient to allow the books to be located almost anywhere, and the design of the new lighting supported this concept while allowing for replanning in the future without major changes being necessary.

Fundamental to all of the planning and design ideas was that the layouts and services would not only suit the needs of the students now, but also seek to design for the future. However, planning spaces suitable for an unknown longer-term future is immensely hard, so we were particularly mindful of designing layouts which could be recalibrated relatively easily, minimising the need for large-scale works in the near future.

Planning and designing spaces at building, discrete space and workspace level

The project considered the desired overall look and feel for the buildings, then how discrete spaces could be created, and finally the design of each desk or study workspace. This layered approach to planning and designing spaces and how it was supported by our research evidence is described next.

Learning spaces at the building level

The design of the learning centres' study spaces needed to ensure that continued provision was made for learners to engage in different activities and to offer a range of attractive environments meeting different preferences. How to provide these different environments and the proportion of space allocated to each were key decisions in the design process. Another overarching principle was to maintain or increase the number of study spaces. The circulation spaces and footprint of the printed stock were also considered, and a balance was reached that allowed for easy movement around the building and access to printed resources while ensuring the desired number of spaces.

Learners expressed a preference for a variety of different learning spaces depending on the task they were undertaking and the environment they found supportive. One key aspect was individual or collaborative study and the related issues of sound and feel. Learners expressed preferences for quiet and silent individual study environments; spaces for individual study in a more vibrant environment which included stimulating background 'buzz' or opportunities for people-watching; and spaces which supported varying degrees of collaborative work. The quantitative arm of our research provided data on the numbers of learners studying individually, in pairs and in groups of different sizes. Learners were also observed undertaking individual work alongside colleagues and friends, which we termed 'working alongside'. The redeveloped spaces were therefore designed to support individual study in silent, quiet and vibrant environments and learners working alongside colleagues, working in pairs and working in groups of various sizes. The research data also highlighted the spaces prior to the redevelopment that were heavily utilised and those which were underutilised. Alongside evidence from space booking statistics, this data contributed to decisions about the proportion of space allocated to each of the different types of environment.

In both learning centres, bookable spaces and open access spaces are now provided, supporting learner preferences for planned study, on-demand study and studying for long periods. Quick access areas near the entrances and printers support the need for short-stay, just-in-time learning activities. The proportion of bookable spaces and open access spaces varies depending on the type of space and the expected levels of demand. For example, meeting rooms are in very high demand, so the majority of these are bookable. In contrast, while some individual silent study spaces are available to book, many are open access.

Having decided on the types of environments required and the proportion of each, the areas of the buildings in which these could be most effectively located were considered.

Discrete spaces within buildings

The experience of our learning centre staff was that it was difficult, if not impossible, to provide a functioning quiet or silent area that was not clearly separated from the collaborative spaces and circulation areas. Prior to the redevelopment project, quiet and silent spaces, particularly in the open-plan Adsetts Learning Centre, were not separated from other spaces and were therefore ineffective, and so improving this situation was one of the aims of the project. The open-plan nature of the Adsetts Learning Centre also resulted in large spaces with no clear identity, where there was little privacy, sound travelled, and circulation routes were unclear. Whilst wanting to keep the spaces as open as possible and provide good lines of sight and natural light, our solution to all these issues was to create discrete spaces, thus providing effective, functioning and attractive areas for the different types of spaces within the buildings. This was supported by our research which indicated that spaces should have a clear identity, a purpose conveyed by the design, and should live up to learner expectations.

The different levels of the buildings were an obvious option for creating discrete spaces. In the Collegiate Learning Centre, floor levels are divided into smaller areas and rooms, offering a ready-made option in most cases. The open-plan nature of the Adsetts Learning Centre presented more of a challenge. To address this, ceiling-height glass walls were used to create discrete spaces for silent areas, quiet areas and group meeting rooms, and to differentiate the main bookable areas from open access areas. Lower height half walls (160 cm high) now break up what were previously large open-plan areas. These also double as whiteboards and places to mount large LCD screens for use by groups of learners. Wooden acoustic walls perform a similar function, providing a barrier to sound and creating discrete learning spaces and, in one instance, a room housing a special collection of print materials. These also provide an attractive design feature; in one location it includes a video wall displaying student work and in another, built-in display cabinets for exhibiting art. Figure 14.2 shows an outline plan of Level 2 of the Adsetts Learning

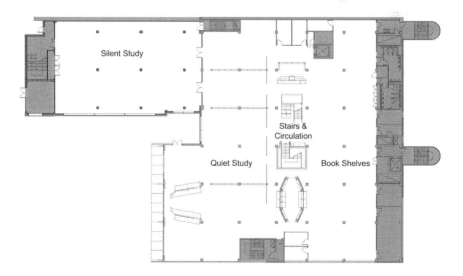

Figure 14.2   Adsetts Learning Centre Level 2 learning spaces showing the additional walls and half walls

Note: Previously walled areas around the perimeters are shaded.

Centre. New ceiling-height glass walls separate the silent study spaces from the quiet area and protect them from the stairs and circulation routes. Half walls and acoustic walls are also used to differentiate spaces and create smaller areas with a more defined feel.

In addition, mobile transparent screens are offered in some areas and further enable learners to create their own discrete spaces.

Desks and study spaces: supporting a range of preferences

One of the key findings from our research was that learners have their own list of preferences and requirements. This applies at the desk and study space level as well as at the more macro level of where to study and preferred environment. To cater for these preferences, a variety of study spaces supporting different activities and preferences are provided. While offering these choices, the look and feel of the overall design has been maintained by using consistent styles of furniture and colour palettes. Examples of study spaces are shown in Figure 14.3 which depicts the furniture layout in part of Level 5 in the Adsetts Learning Centre. This illustrates different shapes, sizes and orientations of tables and desks in an area designed for learners working in small groups or alongside colleagues. Where individual spaces are co-located in a collaborative environment, a range of spaces suitable for working together or in proximity is available. For group work, booths and round tables of various sizes are available to accommodate groups of different sizes.

Further variety in the spaces is provided through chairs of different designs: formal task chairs; relaxed, softer seating; and chairs with and without arms. The vast majority of these desks and chairs are the standard height for a workstation. There is a small number of low-level coffee tables with accompanying seating in waiting and meeting areas on Level 4. This type of furniture was seen to be under-utilised in the research findings, and therefore very limited numbers were included in the redevelopment project.

One of the outcomes of our research was that in spite of the explosion in mobile devices, many learners still expressed a preference for using a fixed PC. The quantitative research corroborated this, showing that spaces with PCs were heavily utilised. The number of spaces with PCs was therefore maintained and in fact slightly increased as part of the project. However, it was clear that laptops and other mobile devices were also being used and were likely to increase in popularity, so spaces without fixed PCs were also provided. These spaces could be used by learners preferring to work with their own devices or with Learning Centre laptops. Some learners expressed a preference for working with papers and books and for space to spread out, and were observed working with a large number of papers or creating large pieces of work such as posters. The desks and tables without PCs also cater to those wishing to undertake this type of activity.

In spaces designed for group work, some are equipped with a PC and a large wall-mounted LCD screen, while others have two fixed PCs. Our research showed that, prior to redevelopment, spaces without power were very underutilised, and

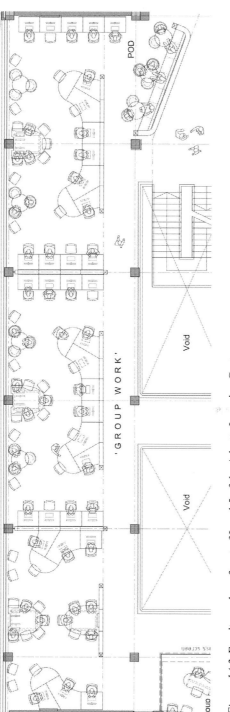

Figure 14.3 Furniture plan of part of Level 5 of the Adsetts Learning Centre

so now every space has easy access to a power socket which is either mounted on the desk or located on an adjacent wall or power pole. Desktop power is provided on desks both with and without fixed IT equipment, thus supporting learners wishing to use a PC in conjunction with mobile devices, as well as allowing for the removal of the fixed IT equipment if mobile devices become the preferred choice in the future.

Many learners expressed a preference for not being disturbed, not disturbing others and not being overlooked. While this preference partly related to sound levels, it also related to privacy. Different levels of privacy are achieved through desks and study places situated behind walls or screens in discrete areas and in locations ranging from out-of-the-way corners to higher traffic areas. Between study spaces, desk-mounted screens of heights between 20 cm and 70 cm also provide different levels of privacy. There are some spaces without desk-mounted screens to facilitate and encourage collaboration. Personal safety was also a key consideration, and so whilst more private spaces were provided, care was taken to ensure that they were visible from the main circulation areas – something judged to be particularly important at night when the buildings are less populated.

The design aimed to provide comfortable, functional and attractive study spaces that did not appear too densely populated and offered sufficient space for learners' needs. The space allocation was one of the key factors in achieving this. Our research demonstrated that learners often use IT and other resources in conjunction, and refreshments and personal belongings are also evident in their learning spaces. During the observational sweeps, it was noted that existing individual desks were too small for all of these possessions to be accommodated comfortably, and so such desks are now a minimum of 110 cm wide and are in many cases wider, providing a more generous allocation without reducing the number of learning spaces. In addition, fixed PCs, where present, are mounted underneath the desks to liberate more space on the desktops. Apportioning a similar allowance for each person in a group work setting would however create tables that would be too big to facilitate collaboration. This principle was therefore only applied to spaces intended for individual study.

Another key preference that the project sought to address was that natural light and ambient, well-lit spaces were important to many learners. The layout of workspaces was therefore designed to make use of natural light, to provide views across the space and to the outside, and to avoid blocking light from windows and other light sources. Brightness was also considered in the furniture selection, and resulted in the purchase of white desks and tables, light-coloured desk-mounted screens between desks, and chairs with mesh backs that allow light through. New internal walls were painted white to reflect light or constructed from glass to allow light to permeate deeper into the spaces. The overall brightness of the learning centres was enhanced through using accent colours of green, orange and blue, reflected in feature walls, large signage and the soft furniture. (Photographs and commentary illustrating the aforementioned aspects of the project can be found on the UX in Libraries website – see http://uxlib.org.)

Typology checklist

In constructing our typology of learning space preference attributes, we aimed to contribute to the dialogue about learning spaces by suggesting that when designing such informal spaces our nine non-hierarchical attributes should be considered. It was also clear that it would be useful to extend the practical usability of the typology by adding a checklist. In part this was driven by the questions we asked ourselves during the design process and recognition that communicating the findings was challenging, and that this may be a way to facilitate this. It is envisaged that the typology and checklist could be used to support future redevelopment projects at Sheffield Hallam University. Furthermore, it is hoped that this tool could be used at other higher education institutions; however, at present it is not known if they are truly transferable. The checklist is presented in Table 14.1.

Table 14.1 Typology checklist

Attribute	Checklist
Destination where learners go to study	• What will be the purpose of the space? • Which learning preferences will it support? • How will the space fit with other spaces available to the learner? • Is the space in a convenient location for the proposed purpose?
Identity the ethos of a space and how a learner feels it should be used	• How should the space 'feel'? • Does the space need multiple identities for different learners, times of the year, etc.? • How will the feel and purpose of the space be communicated? • How will the identity of the space be maintained? • Will learners be able to create their own space, for example by reconfiguring the furniture?
Conversation spaces for collaboration and interpersonal communication	• Is the space for collaborative learning? • How will collaborative learning be encouraged and facilitated by the space? • How will interpersonal communication be encouraged? • How will the space accommodate different group sizes?
Community support and a sense of common purpose which can be found in shared learning spaces	• How will social interactions be encouraged? • How will the space enable learners to support one another and/or take a break together? • How will the space have a sense of common purpose and offer a shared motivational environment? • Will the space engender 'working alongside'?
Retreat privacy and sound levels	• How will privacy be taken into consideration, for example not being overlooked or overheard? • Do personal spaces need to be clearly delineated? • How will learners avoid disturbing others or being disturbed?

(Continued)

Table 14.1 (Continued)

Attribute	Checklist
Timely just in time and on demand	• How will the space support learners undertaking quick tasks, for example printing out an assignment near to a deadline? • How will the space support learners studying for extended periods? • Do learners need to plan to use the space in advance, for example through booking, and/or will there be open access provision?
Human Factors ergonomics of study spaces and their physical attributes	• How will ergonomic and physical factors be considered? Factors include lighting/natural light, outdoor spaces, temperature, sound, desk sizes, seating and accessibility.
Resources access, what and how resources are used	• What fixed technology needs to be provided – PCs, Macs, software, printers, large screens, etc.? • Will laptops and other mobile devices be provided and infrastructure available to support these and/or learners' own devices? • Will it be possible to use fixed devices, mobile devices and other resources in tandem? • Will support from staff be provided? • Is access to print resources required?
Refreshments food and drink	• What types of food and drink will be available for purchase through any outlet and/or self-service vending? • Will food and drink be welcomed everywhere? • Should any catering space support learning and how will it do this?

Conclusion

The research which informed the redevelopment of the learning centres at Sheffield Hallam University was derived from a multifaceted, lengthy data collection and analysis process. In choosing this route, our intention was to provide a strong evidence base which sought to be methodologically robust whilst also offering insights which could be translated into practical learning space design. In this case study, we have explained how we have applied the findings and resultant typology within the context of the redevelopment of the learning centres. The research findings were crucial in providing valuable information to inform the redevelopment project and the creation of the typology of learning space preference attributes enabled us to achieve the aim and objectives of the research.

Moving forward, our learners' behaviours, attitudes and preferences will evolve and our buildings need to stay in step with this. In response, Sheffield Hallam University has introduced learning spaces groups focusing on research, implementation and strategic University vision. These groups are considering the interrelationship of spaces across the University and the blurring of informal and formal spaces. A team approach involving research, planning, design, estates and management will help ensure the University gets the facilities it needs, and the learners the spaces they deserve. Our approach is to be on the side of both the users and the building. To get them both working well together over time, using an evidence-based approach, is critical to bringing these long-term benefits to the University and its students.

References

Alexi Marmot Associates in association with Haa Design, 2006. *Spaces for Learning: A Review of Spaces in Further and Higher Education.* [pdf] A report prepared for the Scottish Funding Council. Available at: <http://www.sfc.ac.uk/web/FILES/learningfiles/Spaces_for_Learning_report.pdf> [Accessed 28 February 2015].

Aspden, E. J. and Thorpe, L. P., 2009. 'Where do you learn?': tweeting to inform learning space development. *Educause Quarterly*, 32(1), pp. 1–3.

Bassey, M., 1981. Pedagogic research: on the relative merits of the search for generalisation and study of single events. *Oxford Review of Education*, 7(1), pp. 73–93.

Beagle, D., 2004. From information commons to learning commons. [online] In: *Leavy Library Conference*, Los Angeles. Available at: <www.usc.edu/isd/libraries/locations/leavey/news/conference/presentations> [Accessed 29 July 2013].

Briden, J., 2007. Photo surveys: eliciting more than you knew to ask for. In: N. F. Foster and S. Gibbons, eds. *Studying Students: the Undergraduate Research Project at the University of Rochester*. Chicago: Association of College and Research Libraries. pp. 40–7.

Bryant, J., Matthews, G. and Walton, G., 2009. Academic libraries and social and learning space: a case study of Loughborough University, UK. *Journal of Librarianship and Information Science*, 41(1), pp. 7–18.

Bulpitt, G., 1996. The Adsetts Centre at Sheffield Hallam University. In: *The Development of Learning Resource Centres for the Future: Proceedings of a Conference Held at the Royal Institute of British Architects*, 10 October 1995. London: SCONUL. pp. 43–9.

Clark, K., 2007. Mapping diaries, or where do they go all day? In: N. F. Foster and S. Gibbons, eds. *Studying Students: The Undergraduate Research Project at the University of Rochester*. Chicago: Association of College and Research Libraries. pp. 48–54.

Denscombe, M., 2003. *The Good Research Guide*, 2nd ed. Maidenhead: Open University.

Dugdale, S., 2009. Space strategies for the new learning landscape. *Educause Review*, 44(2), pp. 1–9.

Elliot Burns, R., 2005. Designing spaces for learning and living in schools: perspectives of a 'flaneuse'. [online] In: *Proceedings 2005 Australian Curriculum Studies Association Biennial Conference 'Blurring the Boundaries, Sharpening the Focus'*. University of the Sunshine Coast, Queensland, Australia. Available at: <http://eprints.qut.edu.au/archive/00004345> [Accessed 5 September 2015].

Foster, N. F. and Gibbons, S., 2007. Library design and ethnography. In: N. F. Foster and S. Gibbons, eds. *Studying Students: The Undergraduate Research Project at the University of Rochester*. Chicago: Association of College and Research Libraries. pp. 20–9.

Harper, D., 1984. Meaning and work: a study in photo elicitation. *International Journal of Visual Sociology*, 2(1), pp. 20–43.

Harrop, D. and Turpin, B., 2013. A study exploring learners' informal learning space behaviors, attitudes and preferences. *New Review of Academic Librarianship*, 19(1), pp. 58–77.

Herbert, E. A., 1998. Design matters: how school environment affects children. *Educational Leadership*, 56(1), pp. 69–70.

JISC, 2006. *Designing Spaces for Effective Learning: A Guide to 21st Century Learning Spaces Design*. [online] Available at: <http://www.webarchive.org.uk/wayback/archive/20140614213943/http://www.jisc.ac.uk/publications/programmerelated/2006/pub_spaces.aspx#downloads> [Accessed 28 February 2015].

Lippman, P.C., 2010. Can the physical environment have an impact on the learning environment? *CELE Exchange*, 2010/13, pp. 1–5.

Matthews, K.E., Andrews, V. and Adams, P., 2011. Social learning spaces and student engagement. *Higher Education Research & Development*, 30(2), pp. 105–20.

Patton, M.Q., 2002. *Qualitative Research and Evaluation Methods*, 3rd ed. London: SAGE.

Payne, G. and Payne, J., 2004. *Key Concepts in Social Research*. London: SAGE.

Roberts, S. and Weaver, M., 2007. Spaces for learners and learning: evaluating the impact of technology-rich learning spaces. *New Review of Academic Librarianship*, 12(2), pp. 95–107.

Robson, C., 2002. *Real World Research*, 2nd ed. Oxford: Blackwell.

Robson, C., 2011. *Real World Research*, 3rd ed. Chichester: Wiley and Sons.

Walton, G., 2006. Learners' demands and expectations for space in a university library: outcomes from a survey at Loughborough University. *New Review of Academic Librarianship*, 12(2), pp. 133–49.

Watson, L., 2007. Building the future of learning. *European Journal of Education*, 42(2), pp. 255–63.

15 Spaces for learning? using ethnographic techniques

A case study from the University Library, Edge Hill University

Helen Jamieson

This case study will outline why Learning Services at Edge Hill University began to utilise user experience methods, what techniques were of most benefit, and how we have made improvements to our library facilities on the back of the evidence we collected.

Edge Hill University was named University of the Year in the 2014 *Times Higher Education* awards. Located in the North West of England, Edge Hill has been delivering higher education since 1885 and achieved University status in 2006.

Learning Services is one of the largest academic support departments within Edge Hill University, with approximately 130 staff based across four libraries as well as a number of outreach centres. Learning Services has been a holder of the Customer Service Excellence award since 2005. It includes libraries, support for ICT, support for students with SpLD (Specific Learning Difficulties), media development, technology-enhanced learning and the Virtual Learning Environment.

In 2012, with a number of library processes becoming increasingly automated, an opportunity arose to restructure the Customer Services division and allow staff to spend more time interacting with customers, gaining customer insight and trying to get to the heart of what makes for a good student experience in our learning spaces. This resulted in the creation of a learning spaces team who, as well as managing the spaces in terms of functionality, aesthetics and housekeeping, were tasked with developing techniques to monitor usage, activity and customer behaviour.

As a library and information service we had always gathered a wide variety of statistical and quantitative data. The data comes from a number of sources including our library management system, the University Virtual Learning Environment, RMS (which is our service desk software) and Ask Us (our customer-facing knowledge base), as well as a number of other in-house mechanisms. We harvest the data about usage of our services, facilities and resources using an in-house library analytics system called MIDAS (Management Information and Data Solutions). MIDAS allows us to quickly see what the data is telling us about customer activity; using MIDAS we can build up a much clearer and more accurate picture of the key characteristics of our customer groups and how they are choosing to interact with us. This data is taken to team meetings, discussed with staff, and used to inform decisions around planning new services. The data from MIDAS also feeds into our service KPIs (key performance indicators) which are based around our core values of customer service excellence, operational excellence and staff engagement. Whilst this is incredibly useful data and integral information for strategic planning, one of the key limitations was that the data collected through MIDAS was only quantitative. We were not, at that stage, capturing qualitative data in a considered way.

Quantitative data is important and does tell us some interesting information about both volumes and types of activity that students are undertaking in our libraries. For a number of years we have conducted seating sweeps and activity counts under the umbrella term 'roving observations'.

The learning spaces team look for a range of indicators to record: numbers of students in the space; students working individually or in groups; the use of technology and whether this was at a fixed PC or via a mobile device; the use of books or print journals; and average group sizes. Whilst this vast amount of information is really useful it can be difficult to digest, and we have found that a good way to present this type of data is to use infographics to help visualise statistics and data for easy understanding. The team produced a large set of infographics to enable wider discussion and to aid decision making and planning for future changes to the spaces. We have made a number of changes to our learning spaces on the back of this data, ranging from small enhancements including installing extra power points on the ground floor of our library to accommodate the amount of students using and wanting to charge mobile devices, to more significant changes including completely removing book stock from our ground floor to make it more conducive to social and collaborative learning with larger group tables.

The type of exercises described earlier generate valuable data, but often the data is one-dimensional. To add context, make the data 'thicker' and construct more meaningful narratives about how students are using our learning spaces, we needed to use a range of qualitative methods including ethnographic techniques.

Investigating ethnographic techniques

Bryony Ramsden's article *Learning Spaces in Academic Libraries: Research and Assessment Methods* (2012) was a starting point for us in terms of looking in more detail at using ethnographic techniques, and we began to reflect on what data we were currently collecting and how it could be improved. We began by testing out a range of ethnographic techniques including exit interviews, scribble sheets and nonparticipant observations.

Exit interviews

On exiting the building, students were asked for their feedback on what spaces they had used and why, the length of their stay and what problems they may have experienced on that particular visit.

Scribble sheets

Large, blank sheets of paper were placed in key areas of our learning spaces and students were asked to comment on their experience of working in these areas. This provided some basic but useful information about how the students felt in that environment. Some of the issues related to comfort (heat/light/furniture), but some entries related more to thoughts and feelings. For example, a couple of our study booths were described as oppressive and 'cell-like'.

Non-participant observations

Our learning spaces team spent time within each of the library zones observing activity and recording what they felt was interesting behaviour. Whilst we weren't overly prescriptive with what we asked them to record, we did introduce the concept of field notes and were happy for these notes to be both a log of activity and some personal commentary about behaviours they observed. Observing activity whilst maintaining neutrality is an ongoing challenge, and when conducting observations staff were encouraged to put their library persona to one side.

Student diary mapping

Whilst the use of ethnographic techniques in libraries is still fairly limited in the UK, reading about the ERIAL (Ethnographic Research in Illinois Academic Libraries) Project and the Library Study at Fresno State (see reference list) inspired us to investigate how we could use student diary mapping to give us an insider perspective direct from the students themselves without the intervention of an outsider (library staff).

This method involved working closely with a number of stakeholders, so a small project group was set up to oversee the process from recruiting and briefing the students, to conducting the semi-structured interviews, to analysing the findings and making recommendations.

Ten students were recruited to the project and were asked to take part in a variety of activities. We wanted students to tell us their personal stories of how they used the library, what made them choose certain areas to work in and what spaces were barriers to – or enablers of –their learning.

Real-time diary entries

Students were asked to write down all learning-related activities undertaken in a 24-hour period from the moment they woke to the moment they went to bed. We were interested in the details of the activity, but also any thoughts, feelings and barriers they experienced. To assist students with their diary entries we provided them with a log sheet with entry slots for time of day and the activity being undertaken. The students were also encouraged to jot down anything they thought may be of interest to us. In this section entries were very personal to individual students and ranged from concerns about how often the keyboards are cleaned, to concerns about noise, to stress levels in relation to availability of resources. Here are a few examples:

> Struggled to find a PC. The one I eventually got was in my least favourite area close to the door, which was constantly opening and banging shut, lots of talking as people came through. Don't like sitting at this PC, too distracting with all the comings and goings behind me, this was annoying.
>
> Sometimes work best at home. Being a commuting student I have to really commit if I am going to go to the Library to work, always worried I'll forget something.
>
> On floor 1 – found the free computer near the Ask desk. Look around to see if anyone is wearing in-ear headphones – no one is. Good. I won't hear anyone else's music so I can concentrate.

Mapping exercises

In a second 24-hour period, students were asked to literally map out their journeys within the University Library learning spaces and record thoughts and feelings along the way. Students were given a detailed map of the learning spaces and asked to plot their journeys, including where they went and why, how long they stayed there, and how the spaces or activities made them feel.

When the exercises had been completed, the team met with the students individually to discuss their diaries and maps. Most of the students gave us very thorough diary entries, so the interviews were an opportunity to engage the students in wider conversations about how library staff contribute to the learning experience. The students brought their diaries to life, talked about their own narrative and provided valuable information in a more informal way. The interviews also encouraged reflection for both the team and the students. For the students it was a chance to engage in some discussion about how and why they are using the learning spaces, and how they manage their transition between academic years, their different modules and the different environments both on and off campus. For staff it was a chance to see things from a different perspective and to reflect on and examine their own beliefs about how the spaces are being used by students.

Visual ethnography

The use of visual media can be a powerful tool in terms of capturing how students are using learning spaces, but again the danger is that these images can be one-dimensional and they do need context and narrative. As part of the student diary mapping project, we asked students to take photographs of things that were important or meaningful to them in relation to their learning, including objects that helped or hindered them. The students took a wide range of photographs, ranging from favourite study spaces within the library to student lockers, technology and even plug sockets, as well as lots of pictures of coffee. Students were asked to annotate the photographs, and at the interview we asked them to talk about what the photographs meant to them.

To complement the data gathered through the student diary mapping project, the team filmed key areas within our main library building. Busy days and times of day were chosen and filming took place for 3 hours per area, which was then condensed to four sets of 3-minute footage. To add context and depth to the footage it was overlaid with commentary from two members of staff. It was fascinating to see how different members of staff observed different behaviours in the same set of footage, and this all added to the rich picture we were building.

Conclusion

From the data we gathered, there was some consensus that emerged around key issues to address, including noise, layout of furniture and the increased use of mobile technologies.

On a practical note, we therefore made a number of improvements to our physical spaces. We purchased desk fans for our 20 individual study rooms so that students would have more control over the temperature within the working environment. In our quiet and silent study spaces we installed additional desk power so that students could plug in laptops without having to move furniture. In an area designated for quiet study, but in quite an open space, we installed desk dividers to allow more privacy and minimise distractions from noise and passing footfall. We now even hand out free earplugs to students who want that extra level of quiet, even though they may prefer to situate themselves in a busy area.

It was very important to us that we made some real changes on the back of our findings, but what was much more interesting was engaging with students on a one-to-one basis and listening to unique stories about our learning spaces, the impact they have on students' behaviour and academic practice, and how they contribute to that student's personal narrative.

From the quantitative and qualitative data we collect we have been able to get a much better insight into how our learning spaces are being used by students. Whilst the use of ethnographic techniques started out as an additional project, it is now fully embedded into the work of the learning spaces team, and we are looking to see where else we can use these techniques across the wider service.

References

ERIAL Project. Available at: <http://www.erialproject.org/> [Accessed 17 September 2015].

Library Study at Fresno State. Available at: <http://www.fresnostate.edu/socialsciences/anthropology/ipa/thelibrarystudy.html> [Accessed 17 September 2015].

Ramsden, B., 2012. Learning Spaces in Academic Libraries: Research and Assessment Methods. In: *9th ALDinHE Conference. Learning Development in a Digital Age: Emerging Literacies and Learning Spaces, 2–4 April 2012, University of Leeds.* Available at: <http://eprints.hud.ac.uk/13277/> [Accessed 17 September 2015].

16 Are you sitting comfortably . . . ?

Elizabeth Tilley

Learning through stories encourages interaction and active listening, building respect, collaboration, mutuality, common ground, and healing through understanding.

(Devine, Quinn and Aguilar, 2014, p. 273)

'Once upon a time a cat drank a bottle of green ink. At once the cat turned green . . .' Thus is a story announced. Thus does it command attention no less firmly than the opening bars of a Beethoven piano sonata . . . Thus does each story hold promise.

(Gabriel, 2000)

Why stories?

Stories command our attention. I cast my mind back to 2005, a conference hall in Oslo and author Linn Ullmann, at an IFLA keynote taking a breath before launching into reading some of her latest work. For 45 minutes she held nearly 1,000 delegates totally absorbed by the power of her story, and the collective sigh and brief silence as she stopped, followed by the subsequent rapturous applause tells its own tale. Linn Ullmann sensed that the impact of a story would be absolutely perfect for this stage of an international library conference, and how right she was. It made my conference experience perfect, and nearly 10 years later her keynote is the only one that I recall in any detail. My immediate response to this memory has been to rush to Amazon to buy her latest offering.

At their most simple, stories connect cause and effect; they are persuasive, personal and thrive on participation; they are a framework and structure within which community learning is facilitated.

Can stories improve users' learning experiences?

We all like a good story. Spend half an hour in the company of friends, family or colleagues and you'll no doubt come away having heard them relate an experience. In fact we do this constantly throughout our conversations.

Instinctively we use stories to help others understand us, to learn more about the situation we are in, to reflect, contextualise, understand and broaden our world knowledge. Someone else's similar experience, or cautionary tale, helps us get to grips with our own current understanding, or future uncharted territory. Many of us spend hours on the Internet looking at hotel reviews and book reviews; they are all stories that help shape our understanding and decision-making processes. And we like to engage with the storyteller by telling another. A friend retelling their experiences becomes the perfect opportunity for us to relate our own. It's not just our own learning landscape we're pushing the boundaries of, but a two-way process that is truly collaborative.

Stories are traditionally part of learning; they stimulate conversation, reflection through dialogue and the ability to assess and reassess our situation, and often lead to changed behaviour. Stories allow us to understand ourselves and each other's lives, to appreciate our own issues better, and they do so in a way that accommodates varied perspectives and realities. Stories bring learning to life. A pub conversation frequently results in sharing memories and life experiences. Sometimes it will result in affirmation ('I was right'), sometimes a new pragmatic understanding ('I hadn't thought of trying that'), and often the acquiring of knowledge critical to subsequent behaviour ('Now I know X, I can try Y'). A visit to a pub might be a cathartic experience, offloading the day's stories, establishing context, receiving wisdom in return and an opportunity to reflect; so too does the use of storytelling in a teaching scenario. The format of a story is one that most audiences identify with in some shape or form; from pub culture to a fireside storytelling scenario, it is familiar territory. So moving it into the classroom, with the focus on reflection and dialogue, is not difficult to imagine.

If we teach, and if we are committed to improving user experience through our teaching, then we need to search for the techniques that have the greatest impact on learning. If stories make for a good tool whereby students learn easily, then making focused, planned use of them in our teaching saves reinventing yet another pedagogical wheel. Brian Hoey (2013) asks, 'Do you get told what the good life is or do you figure it out for yourself?' Stories invite students to follow the telling of a story with the 'figuring it out for yourself' bit – typically this is a process of reflection, and even if the impact of the story is minimal and their behaviour itself remains unaffected, they may themselves retell the story to others. In this way we gain more than we lose by using stories in our teaching.

Storytelling: just an ad hoc approach?

Storytelling, or 'narrative', as it may be referred to, has been on the research agenda of educationalists for some time. Carter (1993) considers the place of story in teaching, and Egan (1989) implores teachers to move away from logical pedagogical planning frameworks to incorporate the student's imagination in learning activities. From work conducted in primary schools (for example work with preschoolers by Vivian Paley [1991]), through to the heightened awareness of librarians with an Information Literacy agenda, stories provide fuel for the pedagogically minded. The basis for using storytelling in higher education (HE) is bound up in the desire to develop quality learning. Biggs and Tang (2011) are well known for their constructively aligned, outcomes-based teaching, where the aim is to find those mechanisms which transform students' learning and behaviour. Bain's research (2004) focuses on defining what the 'best teacher in the world' looks like. The answer is wrapped up in our desire to see transformative learning in students. McDrury and Alterio (2003) create a model of reflective learning which incorporates storytelling as a key tool in the HE context. Thus reflection is seen as a tool allowing us to 'reshape, reassess and reconstruct'. Moon (2010) also considers story within the HE context and tackles it more holistically, emphasising that by its very nature it builds community, is attractive as a 'carrier of information', and acts as an encouragement to vicarious exploration, helping students learn about themselves and reflect on their own learning. Moon comments that 'teaching does not facilitate learning if there is no engagement with learners'; she advocates that storytelling provides the essence of the art of engaging learners. Meanwhile, Devine, Quinn and Aguilar (2014) evoke the sense of how storytelling can complement other teaching techniques through their suggestion that narrative (or story) can 'harness the power of informal learning'. A well-told story is often considered to be a device that improves memory; but specifically for community building, the format of a story is one that is easily assimilated by most audiences (Fawcett and Fawcett, 2011; Gershon and Page, 2001), because at the heart of storytelling is dialogue.

Moon and Fowler (2008) grapple with the inherent slipperiness of defining story. It can be so many things: fiction or reality, personal or impersonal, ad hoc or purposeful. Not only are there problems with definitions, but there are other aspects to consider. Stories are not just about language, they are about the unspoken actions tied in with the telling, or the social understanding of the structure of story. Begin a story with 'Once upon a time . . .' and we all know where we are. The impact of stories frequently depends on our own personal journeys, triggering emotive responses. Amongst all this variety lies the core purpose and impact of story referred to earlier, that of dialogue and communication.

Moon's framework for classifying the range of stories has four main categories; for this chapter we take one of these as our focus:

> 'Known' story told in a communal setting: these are the stories told among people who share experiences, such as . . . learners on an educational programme. The stories are about events or experiences within the common interests of the tellers or listeners. They may be presented and used as case studies, case histories, scenarios or critical incidents.
>
> (Moon, 2010, p. 15)

So using storytelling or narrative as a teaching tool is recognised by many researchers, but what is more elusive to understand is what story actually does, how to use it effectively and how it impacts learning. And with demonstrating impact currently high on the HE agenda, this could be crucial.

The 'stories in teaching' project

Over time, the English Faculty Library has developed an instinctive approach to ethnographic research. We are naturally curious, we want to know more about what the students do and think, and we want to make sure that our services relate directly to the experience of our users. Our approach to acquiring stories has been overtly ethnographic; we are embedded within a faculty and can watch, observe and engage users in conversation many times a day. The opportunities for gathering stories are never more apparent than at (the now famed in Cambridge) 'tea@ three' open house for library users in my office. (For more information about tea@three see: http://libpara.blogspot.co.uk/2013/11/teathree.html.) Storytelling occurs naturally over a cup of tea (just as it does over a beer in the pub). Not only that, but by focusing on our relationships in this way we reap benefits later on, as students and academics consequently provide us with information all the time! Tea@three, alongside our 'walking the floors' observation tactics, has produced a wealth of resource. We've been told stories; observed incidents and experiences; built up layer upon layer of understanding about what makes an English Literature student tick; and charted the changes in student needs over several years. We've also heard plenty of anecdotes about life in Cambridge (yes, we get our fair share of not-always-pretty party stories). This, then, has been our research base – the ethnographic approach that led to the questions that we asked ourselves some years after this mode of research was introduced.

Our instincts told us that if we were to make use of the results of our research within a teaching programme, we needed to be more organised about it; the informal sharing environment needed a formal framework. The stories we were telling our students (often cautionary tales to warn and alert them of impending perils) were fun to use, but was there a noticeable positive impact in using them? And if so, how could we become better at it? We had our stories, but wanted to change the chaotic approach to retelling those stories 'on the hoof', and so chose to investigate what the impact was on student learning. Our questions were fairly simple:

- Is it useful to tell stories? Are they merely helpful memory-joggers?
- Do stories impact learning, and if so, how?
- Could we improve how we use stories in our teaching?
- Building a community with students who move through the system incredibly quickly has always been a priority for us, and storytelling speaks of community. Could we make better use of telling stories to engender a sense of community?

We conducted a small-scale research project in 2014 into the use of stories as part of a teaching programme, in order to evaluate their impact alongside our all-important focus of improving our library services for users. Our Library is open to all members of the University, but primarily serves those who learn, teach and conduct research in English Literature. When teaching students who are all studying the same subject, there are obvious economies of scale: we don't need to talk about a general referencing method, we talk about the specific system the faculty requires the students to use; we don't just talk about general principles of literature searching, we use a specific relevant database, and so on. We're winning already with the tailored content we include when we teach. But we want to do better, and to make sure that students are learning for the long-haul.

Observation is key to ethnographic research, and we made use of our normal practice of co-teaching to observe and record the impact of storytelling. We also recorded our evaluative conversations post-session. Our focus was on exploring whether using stories was likely to improve learning over time, and how to harness stories for repurposing in the future.

Methodology

Workshops with colleagues

To trial using stories in a teaching situation, a workshop with library colleagues provided an opportunity to make planned use of a student story. The training context was to encourage colleagues to consider what our users are like, and was deliberately framed as a scenario:

> Katie, a graduate student, had come along to one of the Zotero workshops that we run every October at the English Faculty Library. She told me that she had enjoyed the session, had come away determined to try the software out, but by March of the following year had not found the time to engage with it sufficiently to use it instinctively, merely reverting back in essay crisis mode to her default position of formatting references in Microsoft Word as she went along.

As a group we spent time discussing and refining what we understood about Katie from the story, and what it told us about graduates. We moved on to problem solving, discussing what we could do to help Katie, or whether we needed to do anything at all. Finally we considered how we could better help the next cohort of graduate students to establish good research habits earlier in the academic year.

Excellent teachers are marked out by their ability to reflect on the knowledge they gather about their students. But did Katie's story make any marked difference? The aim in using it had been to highlight what we needed to learn about our users to be sure of providing appropriate content in our teaching: it was intended to allow the group to grapple with what was below the surface and have a deeper understanding of student lives and our own librarian assumptions. Subsequent feedback from the session indicated the success of employing this tactic. Over and above this, it was clear that stories such as this may provide useful problem-solving scenarios for teaching, and they stimulate interactivity and small-group discussion. Personally, I discovered that I enjoy using stories to teach; timed well, they can add tension and drama or create a relaxed environment.

Incidentally, Katie herself recently told me that by telling me 9 months ago why she hadn't found time to use Zotero, it had prompted her to go back to it and she now uses it all the time. This was a great example of storytelling creating an opportunity for self-reflection and change.

Student dissertation workshops

Dissertation workshops are hands-on and interactive, with a maximum of 12 students and 2 teachers. The session lasts for an hour and is intended to tackle referencing management, awareness of current research and specialist formats/databases, with an opportunity for tackling searches for dissertation topics. Three stories were deliberately chosen to complement these aims.

Abigail and the incomplete reference

> A few years ago, Abigail came to see me just one day before dissertation hand-in day with a query about a quote she was using that was crucial to her argument, for which she had all the bibliographic details, but not the relevant page number. If you were in this situation, what would you do?

This is a real student-story that I use quite early on in the dissertation workshop, typically following the first exercise where students reflect on the previous years' experience of writing a dissertation. Invariably referencing comes up at this point, and the story is wholly applicable; it is told in an off-the-cuff manner, but becomes a problem that I expect them to come up with practical solutions to, on which we can capitalise. Every group of students has wanted to know what Abigail actually did to solve her dilemma; not only that, most groups included someone who volunteered a similar example that they themselves had experienced. We noticed that this relaxed students, often allowed them to air other issues more openly and resulted in better group discussion overall.

A tale of two browsers

> Emily has adopted a simple but really effective mechanism for keeping her work and social life apart. She's used Zotero for managing her references (and a lot more) all the way through her PhD, and it works brilliantly in Firefox. So she decided to use Firefox as her 'work' browser. She deliberately keeps it 'clean' with no social media sites automatically logged in. At the end of the working day, she can happily close Firefox down and bring up her browser of choice, in this case Chrome, to engage with all the social aspects of her life. Her work browser, Firefox, is not her preferred browser, but its interrelationship with Zotero made its choice a no-brainer.

This is a story that I tell when introducing Zotero, and to all intents and purposes I am talking about reference management. But the story is actually more about time management, and for students who have pressurised, short terms at Cambridge, anything that provides advice in managing their workload is useful. Emily co-teaches with me, so the students can use the evidence of her subsequent teaching slot to help form in their minds whether this story is borne out by reality. Anecdotal comments from students after the session demonstrate that they are interested in the problem and will add this approach to their repertoire of 'distraction busters'. On reflection, the telling of the story has tended to be drowned out by the 'wow' factor of seeing Zotero being used, and it would be better situated elsewhere in the session.

Connor's research calamity

> Not knowing about current research can cause you problems. You need to be aware of only using databases like JSTOR that have a 'moving wall', i.e. it does not include the last three years of research. Connor told me about a problem he had by focusing on JSTOR for his topic research. He had come up with a quirky title for his dissertation, and went along to his supervisor pretty pleased with himself. He started talking about the topic, including telling his supervisor about the project title. There was a moment's pause; the supervisor said, 'You're joking, right?' Connor had absolutely no idea what he was talking about. The supervisor said, 'I've *just* published an article in *Journal of xxx*, with almost exactly that same title. Why on earth didn't you find it?' So . . . why hadn't he found it?

This story engaged the students immediately; the narrative gathers pace, the students know that there is some impending doom and they are almost on the edge of their seats waiting for the guillotine to fall. It resulted in the classic 'hands over mouth OMG' response from students. They all hate feeling incompetent and many will have had, or feared they might in the future have, similar experiences. This proved to have been a very important story for students in the self-evaluation at the end of the session.

Evaluation of teaching by students

We ran six dissertation workshops for third-year undergraduates. As the content was largely the same for each, students signed up for the time that best suited them. In four sessions we deliberately planned to use stories, and we then had two further sessions acting as control groups. At the end of the training workshop they completed an online evaluation form. Students were asked to identify three key learning points and the results were intriguing. Irrespective of whether the students had heard the stories or not, approximately the same percentage highlighted the learning outcomes associated with them as one of their top three takeaways.

A second online survey was sent out via a follow-up email 1 month later to all attendees; response was not high, but the results were more revealing in terms of understanding the existence of a correlation between students' longer-term learning and the use of storytelling.

From students who had heard the stories the following responses were recorded:

> I have since started using Zotero.
> I've learnt to become more focused in my note-taking.
> Also found out about JSTOR's moving wall.
> To use other resources outside of JSTOR.
> Finding up-to-date journal articles was a really good tip.
> I've started using Zotero.

When asked about what intended behaviour change they had *not* implemented, most of them referred to Zotero, making the comment that although they recognised it might be useful, they hadn't 'got round to using it'. The most important learning outcome they recorded was the need to use current research; it would seem that the JSTOR 'moving wall' story had clearly made its mark. Curiously however, these same students did not appear to remember the JSTOR story, but when prompted to recall stories told during the session all referred to the story about 'the girl who forgot to write down a page number for an important quote in her dissertation'. Clearly this story was still the one that was most memorable 1 month later, and we were intrigued – an aspect of storytelling I will discuss later.

Student responses from the control groups did not include specific reference to any learning outcomes, especially when compared to the first survey after the workshop. Their responses were more vague, although positive (e.g. the session provided 'help regarding targeted academic searches').

There seemed to be a clear distinction between the two groups; students' responses were clearer and more specific when stories were used. The numbers involved in this study were small and the same research exercise would need to be repeated to be sure of understanding the results and impact on learning. However, initial results of the project indicate that storytelling within the teaching context has an impact on learning and changed behaviour over the longer term.

From our own observations about how the teaching process had gone, we noticed that where we included stories in the sessions, students were more likely to engage in conversation – with apparent digressions during discussion, but usually directly linked to the stories. Generally they engaged well with the teaching and developed a more cohesive group approach. From a teacher's perspective we found it very hard *not* to use stories in the sessions that acted as our control groups. We came to the conclusion that using stories is instinctive, and that proactively planning activities where stories featured was a promising way forward for our teaching programmes.

Gathering and recording stories for reuse

If stories work, then let's use them. But instead of the ad hoc 'I remember a story about . . .' approach when teaching, structure could impose more objectivity, giving a planned focus to using storytelling. In particular, this applies to recording stories for future use. We spend a lot of our time telling students that they need to manage information – the 'can you find it, file it, and re-find it' mantra (Coonan, personal communication, 2014) has become a key feature of information literacy teaching, and we were keen to employ this approach for ourselves.

One of the basics for improving how we used stories was to enable others to use similar stories and to share best practice. That meant capturing and filing story material in such a way that it was refindable and useful. We had several years of ethnographic research results that we were already making use of, and we had the stories that we had observed and collected throughout our teaching between September and October 2014.

We identified several requirements for effective storage:

- Logging the basic story detail quickly and easily;
- Making it accessible by all staff and available to other librarians outside of our own library;
- Ensuring that all recorded material is easily searchable;
- Giving the stories short useful tags for refinding content;
- Adding notes to the stories over time and suggesting context/teaching activities for their use, so if a story worked well (e.g. as a problem-solving discussion), then this additional information could be added, including an indication of the impact and success in using it that way. This would encourage staff to build more evaluation and reflection into their teaching.

Solutions for recording the information we were gathering are not in short supply. We considered wikis, blogs, spreadsheets and Word tables. The ability to tag with short keywords, as well as to add more copious notes, was crucial to refinding and repurposing our stories. Ideally we needed a tool that we were already familiar with using. Access to documents saved in a shared space on a local server would be restrictive; wikis or blogs just didn't provide sufficient ways to capture useful information. Knowing Zotero very well (as teacher and user) made it an obvious choice; any referencing tool would have done the same job, but library staff were already familiar with Zotero (and had a well-developed love/hate relationship with it). Using a Zotero Group seemed the clear way forward: publicly available but with restricted membership (see Figure 16.1). Ethical considerations meant that the decision was taken to remove all student names. (For more on Zotero, see https://www.zotero.org/groups/efl_stories_for_teaching/.)

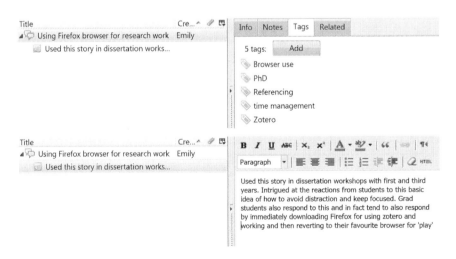

Figure 16.1 Zotero Group use for story recording

This technique for storing stories for reuse and repurposing will be used throughout the academic year 2015–2016 and should allow us to build up a database of useful stories to inform the content of future teaching in the Faculty Library.

Are stories just for the pub or bedtime?

Well, no. This chapter in itself is a story – the story of 'how we observed our users, gathered data, asked ourselves a question, came up with the means to answer that question and produced some initial conclusions'. It has a 'beginning', a 'middle', and (almost) an 'end'. Put this basic story structure into the teaching context and it's obvious that well-planned 'lessons' follow exactly this pattern. Not only is what we do in the classroom built on the characteristics and structures of 'story', but storytelling itself is a useful addition to our teaching repertoires. It gives an opportunity for reflective activity within the classroom; it becomes the perfect segue to group discussion. We maintained at the outset that the use of story is instinctive and should improve our users' learning experiences.

But of course, we wanted to demonstrate that when we put our ethnographic research results (the stories) back into the system deliberately, and tied to specific learning outcomes, that this was more powerful than just including a throwaway story on the spur of the moment. A quick, ad hoc use of story does not usually receive sufficient time in a lesson to make a real impact. However, purposeful use of a story which is deliberately chosen to illustrate key learning points (e.g. 'Connor's Research Calamity'), or to encourage the students to problem- solve or discuss potential outcomes, is more effective, as shown by the results of the longer-term survey, where the 'Abigail and the Incomplete Reference' disaster topped the list of remembered stories.

The 'Stories in Teaching' project has proved to us that it is worth investing our time in making better use of stories. So, yes, we can demonstrate that 'Abigail and the Incomplete Reference' has been more than just a memory-jogger story – the observed discussion in the workshop alongside second survey comments such as 'I've learnt to become more focused in my note-taking' lead us to this conclusion. Yes, we can be confident from the second survey comments that the horror story, 'Connor's Research Calamity', has prompted students to change their behaviour, as they told us they now 'use other resources outside of JSTOR' and remember to use 'up-to-date journal articles'. However, whether or not 'A Tale of Two Browsers' was either overtly memorable or brought about modified behaviours cannot be shown from our data so far. We know we have had some impact by using stories, but we need to further demonstrate this. At the same time we're conscious that variation in learning may occur for some very obvious reasons: the storyteller (or performer) may have a bad acting day and the framing of the story changes; the students are in a post-lunch slump and nothing will stir them into action; or the members of the class may simply be just 'one of those groups', either unwilling or unable to participate in reflective activities. Overall, stories add flavour to our sessions, and we can be even more agile and flexible as teachers when we use them.

Relevance, empathy and community

During the course of this research there have been two further aspects of storytelling using real student stories that have been intriguing and relevant to the student experience.

First, stories often stir us emotionally. Part of this reaction is to do with the truth contained in a case study story. There is an interesting grade of credibility to stories used in all kinds of environments, be that pub, church, lecture hall or TV. If I tell you a story about something that happened to me, it's real, it's credible and will likely provoke a reaction. If I tell you a story about a student I heard about from someone else, it's less credible, and while interesting there is less emotional engagement. Through our research we now more fully appreciate the value and importance of empathy and relevance. There was a direct impact on responses when the story was framed in such a way that group members identified with the student's problem, both empathetically and comprehending its relevance. The emotional response to 'Connor's Research Calamity' resulted in an immediate reaction in the session, but for some, this failed to be highly relevant to them. The 'Abigail and the Incomplete Reference' story resulted in the same empathetic response, but it was also highly relevant so that within the session discussion other student stories were told, and in the longitudinal survey results *this* was the story that made the most impact. So, moving forward with using stories in teaching we should concentrate on bringing both empathy and relevance together to ensure quality learning.

Second, do stories help in building community? Given the earlier argument about personal stories creating empathetic responses and being relevant, surely the logical conclusion is that our students will learn more from the personal story – and where will they get that but from each other? We are almost full circle, and back in the pub. If I could have almost any wish, it would be for our library to have that pub fireplace, some amazingly comfy armchairs, a bar in the background and a group of students who would be there for one of our workshops . . . but I can dream. Given that this is unlikely to happen any time soon, using stories in our teaching is a good compromise to building community amongst our students. It is why we have been co-teaching with graduates and academics for 5–6 years; it is why we use third-year students to help us teach the new freshers. We already believe that we do not have all the answers or stories, and that the telling of the personal story *will* have more impact. We now have some proof.

Conclusion

The small-scale project described in this chapter highlights the long-term impact of storytelling. There are additional variables to consider, but ethnographic research teaches us to observe and to get under the skin of those we study and there will always be endless nuances to this approach. But that is what storytelling is all about as well, and how one person hears a story, and what impact it will have on them, will be different from another. If you have a similar tale to tell, then the impact is different. If the story is superseded by other significant issues, then it becomes an anecdote – not useless, but perhaps simply regarded as what one of our students described as 'good, as it shows we're all human'. So, it seems that using storytelling as a model when teaching will not fail; it is a flexible approach, and although the impact on students may vary purely because of factors such as the time of day, there is an impact nevertheless. Using stories in our teaching directly impacts learning, but they are also helpful in other ways as our students have related: they add a bit of spice; help those attending to relate to the worst-case scenario; make everything seem 'less scary'. Not only that, but they encourage students to recognise that there is help out there. Stories build community and they enhance our teaching. It is our confident assertion that storytelling brings about change in our learners' behaviour and improves their user experience. Building on this work in our local situation and having a planned approach about using stories more effectively will be our goal for the next academic year.

References

Bain, K., 2004. *What the Best College Teachers Do*. Cambridge, MA: Harvard University Press.

Biggs, J. B. and Tang, C. S., 2011. *Teaching for Quality Learning at University: What the Student Does*. Maidenhead: McGraw-Hill/Society for Research into Higher Education/ Open University Press.

Carter, K., 1993. The Place of Story in the Study of Teaching and Teacher Education. *Educational Researcher*, 22(1), pp. 5–18.

Devine, J. R., Quinn, T. and Aguilar, P., 2014. Teaching and Transforming through Stories: An Exploration of Macro- and Micro-Narratives as Teaching Tools. *Reference Librarian*, 55(4), pp. 273–88.

Egan, K., 1989. *Teaching as Story Telling: An Alternative Approach to Teaching and Curriculum in the Elementary School*. Chicago: University of Chicago Press.

Fawcett, S. E. and Fawcett, A. M., 2011. The 'Living' Case: Structuring Storytelling to Increase Student Interest, Interaction, and Learning. *Decision Sciences Journal of Innovative Education*, 9(2), pp. 287–98.

Gabriel, Y., 2000. *Storytelling in Organizations: Facts, Fictions, and Fantasies*. Oxford: Oxford University Press.

Gershon, N. and Page, W., 2001. What Storytelling Can Do for Information Visualization. *Communications of the ACM*, 44(8), pp. 31–7.

Hoey, B., 2013. *What Is Ethnography?* [online] Available at: <http://www.brianhoey.com/ General%20Site/general_defn-ethnography.htm> [Accessed 20 September 2014].

McDrury, J. and Alterio, M., 2003. *Learning through Storytelling in Higher Education: Using Reflection & Experience to Improve Learning*. London: Kogan Page.

Moon, J. A., 2010. *Using Story: In Higher Education and Professional Development*. Abingdon: Routledge.

Moon, J. A. and Fowler, J., 2008. 'There Is a Story to Be Told . . .'; A Framework for the Conception of Story in Higher Education and Professional Development. *Nurse Education Today*, 28(2), pp. 232–9.

Paley, V. G., 1991. *The Boy Who Would Be a Helicopter: Uses of Storytelling in the Classroom*. Cambridge, MA: Harvard University Press.

17 UX in libraries

Leaping the chasm

Andy Priestner and Matt Borg

As we have collated this book over the past 9 months, the value of UX research methods derived from the worlds of anthropology and design has only become more apparent and obvious to us. Better still, it is clear that we are by no means alone in these endeavours. Librarians all over the UK and beyond have started to see for themselves the riches that these techniques can offer, whether they are observing user behaviour, designing new spaces or products (often in direct collaboration with students), or simply connecting with their students more.

Rarely a day goes by without one of us hearing about a new library graffiti wall, a participatory design workshop, or a behavioural mapping project. And, what is more, the excitement around such approaches remains palpable.

Even by our own high standards the UX in Libraries (UXLibs) conference was a great success, igniting as it did interest in UX and perhaps most specifically ethnography in ways that we had not imagined. It has been hugely rewarding to hear that UXLibs attendees have not only gone back to their institutions and presented on what they had learned and run their own workshops, but have also organised regional meet-ups in order to 'keep the faith' and establish informal networks to elicit sharing and collaboration. A simple Twitter search on #uxlibs reveals a hashtag that stubbornly refused to die once our 3-day conference in March 2015 was over, while the number of post-conference reflective blogs was simply staggering. Plans are now afoot for UXLibs II, at which it is hoped delegates will be willing to share their stories of user experience research in action – the successes, the failures, and those unintended insights that these methods often provide. A UX in Libraries community now exists, so it only seems right that it comes together at least once a year.

It would be easy to overestimate the success of UXLibs in terms of reach and lasting impact, or indeed its significance in the library user experience landscape. The reality is that many people beyond our organising committee, speakers and delegates had already grasped the library UX nettle and recognised that it could be applied beyond website usability. *Designing Better Libraries*, for instance, is a US blog which began talking about user experience of libraries as far back as 2007 and is still going strong today (http://dbl.lishost.org/blog/#.Vfso6m-zbIU). Aaron Schmidt, who has written about library user experience of spaces for many years, should also be namechecked here – he, together with Amanda Etches, wrote the highly practical and thought-provoking *Useful, Usable, Desirable* (2014). Their tome, and specifically the questions it encourages us to ask ourselves about our library touchpoints, should be required reading for librarians everywhere.

Elsewhere, Matthew Reidsma collaborated with Aaron and Kyle Felker to found *Weave: The Journal of Library User Experience*, an open-access, peer-reviewed journal for library user experience professionals, in response to the dearth of professional literature in the area. Crucially it calls for a wider definition and application of UX in physical spaces and other contexts. We urge you to read and write for it. Reidsma, alongside several others, also moderates the library UX Twitter chat #litaUX, launched by the Library Information Technology Association (LITA) user experience interest group, which encourages discussion and sharing of challenges, successes, and techniques.

Also Twitter-based and well worth a follow is the fun @HogwartsUXLib account, which uses a Harry Potter lens to illuminate and explore library UX. And finally, although its user experience focus is more digital and features contributions from UX designers rather than anthropologists, we should mention the Designing for Digital conference, which grew out of the US association ER&L (Electronic Resources and Libraries) and looks set to become a mainstay of the US conference calendar. We do not seek to be comprehensive here – there's a great collection of resources on Ned Potter's blog that serves as a great place to start if you want more – but rather hope to illustrate that 'the time is now'. There are more than enough of us engaging with library user experience to get it on the library profession's radar and ensure it stays there.

As the UXLibs conference sought to demonstrate, vendors also need to be part of this conversation. If they are to provide the products our users need, then they must go beyond excellence in interface design and usability testing. Ideally vendors should be considering how their offering fits into a wider learning experience and research how today's user behaviours and routines might directly influence the product design choices they make. Like us, vendors are ultimately seeking to offer services that users adopt which enhance and support their academic experience, but they can only achieve this if they conduct the necessary research and embrace these methodologies.

If we were to map library UX against a model like Moore's Technology Adoption Life Cycle (1991), one could argue that UXLibs attendees are the 'innovators', and that they have returned to their home institutions to work with 'early adopters'. It is important, however, not to underestimate the 'big scary chasm' that lies between these early adopters and the 'early majority' (see Figure 17.1). The latter may accept that users come first, but they will not necessarily accept that engaging with our users and understanding their motivations and experiences should be the building blocks of everything we undertake in our professional roles – that represents quite a leap across the chasm.

Demonstrating the power of these techniques and the solid evidence of user experience they offer will help get the early majority on board, but we are still a long way off securing the understanding and attention of the 'late majority' and the 'laggards'. These latter groups probably consider the current explosion of interest

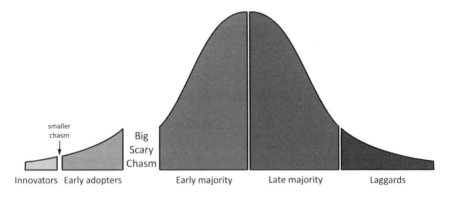

Figure 17.1 Technology Adoption Life Cycle

Source: Adapted from Geoffrey Moore's *Crossing the Chasm* (1991).

in this type of research a fad that they can safely ignore, failing to recognise that we are actually embracing methods that have been around for almost a hundred years and that they operate libraries containing countless tomes describing these tried-and-tested techniques. Perhaps they just need to shelve in their social science research methods sections more regularly?

We have noted that many librarians have recognised that UX research techniques can easily be implemented on a small scale for discrete projects when insights are needed quickly, demonstrating how simple they are to understand and conduct (Margaret Westbury's case study emphasises this clearly). However we have also observed their large-scale adoption. The fieldwork in Cambridge University's libraries that took place as part of the UXLibs conference proved very valuable beyond the event, validating ideas and concepts that had already started to be derived as part of FutureLib – a pan-Cambridge libraries innovation programme grounded in ethnographic research and human-centred design (see Chapters 8 and 9). One idea, presented by team 'Blue Steel', was for a tool that would connect students with available study spaces; another suggested by 'Purple Haze' was that of a well-designed library space in the centre of Cambridge with 'barista librarians' (the concept which eventually triumphed at the conference). In fact both had already been more or less formally proposed as part of the FutureLib programme and are now set to become a reality. However, the research phase for the latter still has a long way to go and that will of course prove to be the most crucial stage of the process. What FutureLib has shown, like the participatory design work undertaken at Manchester (detailed in Chapter 11), is that these UX efforts can be employed on a large scale. They can be implemented institution-wide if senior management and governing bodies choose to resource them.

An issue that is regularly discussed when adoption of UX techniques is on the table is whether the research should only be conducted by anthropologists and/or human-centred designers, or whether librarians can fit the bill themselves. There are solid arguments on both sides. Trained anthropologists like Donna Lanclos and Andrew Asher live and breathe ethnographic method and possess a rare understanding of its application in the context of libraries. Rarer still is the situation of their employment as 'library ethnographers' funded by university libraries in the US. While many UK libraries have certainly employed anthropologists for short-term projects, there do not appear to be many permanently funded equivalents of Donna and Andrew. We therefore do not have access to the same on-tap talent and are relying on anthropologists who instead have to hit the ground running and understand all things 'library' in the short space of time for which they are engaged. Cambridge University Library chose to employ a designer as Head of Innovation (Paul-Jervis Heath) in an attempt to ensure that a culture of continuous and quick innovation, underpinned by ethnography and human-centred design, might be embraced within the institution. It was a bold move that served to further ignite the existing local interest in ethnography in Cambridge libraries, and although Paul moved on to set up his own design consultancy, his employment helped embed an appreciation of the value of these methods and their position high up on Cambridge University Library's strategic agenda, and in turn led to the birth of the current FutureLib programme.

Donna, Andrew and Paul (and we are certain there must be others not on our radar) are all examples of UX experts whose employment has ensured that anthropological approaches are being very taken seriously at a high level within their respective universities, but the model is unusual. Perhaps it is a situation that will change as the burgeoning interest in user experience grows, but if it does not, is it up to librarians to fill the gap? And if so, are we up to the challenge? Librarians are naturally passionate about meeting user need and, in line with Ranganathan, would always consider their users as their number one priority. In terms of motivation alone, then, the embracing of research methods to attain a deeper understanding of the user experience of our libraries seems an obvious next step. However, as we explored in Chapter 1, this will involve putting much less store by our intuition and focusing on the complex needs and behaviours of our users derived from actual research. This means trying to get into the shoes of our users more and, if possible, participating in their environment rather than just behaving as detached observers. It involves accepting that we are not our users and accepting that their way of fulfilling a task may seem alien to us, or even foolish, but that it doesn't make their methods broken or wrong. Instead we should be acknowledging their behaviour and actively seeking to learn from it. This isn't to say we shouldn't try to influence this behaviour by offering better designed touchpoints (those moments when users interact with us), but we help no one, including ourselves, by simply dismissing and condemning it.

As for the skills needed to carry out the techniques themselves, librarians are arguably more than capable of conducting this type of research; provided, that is, that they have sufficient grounding in, and understanding of, its purpose and value. This purpose and value, put simply, as we hope the chapters of this book have demonstrated, is to uncover a more holistic and complex picture of our users' lives; a picture that crucially recognises the library as part of a wider research landscape or social taskscape. It is about a hunger for detail, for data, for information. . . . Who better then, than librarians, to take on this task?

Perhaps the biggest barrier to adoption of user experience research is the perceived or actual lack of existing resource and capacity to undertake this type of research. No one would disagree that to do this work well significant time must be devoted to the activity, but we would argue strongly that it is time very well spent. User experience research promises to reward a library service, and more specifically its users, far more than many of the tasks we currently undertake. Tasks which it could be argued do not directly improve the experience of our users, such as constructing collection development policies, updating largely unread web pages, conducting detailed cataloguing, or the taking of statistics. These and other activities like them may indirectly benefit our users, but are they more valuable than time allocated to actual research into user experience? Many larger libraries have user research teams that explore the usability of their digital collections and resources (e.g. Stanford), but how many have staff dedicated to exploring how users find and behave in our spaces or how the library fits into their research process? User research should have a far broader definition than it currently enjoys, and be conducted by staff members dedicated to exploring this behaviour and experience beyond the use of digital resources. It is a research trajectory that could be very beneficially applied and feasibly lead us to reprioritise the work we do and the choices we currently make as librarians, refining and ensuring our ongoing relevance to our users and fellow support departments. We have the opportunity to be in the vanguard here – leading the way just as we have done in recent years with social media, showing our colleagues in student services, IT, and employability how UX research is actually done and the rich information and evidence that it offers.

In today's highly complex, multilayered world of learning and information it is sorely tempting for us to seek black-and-white, quantifiable answers to the many problems and issues set out before us – to seize upon solutions that will turn situations around, and sometimes to just seize upon one absolute solution as the answer we need. UX research methods do not offer this. Indeed they are often not so much about providing solutions as helping us to formulate and ask better questions – questions that we need to ask if we have any hope of understanding the behaviours, choices and culture of our users. We need methods that will help us to illuminate that complexity – to consider our users and their learning landscapes, of which libraries are only a part, in more detail than we have ever considered before.

No doubt we will encounter more and more discussion, analysis and debate about the value and application of user experience research in libraries. It will be a topic for the literature for many years to come. If past experience is anything to go by, we will be in danger of overanalysing the implications in terms of policy, in terms of senior management, in terms of everyday practice before we've even begun. So let's just pause to reflect here and now on what this is all really about: it is about observing and listening to our users; it is about understanding them in richer ways than we have previously encountered; it is about seeking a deeper and wider meaning of libraries and learning. Whether you and your library colleagues are on board with these methods yet or not, enthusiasm for ethnographic approaches, usability research and human-centred design is certainly growing, and we feel sure that this can only lead to a superior user experience of libraries – and that just has to be the best objective of them all.

References

Designing Better Libraries blog. [blog] Available at: <http://dbl.lishost.org/blog/#.Vfso6m-zbIU> [Accessed 17 September 2015].

Electronic Resources and Libraries (ER&L). *Designing for Digital Conference*. Available at: <http://electroniclibrarian.org/category/designing-for-digital/> [Accessed 17 September 2015].

Moore, G.A., 1991. *Crossing the Chasm: Marketing and Selling Technology Products to Mainstream Customers*. New York: HarperBusiness.

Potter, N. UX in Libraries Resource List. *Ned Potter's blog*. [blog] Available at: <http://www.ned-potter.com/ux-in-libraries-resource-list/> [Accessed 17 September 2015].

Reidsma, M., Schmidt, A. and Felker, K. (founders). *Weave: Journal of Library User Experience*. [online] Available at: <http://weaveux.org/> [Accessed 17 September 2015]. Ann Arbor, MI: Michigan Publishing.

Schmidt, A. and Etches, A., 2014. *Useful, Usable, Desirable: Applying User Experience Design to Your Library*. Chicago: American Library Association.

Index

Printed in Great Britain
by Amazon

56789576R00127